# HITLER'S
## CHILDREN

GUIDO KNOPP

# HITLER'S
## CHILDREN

———————

## GUIDO KNOPP

*Translated by Angus McGeoch*

SUTTON PUBLISHING

First published in 2000 by C. Bertelsmann Verlag GmbH, Munich
under the title *Hitlers Kinder*.
This English translation first published in 2002 by
Sutton Publishing Limited · Phoenix Mill
Thrupp · Stroud · Gloucestershire · GL5 2BU

This paperback edition first published in 2004

In collaboration with Stefan Brauburger, Christian Deick, Jörg
Müllner, Ricarda Schlosshan, Stephan Wiehler

Research: Alexander Berkel, Bârbel Schmidt-Šakić
Translation: Angus McGeoch

British Library Cataloguing in Publication Data
A catalogue record for this book is available from the British
Library

ISBN 0-7509-3780-7

Typeset in 10/12.5 Galliard.
Typesetting and origination by
Sutton Publishing Limited.
Printed and bound in England by
J.H. Haynes & Co. Ltd, Sparkford.

# CONTENTS

# PICTURE CREDITS

# INTRODUCTION

This is the story of a generation who had no choice. They were not the ones who voted for Hitler. Their parents did. Those boys and girls who grew up in the 1930s and 1940s were taken over by the state as no generation of Germans before or since. 'This youth of ours', Hitler proclaimed in 1938 with an almost contemptuous undertone, 'is going to learn nothing but how to think German, how to act German.' At the age of ten, the dictator went on, they join the *Jungvolk*, at fourteen the *Hitlerjugend* (Hitler Youth), then the Party and labour service. 'And after military service we immediately take them into the SA, the SS and so on, and they are never free again for the rest of their lives.'

On 20 April every year, the Führer's birthday, millions of young Germans – 'Hitler's Children' – were sworn to follow the mania of the *Übervater*, the 'Supreme Father'. The writer Erich Loest, born in 1926, recalls how he was ceremonially accepted into the Hitler Youth. 'I was ten years old. It said in the papers at the time that the German people had made a gift to the Führer of a year's crop of children. We were a present for the Führer.'

❖ ❖ ❖

The nightmare only lasted twelve years, yet its consequences can be seen to this day. Many people who were young at the time are only now, decades later, feeling the suppressed trauma of having been abused for the sake of a criminal regime. They have 'scars on the soul', as the screen actor Hardy Kruger, a *Hitlerjunge* in those days, puts it. This generation is still very much alive. It can still bear witness to a time when human beings were looked upon as raw material, not as individuals.

It is true, there was no such thing as *the* Hitler Youth. There were the very enthusiastic ones, some of whom even today talk of the 'great times' in the *Hitlerjugend (HJ)* and its female counterpart, the BDM (*Bund Deutscher Mädel*, or 'League of German Lasses'). There were those, perhaps the majority, who kept a low profile, managed to get through the period, and in the war were mainly concerned with their own survival. And then there was the small group of rebels, who attempted to resist the demands of the regime. Every case is different: a young man born in 1923 had a different experience from someone born ten years later. There were also marked regional differences: in big cities like Hamburg, Munich, Cologne or Berlin, life for young people was different from that in the Black Forest, Pomerania or East Prussia.

And yet, as more recollections are gathered, the more similar they become. Over 1,000 interviews were carried out for this book, with people who at the end of a long working life often for the first time found the strength and even the courage to remember. During the war the young men of that generation were led to the slaughter, the young women at home had to endure the bombing raids; and the defeat in 1945 meant flight and homelessness for millions. Those who survived the terror of total war had lost precious years of their lives – and the harsh conditions in postwar Germany did not make a new start easy. The burden of rebuilding a nation fell on the shoulders of that generation; in their memory lay the recollection of fear and misery, hunger and death – but equally of a time when the dictatorship had not only violence to offer, but also seduction.

It often began in an apparently harmless way. Any young man in Hitler's Reich who wanted to enjoy life found an attractive range of leisure activities on offer in the Hitler Youth: camp-fires, the romance of the outdoors – it all meant adventure and experience, it created a sense of belonging. 'We really had to freeze and swelter, we had to get soaked in our tents', one of them recalls. 'But then there was the feeling of being in a group, going on hikes, the exertion. In the evening we all sat around the fire. And then we sang together. It was dark. The stars above me. It was very moving, something one never forgets.'

Where emotions can be deliberately released in order to control the mind, children are easy prey. For the first time young Germans had the feeling that they were important. Never before in German history had the young been so courted – and never so abused. Seduced by the feeling of being something special, 'not the hope, but the fulfilment of that which we hope for', as the dictator once put it, the young were, often unknowingly, initiated into a vision of the world which broke with the values of a humane society. 'Humanity and humanitarian values were quite simply drummed out of us', one eye-witness recalls. What was sought was the active, disciplined youngster who adapted to the rules of a dictatorship with enthusiasm, and without asking awkward questions. Willing new recruits were needed – cannon-fodder for Hitler's war.

Some were trained for command. They were to be the new stratum of leaders issuing orders to a German world empire – as *Gauleiter*, military commanders, in fact leaders in every field and every profession. Tough and peremptory, able and efficient was what they had to be: managers of power in a modern tyranny.

It was in Hitler's schools for the elite that his insane scheme for breeding the new German master-race was to become a reality. In the so-called Adolf Hitler Schools, in establishments for instilling nationalist policies and in the Reich School of the Nazi Party, at Feldafing, near Munich, the regime intended to raise able enforcers, who would inherit the future as the heirs of Hitler. Even as children they were subjected to military-style drill, and in class it was important that they should absorb the correct *Weltanschauung*, or world view, along with their academic knowledge. 'To believe, obey, fight' was their duty as political soldiers. Lured by the rich variety of sport and leisure activities, and by the prospect of impressive careers, they enrolled in the elite boarding-schools which bound them to unquestioning loyalty. During the war brought about by their Führer, these victims of their education were among the most fanatical Nazis. Only half of them survived to the end.

Nonetheless, an astonishing number of graduates of those forcing-houses made careers in postwar democratic Germany – in business, journalism, politics and diplomacy. Without inhibition, alumni of the elite schools tell of the life they led there – men like the former publisher of the newspaper *Die Zeit*, Theo Sommer, or the ex-chief editor of *Eltern* (Parents) magazine, Otto Schuster.

Some still emphasise the advantages of their education, which demanded toughness on oneself and on others: 'We were educated well for a wretched cause.'

And what about the girls? They too were taken in hand, drilled and comprehensively lied to. 'German lasses' were meant to be hard-working to the point of self-sacrifice, obedient and above all prepared for their role as mothers of future soldiers – machines for producing human reinforcements. The national leaders of the *Bund Deutscher Mädel* fostered this attitude, but the initials BDM soon became corrupted, standing instead for *Bald deutsche Mutter* (soon to be German mothers) or *Bubi drück Mich* (Squeeze me, babe).

'They were the most wonderful days of my life' – many of those who lived through that time still have difficulty today in reconciling their subjective memories with historical truth. Even if they succeed, 'then it is terribly painful', as one former BDM girl admits, 'to acknowledge that one had believed in something so wrong'. One of those we interviewed admitted: 'I can't get the sunshine out of my memories.' Nevertheless, at the end of the twentieth century there is an obvious willingness to provide evidence of youthful desires and mistakes. Today, Hitler's 'lasses' are grandmothers, a number are even great-grandmothers. After the war they did their bit, in both Germanies, east and west, to create from the ruins the now reunited country in which they live. It took decades for them to realise that they had been forced into a stereotyped role, from which they could not escape. Is it possible that their 'relationship' with Hitler had something to do with this? A sizeable number of the one-time 'lasses' now admit to a good measure of emotional involvement: 'He was the *Übervater*, our supreme father'; 'It was really a deep and intense love'; 'I felt exactly the same for him as I did for God.' Even young girls were among those who wrote the thousands of love-letters which arrived at the Reich Chancellery ('Sweet Führer, I want you to give me a child') – these may be bizarre examples, yet they bear witness to an underlying collective emotion.

During the war Hitler's children were a necessary support for the regime. Without the tireless and versatile commitment of the

Hitler Youth, society and the economy in Germany would have collapsed much sooner. Through their active involvement the youth contributed significantly to the prolonging of the war. A 9-million-strong army of cheap labour plugged the gaps left by the men called up to the Front. Hitler's children darted through the cities as messengers, were put to work as harvesters, air-raid wardens and couriers, issued ration-cards and distributed propaganda material. In large families the girls helped with the housework, others did junior jobs with the Red Cross or the local authorities. Older boys served as firemen in burning cities or went to a 'military fitness camp' for a final polish before enlisting in the Wehrmacht.

More than one-third of those born in the years between 1921 and 1925 were slaughtered on the battlefields of the Second World War, or fell victim to Allied bombing on the Home Front. From the Atlantic coast to the Black Sea, from the Arctic Circle to North Africa and back through Kaliningrad and Wroclaw to Berlin their graves bespeak the erring of a seduced generation, whom Hitler cheated of their youth. Indeed many were both victims and perpetrators. Hitler Youth leaders were involved in almost all the atrocious measures initiated in the eastern territories by the *Gauleiter* and SS. They too made decisions about resettlement or expulsion, life or death. And in the final chaotic weeks of the war, HJ members sometimes had to take part in the shooting of Jews.

Yet for a long time before this they had had to make the final sacrifice for the man to whom they had sworn allegiance. Certainly many gave themselves of their own free will: 'To die for Führer, *Volk* and Fatherland was of course an honour and a duty, or so they had taught us.' Hundreds of contemporary witnesses give this as the reason why they went off to fight a senseless war without complaint – at the age of fourteen, fifteen and sixteen. Those who survived only discovered after the war what kind of Fatherland it was that they were supposed to sacrifice themselves for.

What conclusions can be drawn from this? For this generation 1945 was more than just total defeat. It marked the collapse of an entire value-system. For the young Germans of 1945 there was no past to reach back to and pick up again. They knew nothing but

National Socialism and war. Nazism had prepared them for war. Both came to an end in 1945.

For the first few years at least, many of the young found it hard to come to terms with democracy. They put all their energy into the economic recovery and into raising families. In 1968 the sons (and some of the daughters) of this war generation rebelled against their fathers, confronting them with hard questions. That debate is not over yet.

Hitler's children did not seek out their 'father' themselves. It was *their* parents who were responsible for that, through their unwillingness or inability to prevent him from becoming a dictator. This generation is no better and no worse than the generations which preceded and followed it. It is just that they had more to endure. Seduced, dragooned, betrayed and abused, they can now look back once more, as we enter a new century, to the life and death of their youth.

This book directs its attention to those who were led and who for a long time and in good faith allowed themselves to be led. Many simply accepted their destiny, others were filled with the ideals of duty and patriotism. Or even with fanaticism – determined to do more than was demanded of them. Others again went along with it, but with misgivings, unspoken defiance and inner reservations. We hear, too, from men and women who in their youth were able to escape the influence of the Nazi regime. Today they tell of those years. Some of their judgements may seem to have mellowed in the long intervening period, but their first-hand experiences deserve to be brought before a wide audience. Thus *Hitler's Children* knowingly accepts the subjectivity of these statements. They are like personal memoirs, which, placed alongside and combined with documentary evidence, are an integral part of the historical record – the legacy of a generation which, without ever being asked, was made by history into 'Hitler's Children'.

This generation is still living. It can still tell us about the past. And we can still draw lessons from their fate – and spare our own children from it.

# CHAPTER ONE

# SEDUCTION

## KNOPP/WIEHLER

When you were little lads and lasses you chose to stand up for this new Germany. You have remained loyal to your Germany, and this memory of your age will carry in it the reward which today no-one is able to give you.

*Adolf Hitler, 1932*

I don't believe that every single one of my generation became infected by National Socialism, but we grew up in an atmosphere that was conditioned by uniforms.

*Klaus Bölling, born 1928*

Adolf Hitler, we believe in you; without you we would be individuals, through you we are a nation. You give us the experience of our youth.

*Baldur von Schirach, 1934*

The feeling was instilled in us that to die for the community, the nation or the Führer was in fact the highest thing in life.

*Hans-Jochen Vogel, born 1926*

The young will, I know, place themselves with passion and unbounded enthusiasm in the service of the cause.

*Hermann Göring, 1939*

They enticed us for their own ends, but we were glad to go along with it. Many like me did absolutely nothing to resist, we saw no reason to resist, and in turn, when we became leaders, we enticed the others.

*Erich Loest, born 1926*

The whole work of education and training in a national state must find its culmination in burning into the hearts and minds of the youth in its charge, a sense and feeling of race that is both instinctive and rational.

*Adolf Hitler, Mein Kampf*

The Hitler Youth trampled on human worth, whenever a person belonged to a different race, came from a different country, followed a different religious faith or held different political beliefs.

*Hanns-Peter Herz, German Jew, born 1927*

We are looking for the ideal embodiment of National Socialist achievement, National Socialist character and a National Socialist attitude to the world. The task has been set; youth of Germany, go to it!

*Joseph Goebbels, 1935*

Of course, they were so cunning in the way they presented things then – they didn't say right at the start: we want to make you into good Nazis.

*Hans Müller, born 1923*

Your child already belongs to us today. What are you? You will pass away, but your descendents already stand in the new camp. In a short time they will no longer know anything else.

*Adolf Hitler, 1933*

Naturally, young people are impressed when they are told, they are the future, they are what matters, that the old will be gone one day anyway.

*Hans-Jochen Vogel, born 1926*

Here, at your command, *mein Führer*, stands a young generation that knows nothing of snobbery and class-consciousness.

*Baldur von Schirach, 1934*

Generation will succeed generation in the tasks and their fulfilment, and again and again here in this city a new group of young people will step forward. They will be ever stronger, ever more powerful and ever healthier and they will give to the living national family ever greater hope for the future.

*Adolf Hitler, 1936*

The young can be led astray because their knowledge cannot yet be great enough to give them a completely clear picture of events. They develop a longing. It is a longing to believe in something, and we all carry it within us.

*Imo Moszkovicz, German Jew, born 1925*

❖ ❖ ❖

The nation's future rode on the back of trucks or arrived on special trains of the Reichsbahn. Only the chosen ones came on foot. They marched for hundreds of miles across Germany. They filled the roads with their drums and bugles, and carried their banners, singing, through towns and villages. Many of them had been on the move for more than a month. They spent the nights in tent camps or in haystacks. Year after year some 2,000 *Hitlerjungen* enthusiastically obeyed the call of the Reich Youth Leader, Baldur von Schirach: 'We are marching to the Führer – and if he so wishes, we will march *for* him as well.'

On the morning of 14 September 1935 the participants in the 'Adolf Hitler March' had reached their destination. With them 54,000 boys and girls from all over Germany had entered the Nuremberg stadium for the 'Roll-call of Youth'. The directors of this mammoth Nazi production had arranged them into vast blocks of humanity for the 'Reich Party Freedom Congress': they were mere extras in this heady geometry. In front of the main podium with its rows of notables from the Party and the Wehrmacht the uniformed youngsters waited tensely for the arrival of their *Übervater*.

To us he was like a god. He was the idealised figure who was in charge of everything, and to whom everyone turned.

*Kurt Heindorf, born 1925*

At last the ruler made an entrance among his young people. The leading Hitlerjunge in the Third Reich stepped forward and stood to attention. Proudly Baldur von Schirach reported his contingent present. Then he gave the command: 'Stand at ease!' And, as one, 10,000 adolescent voices broke the silence of the stadium with a shout of 'Heil Hitler!' The pent-up tension was released in several minutes of cheering, before drum-rolls and fanfares brought the calculated outburst of feeling back into the discipline of the party rally. The loyal army of young joined their voices in a collective confession of faith: 'We are the Reich's young strength, a single brotherhood . . .'

With his own particular tendency to overwrought emotion, the 28-year-old Reich Youth Leader invoked the spirit of self-sacrifice in the assembled mass of youth. 'Here before you stands the entire young generation of our nation. When we look here upon these cheerful young people, I see, however, among them the twenty-one pale faces of those dead comrades who sacrificed themselves in order that we may live in such communal harmony. These comrades, *mein Führer*, died believing in you. The whole youth of Germany lives in this same faith. We have learnt from the heroic example of these, the best of our number, and know that loyalty to you is the gateway to our immortality.'

It was an initiation into a cult of death: with missionary zeal Schirach preached to a whole generation of young Germans the catechism of a National Socialist religion, which declared that to die for the Führer was the way to the eternal life of his youth movement. With his faithful gazing in rapture at their almighty idol, Adolf Hitler pronounced his vision of the supposed New Man: 'What we want from our German youth is something different from what was wanted in the past. In our eyes the young German must be lean and lithe, as fleet as a greyhound, as tough as leather and as hard as Krupp steel.'

In the 'Year of Conditioning' Hitler called upon his young listeners 'to arm yourselves; steel yourselves physically and prepare yourselves mentally'. The adolescent lads had yet to discover what marching-orders the regime was planning for them, but there was no doubt about who would decide them: 'Nothing is possible, if there is not one will commanding, a will which the rest have to obey, from the top down and only ending at the lowest.' That was the lesson of blind obedience in the Führer-state. As an example to the whole ethnic community Hitler assigned an educative task to the youth themselves: 'We must instruct our entire people, that whenever and wherever someone is placed in authority, the rest recognise his authority and obey him, because at any moment they themselves may have to give orders and likewise they can only do this if others show obedience. Let us never forget that only the strong earn friendship and only the strong bestow it. And so we want to make ourselves strong; that is our watchword. And it is you who are responsible to me for the fulfilment of this wish. You are the future of the nation, the future of the German Reich.'

> Our nation is becoming visibly more disciplined, more erect and sturdier, and it starts with the young.
>
> *Adolf Hitler, 1935*

At the end of the speech the Great Seducer was intent on immersing himself in the throng of his cheering supporters, whom he had committed to soldierly discipline and pitiless harshness towards the weak. Where the required endurance was still lacking, help would be given. 'While Hitler spent a good half-hour walking through our ranks, we had to keep our arms raised in the Nazi salute. That was very exhausting', recalls Hanne Beer-Page, who had made her pilgrimage to Nuremberg with a deputation of the *Bund Deutscher Mädel*. 'In each rank two *Hitlerjungen* made sure that we kept our arms raised. And every time a tired arm drooped somewhere, they flung it up again.'

While the new young Nazis – at once exhausted and elated by the exertions of the 'audience' with the Führer – made their way homeward the following day, the 'Reich Party Freedom Congress' endowed Hitler's murderous racial mania with the force of legally regulated injustice. With the promulgation of the *Reichs-bürgergesetz* (Reich Citizenship Law) and *Blutschutzgesetz* (Blood Protection Law) the Jews in Germany were deprived of their civil rights. Clauses which were an infringement of international law paved the way for the inhuman selection process, which ended in the gas-chambers of Auschwitz.

Yet the returning onlookers of Nuremberg had nothing to report to their parents about these grim measures. Back home they only enthused about the marching columns of Party soldiers, the waving sea of swastika banners in the decorated streets, and the rousing sounds of the ceremonial processions. Proudly they related the adventures on their journey, the romance of outdoor life and evenings around the camp-fire. To many, wearing the uniform of the HJ gave the feeling of being part of a great movement, which had placed upon them the responsibility for the future and destiny of the nation. It was considered an accolade to be allowed to take part in the annual pilgrimage to the spectacle of the massed brownshirts. 'It was an honour for us *Hitlerjungen* to attend the Reich Party Congress. The ones who were not allowed to go felt left out', recalls Klaus Mauelshagen.

> He was almost a saint really. We wouldn't hear a word against the Führer. And I can still remember completing my duties – it ended every time with a triple '*Sieg Heil*' to the Führer Adolf Hitler, whom we loved above everything. It was even the case, as was said at the time – that we loved him more than our own parents.
>
> *Karl-Heinz Janssen, born 1930*

Standing to attention for the Führer was a matter of honour for many of the almost four million children and adolescents who, since the beginning of 1935, had been marching with the Hitler Youth. This meant that fully half of all young Germans between the ages of ten and eighteen had been dragooned into the Hitler Youth. But this did not satisfy the ambitions of the Reich Youth Leader. He wanted to place the entire youth of Germany in the service of the Führer. In his New Year appeal Schirach solemnly proclaimed 1936 to be the 'Year of the German *Jungvolk*'. For the first time every boy born in a particular year was to be taken into the junior wing of the Hitler Youth. Under the slogan 'The whole of youth for the Führer,' a massive advertising campaign was rolled out. On radio and in the cinema, on posters, in schools and at sports events it wooed the youngest generation of 'compatriots'. Officially, as Schirach insisted, the propaganda was to spur the children into 'voluntary' entry to the Hitler Youth. In order to make good his claim to encompass all ten-year-olds, he enlisted the state and local government in his ruthless round-up. Communal registers – where available – provided him with the addresses of all boys and girls born in 1926. The parents were enjoined to enrol their children in the *Jungvolk* or *Jungmädel*. Even the Minister of Education, Bernhard Rust, who feared that Schirach's growing power over the youth would make inroads into his own department, gave his support to the Reich Youth Leader and arranged parents' evenings in the schools, at which teachers and local HJ leaders recruited the children into the organisation.

> The HJ is not something established by the state for its youth, but established by the youth for the state.
>                                            *Baldur von Schirach, 1934*

The teaching staff in primary and secondary schools were meant to persuade their pupils to join the *Jungvolk* with every means at their disposal. 'I was in my first year at high school, and one day the head was waiting for me at the entrance. He asked me why I wasn't in fact a member of the Hitler Youth', recounts Hans-Jochen Vogel, the former chairman of Germany's Social Democratic Party. 'I explained to him that we had moved and now lived quite a long way out of town. He said that wouldn't do, and as I was ten years old, I had to join. It created problems for the school as well, if someone didn't join. So I became a member. I can't remember anyone at our school who did *not* join the *Jungvolk* and then at the age of fourteen, the Hitler Youth. It was just a matter of course and no-one discussed it. There was virtually no alternative for young people.'

In order to ensure the greatest possible success for his enterprise, Schirach adapted his youth organisation to the regional structure of the Nazi Party. Up till then the girls and boys had been free to choose which unit they wanted to serve in. Now, however, the children were grouped in residential districts which corresponded as far as possible to the *Ortstruppen*, or local troops, of the Party. Approximately 150 boys aged between ten and fourteen made up a *Fähnlein* ('company'), and the same number of girls formed a group within the *Jungmädel*. The smallest unit, the *Kameradschaft*, comprised ten boys; and ten girls made up a *Jungmädelschaft*. It is true that links with the Party were still loose, but when necessary the HJ leader could count on the protection of the *Ortsgruppenleiter*, the local Nazi official – a man as influential as he was feared. With processions, leaflets, parents' evenings and community singing, the children already wearing the uniform of the Hitler Youth drummed up enthusiasm for local recruitment campaigns.

> But we were rather glad that we didn't have to join this compulsory uniformed organisation and that we weren't forced to march in any parades or processions.
>
> *Hanns-Peter Herz, German Jew, born 1927*

For four weeks the signing-up process continued at full tilt. On 19 April 1936 Schirach was able to report its completion to his Führer in a radio broadcast: 90 per cent of all ten-year-olds were under his command. For their enrolment into the *Jungvolk* he had, as every year, summoned hundreds of children to the castle of Marienburg in West Prussia. On the eve of Hitler's birthday the novices entered the Gothic halls of the ancient fortress of the Teutonic Knights to take their solemn vow. 'The entire youth of Germany is today a chivalric order, bound by an oath of fealty.' The Reich Youth Leader's words echoed around the gloomy vaults. Relayed by every radio station the sounds of this initiation rite boomed out from *Volksempfänger* in homes throughout the country. By the light of flaming torches the children gave voice in the hymn '*Wir geloben Hitler Treue bis ins Grab*' (We vow loyalty to Hitler to the very grave), and many of them were seized by the awesome yet uplifting feeling of belonging to a 'company of blood-brothers'. 'Many thousands of *Volksgenossen* (compatriots) from all sections of our population send the Führer their gifts on his birthday. But the young give themselves', Schirach declared enthusiastically.

> In those days the flag was quite simply the most important thing to any of us.
>
> *Werner Hanitzsch, born 1929*

On the following day, throughout the Reich, the newly recruited members took their oath: 'I promise in the Hitler Youth to do my duty at all times, in love and loyalty to our Führer and our flag. So help me God!' The invocation of God's help was later removed. 'Love and loyalty to the Führer' was thought to be sufficient salvation for the soul of Germany's youth. The last oath was sworn on 20 April 1945, by those born in 1935 – to a Führer who ten days later shot himself in the bunker of the Reich Chancellery beneath the ruins of Berlin. Many of the children who paid lip-service to Hitler by joining the *Deutsches Jungvolk* only recognised in retrospect how sorely they had been abused.

> As you stand before me today, so year by year in centuries to come will the young generation stand before future Führers. And again and again they will profess their faith in the Germany which we have fought to create today.
>
> *Adolf Hitler, 1937*

Tirelessly Schirach pursued his goal, to achieve sole command of the youth of Germany. Hitler rewarded his Pied Piper with ever greater authority. With the 'Law on the Hitler Youth' of 1 December 1936 he promoted Schirach to 'Educator of the Nation': 'Apart from in the parental home and at school, the entire German youth is to be brought up physically, spiritually and intellectually in the Hitler Youth, to serve the people and to be part of the ethnic community.' Initially this was no more than a declaration of intent, yet for Schirach it was an important stepping-stone towards his ambition to make the Hitler Youth into the 'state youth' of the Third Reich. The Reich Youth leadership became a 'Supreme Reich Authority'. As 'Youth Leader of the German Reich' Schirach moved up to the rank of secretary of state and henceforth was answerable to Hitler alone. From now on the Nazis' guardian of youth embodied the office of state and the Party function in one person. In future no young German would be able to escape from his power.

This meant that, alongside family and school, the Hitler Youth became the third officially recognised bearer of educational responsibility – an instrument of state power with which to imbue the adolescent generation with the spirit of National Socialism. 'The struggle to unite the youth of Germany is over', crowed Schirach. As the former *Hitlerjunge*, Paul Stüben, saw it: 'Parents gave up the right to educate their children when boys joined the Hitler Youth – that's to say the *Jungvolk*. That was the actual purpose of it. Because now boys could be made to do what the grown-ups were already doing: march through the streets.'

Before long the Hitler Youth was deciding how its members should spend almost every free moment of their lives. Schirach's total takeover of boys and girls was exactly what dictatorship required, a dictatorship which was to encompass 'not only the whole young population but also the entire personal life of every young German'. The introduction of a 'state youth day' allowed HJ members to skip school on Saturdays. They had to report for duty which, in the summer, could last up to twelve hours. Meanwhile the others were submitted to 'at least two hours of National Socialist indoctrination in class'. 'Twice a week we had HJ service', recalls the writer Erich Loest, 'and as I soon became a Leader, there were extra leadership duties on Mondays; and on Sundays we had shooting, or we went bicycling somewhere, or we had a parade. So for four or five days a week I was busy with the Hitler Youth. We had no time to think about what we were actually doing. The next thing was always coming up. It was non-stop action.'

> We heard about it from older pupils who were all very
> enthusiastic. And all of us desperately wanted to be ten years
> old as soon as possible, so we could join the *Jungvolk*.
>
> *Kurt Richter, born 1928*

Even outside duty hours the young did not remain unsupervised.
From 1935 onwards additional control was in the hands of the HJ
Patrol Service, a special force with quasi-police powers. The young
upholders of law and order patrolled public events and around
bars and cafés. They monitored the ban on smoking and alcohol
and checked the identity papers of any young people whose
behaviour attracted attention. Any anti-authoritarian attitudes or
criticism voiced against the regime were reported by the HJ
patrols to the police and the Gestapo.

It is true that membership of the Hitler Youth remained
voluntary until 1939, but very, very few children could stand up
to the all-pervasive pressure and the lure of belonging to the great
community. If in the Kaiser's day it was the army that was seen as
the 'school of the nation', now the Nazi state drilled into even the
smallest citizens a soldierly *esprit de corps* and zeal to serve, true to
the motto: 'You are nothing, the *Volk* is everything!' Many six-
year-olds at infant school looked up with envy and admiration to
the older ones who marched to their duties in uniform with their
sheath-knives, while they themselves had four long years to wait.
Baldur von Schirach saw the children as no more than a civilian
reserve: 'We use the word "children" to decribe those not in
uniform, who have never taken part in a sing-song or a parade.'

The children could often hardly wait to be accepted into
the great 'Movement'. The former *Hitlerjunge* Hans Jürgen
Habenicht speaks for many who feverishly awaited their enrolment
in the *Jungvolk*: 'I really longed for the day and was proud when it
finally arrived. My elder brother was already in the Hitler Youth. I
too wanted to belong one day to that organisation, which was
bound up with ideas like comradeship, Fatherland and honour. In
uniform you felt you were taken more seriously. Now I was one of
the big boys.'

'To wear the uniform was an honour', says Jobst-Christian von Cornberg. And Klaus Mauelshagen elaborates: 'Brown shorts, brown shirt, a black triangular kerchief held together by a brown leather toggle, leather shoulder-straps, and a leather belt with a buckle that had a runic symbol on it. Then we wore white knee-socks and brown shoes. To round it all off we had a brown forage-cap which we wore tilted over one ear. Very cocky; we were proud of that. The girls admired us.' Any boy who was finally allowed to don the coveted *Jungvolk* garb felt he was part of the nation's uniformed community – and ready for mighty deeds: '"*Bin ich erst mal gross und nicht mehr klein, werd' ich Soldat des Führers sein.*" (Once I'm big, and small no more, I'll be the Führer's soldier!). These were the words which captivated me at that time', recalls Albert Bastian. 'I realised that when my mother said: "But they're still only kids!" Then I thought to myself: "I'm certainly not a kid any more, I'll soon be a soldier!" '

In the increasingly monolithic and disciplined Nazi society the Hitler Youth appealed to children's self-esteem and urge for recognition. They saw themselves valued more highly through serving the people and the Fatherland. Hundreds of thousands of uniformed boys and girls swarmed the streets every year with collecting tins, asking for donations to the 'winter relief', the programme of aid for 'needy compatriots', which was driven by huge propaganda expenditure. The Hitler Youth continually organised the collection of second-hand clothes and other goods, and the most industrious of them received awards. 'I was needed! The feeling of being a necessary part of a whole, no longer having to stand by and watch – this feeling was new to me and it was like a drug', is how Renate Finhk describes the farewell to her 'civilian' childhood in Nazi Germany. 'So it was a good thing there was the youth service. There I counted for something. And in serving the Führer I also felt I was on equal terms with my parents.'

---

I knew of no other youth group that one could have joined – everyone was in the *Jungvolk* and the Hitler Youth and we just went along with it.

*Günther Sack, born 1920*

'Youth must be led by youth' – Schirach took up Hitler's slogan and elevated it to the dogma of his youth organisation. Even the company leaders in the *Jungvolk* were often only a few years older than the *Pimpfe*, as their diminutive troops were known. This gave the children an additional incentive to emulate the bigger boys. Those who were selected to lead a unit themselves, even if it was only a ten-strong *Jungenschaft* or *Mädelschaft*, were pleased with the trust that had been placed in them. They were filled with pride at the responsibility they carried. Admittedly, it was the adults who decided what models the youth of Germany should follow. To guide his young brigades along the course of National Socialism, Schirach put 12,727 HJ leaders and 24,660 *Jungvolk* leaders through 287 training courses – and that was just in eight months up to August of 1934, designated by the Reich youth leadership as the 'Year of Schooling'. In the years that followed, the youth leadership developed an elaborate system of leader schools. The instruction in them followed fixed guidelines and gradually the new professional image of the Nazi youth-leader was forged. Schirach demanded of the prospective HJ leaders that 'the youth-leader and educator of the future must become a priest of the National Socialist faith and an officer in the service of National Socialism'.

Sport was the first compulsory subject in the timetables of the Hitler Youth. In his book *Mein Kampf* Hitler had already declared 'physical conditioning' to be the highest precept of National Socialist youth culture: 'The national state must focus its entire educational effort not principally on the inculcation of mere knowledge, but on the rearing of thoroughly fit and healthy bodies. Only in second place comes the development of mental faculties and last of all academic schooling.' No sooner had Hitler sneaked into power than the HJ began to impose its influence on youth sport in Germany. From now on, for children under fourteen, physical activities were only available in the Hitler Youth. Young people could only join gymnastics and sports clubs if they were also members of the HJ. Sports supervisors and coaches were trained in specially created Reich sports schools. 'Praise be to that which toughens!' Hundreds of thousands of young people competed in countless sporting events for the HJ's performance awards. Unflaggingly they dashed from one local or regional sports meeting to the next, went on cross-country runs in the spring, and took part in winter sports and 'Führer-decathlons'. Faithful to Nazi racial ideology, which claimed that only the strongest would prevail in the 'struggle for existence', the HJ sports service forcibly imposed the 'selection of the fittest'. The climax of this display of 'Aryan' performance came with the 'Reich Sports Contest of the HJ', which was intended to serve as a powerful demonstration of Germany's 'strength and invincibility'. Hitler, who had never even learned to ride a bicycle himself, expected the physical steeling of his youth to bring about the 'rebirth of the nation, through the conscious breeding of a new kind of human being'. With slogans such as: 'Your body belongs to the nation' or 'You have a duty to be healthy', the HJ propagandised for the racially motivated 'Duty to be physically fit'.

As soon as they joined the *Jungvolk* the children had to face tough challenges. In the first months of their service the ten-year-olds prepared for their *Pimpfenprobe* or test for novices. Generally the children had to get through a triathlon: a 60-metre sprint in 12 seconds, a long-jump of 2.75 metres, and a baseball throw of 25 metres. Frequently, however, the *Jungvolk* leaders also demanded 'tests of courage'. Klaus Bölling, today a Social-Democrat politician and journalist, recalls: 'At the Reich Sports Field in Berlin we had to go to the swimming-pool. There each of us had to jump into the water from a five-metre high tower – quite a height. That needed a great effort of will.' Alongside all this, the youngest boys had to learn the words of the 'Horst Wessel Song' by heart during their 'social evenings', and familiarise themselves with the career of Adolf Hitler, carefully purged of its seamier details. Together they intoned the 'sword-words' of the *Jungvolk*: '*Jungvolk* boys are tough, discreet and loyal. *Jungvolk* boys are comrades. For a *Jungvolk* boy honour is supreme.' Having passed their *Pimpfenprobe* the new intake were given their coveted sheath-knife with the inscription '*Meine Ehre heisst Treue*' ('Loyalty is my Honour'). Only then were they fully fledged members of the *Deutsches Jungvolk*.

It is never too soon to bring up the youth of Germany to feel themselves to be, above all else, German.

*Adolf Hitler, 1932*

Together with physical exercises, military-style drill dominated the daily routine. At every parade the adolescent *Jungvolk* leaders made their *Pimpfe* form ranks and columns. With hours of drill, roll-calls and parade-ground marching, the children were to be imbued with soldierly discipline. Any slackers were soon made to suffer for it: 'I was put on punishment drill', remembers former *Jungvolk* boy Rudolf Hiemke. 'It was like being in the army. On the ground – down! On the feet – up! Quick march, quick march! For fifteen solid minutes, so as to drum some sense into me.' The future of the nation: a generation marching in step. At weekend and holiday camps the boys played war-games against each other, set off with map and compass through unknown territory, practised giving reports, identifying targets and judging distances. A military regime was imposed in the camps from reveille to lights-out. This preparation for army service reached its peak when the fourteen- to eighteen-year-old *Hitlerjungen* were taught to handle small-calibre firearms. By 1938 1.25 million youths in the Reich had completed their HJ weapons training. Of those, 20,000 acted as *Schiesswarte* (shooting supervisors). The best were awarded badges as marksmen and master-riflemen. 'As the years progress', declared Schirach's military training officer Helmut Stellrecht, 'we want to reach a point where German boys hold a gun with as much assurance as a fountain-pen. The liberals wrote above the school door: "Knowledge is Power". But we learned during and after the war that the power of the people ultimately rests in its weapons alone, and with those who know how to use them.'

'In place of young people who were previously brought up to enjoy themselves, a generation is now coming of age, brought up to privation, self-sacrifice and above all to the development of a healthy, resilient physique. For we believe, quite simply, that without such a physique, in the long run the nation will not be in possession of a healthy mind either', Hitler declared to his youth at the 1937 NSDAP Party Congress. He went on: 'The wonderful thing is that in you the first link in the chain of national education is completed. It begins with you and not until the last German descends into the grave, will it end!' Previously, in 1936, the dictator had noted with satisfaction: 'A magnificent new physical type has come into being. No longer is the corpulent beer-lout the exemplar of our age, but the lean, lithe youth, who stands firmly on this earth with legs astride, healthy in body and healthy in soul.'

> National Socialism is shaping an ethnic community which begins with the child and ends with the greybeard. No-one can silence this tremendous symphony of German life.
>
> *Adolf Hitler, 1932*

In fact, of course, the Hitler Youth poisoned the soul of an entire generation with the notions of an irrational ideology. Systematically and comprehensively the leadership of the HJ subjected its under-age ranks to brainwashing, intended to shape the youngsters into 'right-thinking' Nazis. No weekly parade, no camp, no expedition took place without 'attitude training', without the incantatory indoctrination of an ideology which defied all common sense. The age-related curriculum drawn up by the Reich Youth Leadership held closely to the precepts of Adolf Hitler, who had elevated the bedazzling of the young to an official programme: 'The whole work of education and training in a national state must find its culmination in burning into the hearts and minds of the youth in its charge, a sense and feeling of race that is both instinctive and rational.'

When the boys assembled for their duties each Wednesday, or foregathered in specially built HJ hostels for weekly 'fireside evenings', they revelled in epic tales of Germanic heroes. Through the narrow Party perspective on German history they came to know Arminius, king of the Cherusci, Frederick the Great and Bismarck, but only as historical ancestors, who prefigured the Führer and prepared the way for him. They listened enthralled to readings from battlefield literature, those heroically uplifting accounts of sacrifice and courage in the face of death amid the carnage of the First World War. These were drawn from the works of Ernst Jünger, Werner Beumelberg, Franz Schauwecker or Friedrich Hielscher, whose books had sold in huge numbers in the

1920s. The young disciples heard the myth of 'Stab in the back of the front-line army, undefeated in the field', the torrents of hate against 'the arsonists of international Jewry', the message about 'preserving the purity of German blood', and the call for 'living-space in the East'.

These *Heimabende* or hostel evenings were a compulsory element in the timetable of the Hitler Youth. Anyone who was absent had to produce a written explanation from their parents. If the evenings were repeatedly skipped, the parents could expect a visit from the HJ leader who made it very clear to them that they were responsible for their children's attendance. As a rule, this degree of pressure was enough to make the offenders see the error of their ways. Whether, on the other hand, the 'ideological training' produced the results desired by the regime and educated the boys to be convinced Nazis, is open to doubt. To many *Hitlerjungen* the *Heimabende* were just tiresome extra classes which they attended with only half an ear open. Boredom was widespread. 'We considered the *Heimabende* a necessary evil', recounts Jobst-Christian von Cornberg. 'The *Jungvolk* leaders, who ran these evenings, were hardly any older than the boys they led. So a fourteen- or fifteen-year-old was not really in any position to present a subject as well as a history teacher at school. These schooling sessions suffered from that, of course. On the one hand, the principle that "Youth must be led by youth" applied, but when it came to dealing with ideological topics, things got very difficult. Then, when people came along who had only been through elementary school, the rest of us nudged each other and giggled, and asked one another: how much more of this do we have to listen to? Of course, the Reich Youth leadership recognised this problem and started handing out training briefs every fortnight, in which the *Heimabend* was planned minutely, with introduction, songs and texts on a given subject. Later these training booklets arrived every week, so that the leaders could use them as models. That way, they couldn't go far wrong; if the worst came to the worst, they just read it aloud word for word.'

These occasions proved to be trials of patience for the listeners, though they were allowed to intersperse the ideological lectures with songs and poems: 'The world belongs to those who lead;

those who follow the sun. And we are the marchers; none can halt us. The old world totters, the crumbling walls fall down. We are the young stormers, we are victory! Leap up, march, march! Raise the banner atop the tower!' Critical discussion of the subjects on the agenda was not called for in the Führer-state. 'The pattern of the *Heimabend* was strictly laid down, all creativity was suppressed. There was no debate, everything was dictated and organised on military lines. We had absolutely no opportunity to express ourselves freely and dared not offer any criticism', says Rudolf Hiemke.

> It is not hard to imagine how this boy's breast swelled: one day he will be a leader. It's thrilling, it's a wonderful dream – hence the total disillusion later, when it all lay in ruins.
> *Sal Perel, born 1925 (author of* Hitlerjunge Salomon*)*

Yet Hitler's Party youth organisation had far more to offer than parade-ground drill and wearisome political lectures. Baldur von Schirach, the Pied Piper, knew the needs of the youngest 'compatriots' who sought, in the company of those of their own age, independence from the parental home and the adult world. He enticed with sounds which were music to the ears of many children. The Hitler Youth channelled the urge for action in the young and opened up to boys and girls the kind of leisure pursuits which had hitherto only been available to the offspring of well-to-do families. Tours all over Germany, hiking, cycling and camping – all held the promise of excitement and adventure. 'Usually the children didn't have much to do in the holidays', explains former *Hitlerjunge* Karl-Albert Schlüter. 'If they were very lucky, they might have a Granny with a farm in Mecklenburg, where they could go. But that was about it. Then suddenly the kids could go on holiday for two or three weeks, and they were off like a shot. Travelling was something they had never known.'

The best thing on offer each year with the Hitler Youth was the summer camp. Hiking through the countryside with people of one's own age made an attractive change from the monotony of home life: 'For us what mattered was being in a boys' community. The group experience, the expeditions, the exertion', says Wilfried Glatten. 'We really had to swelter and freeze, we had to get soaked in our tents. We might curse about it, and it might bring out our nastier side, but we always came back to the communal group; that was very important.' The romance of the camp-fire made the children's hearts beat faster: 'In the evening we all sat around the fire. And then we sang together. It was dark. The stars shone above us. It was a thrilling feeling that one never forgets,' says former *Pimpf*, Peter Löhrer.

On ceremonial occasions, when we sang solemn hymns, we felt we were bound together as a community. At that moment one could have died for the Fatherland.

*Lothar Scholz, born 1928*

The children sang songs together in choirs, learned to play instruments and marched in musical processions. Those with theatrical talents joined drama groups and put on plays. The 'performance education' of the HJ used numerous badges and awards to raise the motivation of the children who put their abilities to the test in 'Reich Music Days' or 'Reich Theatre Days', as well as in sports and skill contests.

Among the older boys, who moved up from the *Jungvolk* to the HJ at the age of fourteen, the HJ 'special units' were particularly popular. In the 'Reconnaissance HJ', the 'Motorised HJ' and the air-force and naval HJ, the youths were made familiar with the different branches of the Wehrmacht and prepared themselves for future duties in the army and the *Waffen-SS*. 'How many boys would normally have the chance to learn gliding, as they did in the *Flieger-HJ*?' wonders the writer Walter Kempowski. 'In the *Motor-HJ* kids were suddenly allowed to ride motor-bikes; and in the *Marine-HJ* they could run around in those smart uniforms and crew on sail-training ships. What a break for kids who hardly got a square meal at home. It was a very attractive proposition for many of them.'

By keeping them constantly occupied and challenging their thirst for action, the Hitler Youth aimed to develop the young into Nazi conformists: the regime wanted active, physically fit, skilled, competent and disciplined boys, who adapted to the dictatorial system without questioning it. The model member of the Hitler Youth had to be deliberately differentiated from the 'romantic', 'awkwardly intellectual', or even 'socialist revolutionary' type, which was how the HJ characterised the young people of the detested Weimar republic. The purpose of educating the young as activists who uncritically accepted Nazi ideology was to increase the nation's preparedness for war, as a leading HJ propagandist made clear: 'A youth that has been brought up to be activists cannot help but go into the war with the insatiable desire to have as many duties as possible placed upon them.'

In selecting its methods of seduction, Hitler's youth organisation harked back to the tradional features of pre-1933 youth movements: uniforms and national costumes, flags and banners, expeditions and hiking – these were the stock-in-trade of countless groups and associations, which millions of young people joined in the Weimar years, before they were banned and then dissolved under National Socialist rule.

> They wear the same brown shirt. No-one asks about their background. And they all look as if they have come from the same mould. There are working-class children, middle-class children, children of employers and employees, of farmers and so on. But to look at, they are all identical.
>
> *Adolf Hitler, 1937*

The self-confidence of youth had increasingly been stirring since the beginning of the twentieth century. Patriotism notwithstanding, the younger generation did not always feel at home with the narrow, petty-bourgeois authoritarianism of the Kaiser's Germany. Under the Wilhelmine empire, the Establishment was firmly in the saddle. An anachronistic order prevailed through the parental home, school, church and state bureaucracy, while at the same time headlong industrialisation was bringing about profound changes in society. From the upper middle class to the small businessman, a wide swathe of the population benefited from the feverish atmosphere of economic boom, and even the new class of factory workers had far less to complain about, under Wilhelm II, the *Industriekaiser*, than did their counterparts in Britain or America, for example.

Yet it was chiefly among the well-off children of Wilhelm II's economic miracle that critical voices were raised against the ossified authoritarianism and bureaucracy of a state in which their parents had done very nicely. Middle-class youth broke out of the strait-jacket of their parents' narrow, rule-bound world. In their search for a separate identity, the young directed their protests at the growing materialism and unwavering faith in the limitless progress of science and technology. It was precisely the epoch-making processes of modernisation that plunged many young people into deep insecurity. On the assembly lines of the Machine Age they saw the destruction of individual liberty in progress. A vast number of critical writings warned against the human consequences of the anonymous 'mass society', which in the view of many was actually heralding the 'the end of western civilisation'. Young Germans developed their own philosophy of life, directly opposed to industrial rationalism and the ornate façade of Wilhelmine culture. Instead of meeting the challenges of their era, quite a number of young people took refuge in a romantically imagined past.

Many others saw the military, of all things, as an alternative to the dehumanising of the individual in the mechanism of modern industry. In the army, with its clearly defined hierarchy and compulsory code of behaviour imposed through command, obedience and discipline, they saw a secure community, which stood in stark contrast to the 'anarchy' of industrial society and the free market economy. Others again wallowed in ideals of a nation which, according to preference, would arise as a 'Third *Reich*', or empire, a socialist republic, the 'kingdom of God' or simply as the 'realm of the young'. In taking their stand against the rigid educational methods of the Kaiser's empire, some young people found their position confirmed in the writings of Julius

Langbehn, who emphasised the role of race by claiming that a person was determined by his blood, and that innate qualities were more important than acquired ones. The scholar Paul de La Garde longed for an 'organic substance' to fill what he saw as the hollow shell of the new Fatherland. He expressed young Germany's deep sense of mission when he wrote: 'If only there were conspirators among us, a secretly accessible fellowship, which would plan and bring about the great Tomorrow, and to which, even though the great mass would not understand it, everyone could belong – all those whose unexpressed longings it would give voice to. We are weary of being fobbed off with the ready-made, with the legacy of others: we want what is the new-born, something we can grow up with, on terms of Thee and Thou. But the spirit has not yet come riding over heath and hill.'

However, this youth movement still lacked the inspiring leadership that would have been able to unite its diffuse aims and visions into a single force. Yet ever more young people began to express their desire for autonomy in an independent lifestyle. In the closing years of the nineteenth century a small band of schoolboys and students foregathered at a high school in the Berlin suburb of Steglitz and went on occasional hiking expeditions into the surrounding countryside. On free weekends they turned their backs on the hectic bustle of the metropolis in order to enjoy the 'beauty of nature' together. During the holidays they went on longer expeditions on foot through the Harz mountains or along the Rhine. In shorts and dark shirts, with hob-nailed boots and knapsacks on their backs they carried on the tradition of the itinerants and tramps, revived forgotten customs and sang folk-songs to the accompaniment of guitar or harmonica. Using public transport was frowned upon; 'Shanks's pony' was the normal means of travel. These weekend vagabonds went out in all weathers, and preferred to sleep in haystacks than freshly made beds. Instead of clicking their heels and bowing, they greeted one another by raising their right arm and shouting '*Heil!*' (The word is normally translated as 'Hail!', as in 'Hail, Caesar!', but it has a range of meanings such as 'benefit', and 'salvation', and as an adjective, 'safe', 'unharmed'. Cf. English 'hale'. *Tr*). Within a few years the example of the lads in Berlin, who called themselves

*Wandervögel* (birds of passage), had captivated tens of thousands of youngsters. It grew into a mass cult which had imitators throughout Europe.

> What can befall a people whose youth gives up everything to serve its great ideals!
>
> *Adolf Hitler, 1932*

With the advent of the new century the long-hoped-for Age of Youth seemed to have arrived. Beside the *Wandervögel* movement, very soon the *Bündische Jugend* (Youth Alliance) made its appearance. Everywhere youth groups formed, each aggressively supporting their cause. Their demands ranged from a ban on nicotine and alcohol to freedom for nudism. But apart from open opposition to existing values and institutions, most young people kept out of day-to-day politics. In their contempt for parties and the parliamentary system, the majority of the youth movement showed themselves to be in tune with the prevailing atittude of the lower middle class, who regarded politics as a dirty business, and nothing more. The young rebels knew what they did not want, but were not clear what direction to take. The Children's Revolution was heading into emotional vagueness.

The youth movement reached its apogee in Leipzig in 1913, at the centenary of the Battle of the Nations. While imperial Germany prepared with patriotic pomp for the celebration of the historic victory over Napoleon and the unveiling of a monstrous memorial, the young saw their opportunity to demonstrate their own national unity. In October 1913 some 2,000 members of youth groups assembled for a festival on a hill named Hoher Meissner, south of Kassel, on which according to ancient legend 'Frau Holle' made her home. (There is an old German saying that when it snows, Frau Holle is plucking her geese. *Tr.*) In a joint resolution the participants announced their claim to self-determination and signalled for the first time that organised youth, at least, was emotionally united and that social and confessional differences were no longer to remain unbridgeable: 'The free youth of Germany intends to shape its own life on its own terms, on its own responsibility and with inner honesty. Under all circumstances it will stand up for this freedom with united ranks.'

Only a few months after the Hoher Meissner declaration the youth of Germany was marching enthusiastically into the First World War. Millions of young men volunteered for the armed services in August 1914 and exchanged their hiking gear for soldiers' tunics. Amid the cheers of the population, thrown into a frenzy of nationalistic euphoria by the outbreak of war, they headed for the battlefields of Europe. The young imagined they had reached the object of their dreams. For them the hour had struck, when their ideals would be brought to fruition and the old wielders of power would be swept away. In the field-grey army of millions, young Germany glimpsed their longed-for 'community of destiny'. Here the old barriers of class and status seemed to have been removed, and the social conflicts of the past reduced to petty squabbling. Out of the baptism of fire in war young idealists hoped for the birth of a new breed of man, who would found a true nation based on a great 'ethnic community'.

Later, the Hitler Youth taught those born after the war the myth of the self-sacrifice and courage of the young regiments who, west of Langemarck in November 1914, charged towards the enemy lines singing '*Deutschland, Deutschland über alles*'. Yet the staccato bursts of machine-gun fire and the thunder of artillery exposed the dreams of youth as a fatal illusion. Death had raged too brutally, the slaughter had cost too many lives for the war to offer any sense of a better future. Instead, the war produced its own 'society'. Those who survived it now formed the 'aristocracy of the trenches' – a sworn brotherhood, who felt bound to each other in life and death. Thus the artificial hierarchy of the garrison and the barrack-square gave way to a natural ranking, in which the class differences between officers and men, former students and former workers, became blurred.

The loss of the war left the young men of the front line generation in a state of intellectual rootlessness. Many of them looked in vain for a way back into civilian life, with which they had long since lost contact. Weighed down by the bitter defeat, their comfortable pre-war existence swept away in the 'storm of steel' that had destroyed national resources, they plunged into the chaos of revolution and civil war which shook the young Weimar Republic to its foundations. The writer and veteran of the trenches, Ernst von Salomon, wrote: 'The war drove them, the war dominated them, the war will never let them go. Never will they be able to return home, never quite belong to us; they will always carry the Front in their blood, the closeness of death, the preparedness, the horror, the thrill, the iron. What was happening now, this invasion, this adaptation to the peaceful, ordered, comfortable world, was a transplantation, a pretence that could never succeed. The war is over, but the warriors are still on the march.'

In their militant, nationalistic-cum-revolutionary stance, numerous young men returning from the war rejected the Kaiser's empire that had just collapsed as much as they did the Weimar democracy, which they nevertheless exploited. In the postwar confusion of the still insecure republic many of them joined forces in *Freikorps* units, with whose help the Supreme Army Command crushed the Red revolution and fought bloody frontier battles against the Poles in Upper Silesia. The one-time front line soldiers became professional revolutionaries. They marched with the illegal 'Black Reichswehr', or wore the brown shirts of *Oberleutnant* Gerhard Rossbach's *Freikorps*, strengthened the 'Special Police' of *Fähnrich* (Ensign) Heinz Oskar Hauenstein or served in *Hauptmann* Hermann Ehrhardt's 'Marine Brigade' under the very swastika that would soon become the symbol of a *coup d'état*. Everywhere young men were joining paramilitary organisations and terrorist groups, blowing up bridges in the French-occupied Rhineland or carrying out assassinations, like that of the Foreign Minister, Walter Rathenau. 'Later I thought a lot about those in my age-group. What sort of men were they really?' the novelist Gerd Gaiser wondered. 'Well, some were born with a silver spoon in their mouth and had airy-fairy ideas. Very dangerous. Others knew where a crate of hand-grenades was buried, or an aircraft engine. Almost as dangerous. The most dangerous was a combination of the two.'

The hideous experience of the First World War was etched in the faces of the young war veterans and changed the German youth movement permanently. New alliances merged into larger communities, groups modelled on chivalric orders organised military-style camps and war-games in the countryside. Wherever the youthful survivors of the war returned to their professions, to universities, to trade unions, or into church or political organisations, they imposed their mindset on the new society. As 'Young Conservatives', Young Democrats', 'Young Protestants' or 'Young Socialists' they made their opinions heard in almost every sphere of the Weimar republic. The political spectrum of the youth movement ranged from the semi-communist 'Free Proletarian Youth' through the 'Socialist Workers Youth', the 'New Pathfinders' and the 'Alliance of Youth' to the right-wing 'Young Nationalists' and the youth formations of the paramilitary 'defence' forces and *Freikorps*. The ideological directions and interests of the young generation were too diverse to make it possible for the Weimar republic and its leaders to involve the young in the building of the new state. One observer soberly summed up the lowest common denominator, down to which young postwar Germany could be brought: 'In an age when democracy was sweeping the whole world, when the masses were intent on governing, the notion of loyally following a Führer once more came to life in the youth movement.'

The thirty-year-old painter of postcard views, who in September 1919 joined one of the countless tiny nationalist parties in Munich, cared little about the provenance of the hazy ideas about a 'Third Reich' or a 'National Socialism', which were floating about in many heads at the time. With more adroitness than anyone else around, the power-hungry regimental runner from the First World War juggled with fashionable concepts, swore to avenge the 'dictated peace of Versailles' and promised satisfaction for the punch-drunk nation. In July 1921 Adolf Hitler took over the leadership of the party which now called itself the NSDAP (National Socialist German Workers' Party). Thanks to the rhetorical gifts of its demagogue, the party saw members come flooding in. Its *Sturmabteilung* (Assault Division) known as the SA, brought together many militant desperadoes of the war generation who threatened public safety with their brutal assaults on political opponents. The eighteen-year-old Adolf Lenk was one of those moved to join the NSDAP after hearing some of the speeches made by its 'Führer'. At first this young piano-maker was refused entry because he had not reached the required minimum age of twenty-one. But Lenk was undeterred and asked if the party had a youth section. Since, up to that time, there had not been such a thing, he himself was given the task of setting one up. In February 1922 Hitler decreed: 'The organisation of the Youth Section will take place under the auspices of the *Sturmabteilung*.'

In spite of his organisational talent Hitler's first youth supervisor at first found it difficult to win young people over to the cause. It is true that there was a good attendance at the meeting in Munich's Bürgerbräu beer-cellar, which had been called by Hitler, Lenk and the then head of the SA, Johann Ulrich Klintz, on 13 May 1922, to announce the founding of the *Jugendbund* (Youth League) of the NSDAP. However, the mere 17 youngsters who turned up were lost in the crowd. Nevertheless, in the course of the year the number of members rose to about 250. As well as in Munich, local groups were established in Nuremberg, Dresden, Hanau and Zeitz. Lenk was encouraged to start building up a national network of the *Jugendbund* and by October 1923 there were already 23 provincial associations with 120 local groups. Lenk divided the *NS-Jugendbund* into two groups: the first was for boys aged fourteen to sixteen, and the second was made up of sixteen- to eighteen-year-olds and bore the name *Jungsturm Adolf Hitler*.

Wearing the brown shirts of the SA the youths paraded at the first Party Congress of the NSDAP on 23 January 1923 in the Marsfeld park outside Munich. During the dedication of the SA colours Hitler solemnly presented the *Jungsturm* with their own banner – a blue anchor on a white background. Their joy at receiving their own insignia from the Führer in person was admittedly shortlived, for on 15 July that year a demonstration at the German Gymnastics Festival ended in a street battle in which the police confiscated the banner of the *Jungsturm Adolf Hitler*.

Hitler's unsuccessful attempted putsch of November 1923 finally sealed the fate of the *Jungsturm Adolf Hitler* as well. The ban on the NSDAP and its subsidiary organisations forced the National Socialist youth movement underground. While Hitler, convicted of treason, tried his hand as a writer in his cell in

Landsberg Castle, and dictated his *Mein Kampf* to his amanuensis, Rudolf Hess, the nationalist camp was splitting up. In defiance of Hitler's veto, the Party *Gauleiter* in Lower Bavaria, Gregor Strasser, together with Ernst Röhm, who later became head of the SA, founded the 'National Socialist Freedom Movement'. In the national Reichstag elections in May 1924 the new splinter party managed to win thirty-two seats. Meanwhile, the *Grossdeutsche Volksgemeinschaft* (Greater German National Community) was formed by Julius Streicher, founder of the anti-Semitic smear-sheet *Der Sturmer* and chief editor of the Nazi Party newspaper *Völkischer Beobachter* (National Observer), along with the racial theorist Alfred Rosenberg and several others. In the spring of 1924 they set up the 'Greater German Youth Movement', of which Adolf Lenk soon became the leader. The youth wing of the Party broke up and dispersed in groups which continued their activities independently under various cover-names. Hitler's fellow-conspirator, Gerhard Rossbach, who had fled to Salzburg after the failed coup, established, in his Austrian exile, the *Schilljugend*, named after Ferdinand von Schill, leader of one of the uprisings against Napoleon more than a century earlier. Ernst Röhm added a *Frontjugend* to his paramilitary *Frontbann* organisation. Other groups combined to form the *Deutschvölkischer Jugendbund York von Wartenburg* and the *Schlageter-Jugend*, named after the SA member Albert Leo Schlageter. An early martyr of the brownshirt movement, Schlageter was leader of a sabotage group in the Ruhr and was condemned to death and executed by the French occupation authorities in May 1923.

Meanwhile a law student named Kurt Paul Gruber from the Vogtland district of Saxony emerged as a skilful promoter of the brownshirt movement among the young. He himself was one of the rootless young postwar generation seeking a new purpose in life and finding it in National Socialism. As a youth he had signed up with a *Freikorps* but was too late to see any action. In the autumn of 1922, at the age of eighteen, he founded a local group of the NSDAP's *Jugendbund* in his home town of Plauen. The tiny band initially comprised just six boys aged fifteen and sixteen, but thanks to Gruber's organisational skill it was the seed of what later became the Hitler Youth. Disguised as the *Wandersportverein*

*Vogtland* (Vogtland Ramblers Club), the group survived the period of the ban on the Nazi Party, a ban which merely fired its leader's ambition and the youthful zeal of his little troop of supporters, spurring them on to conspiratorial activity. Gruber gained the favour of the Saxon textile manufacturer and later *Gauleiter*, Martin Mutschmann, with whose financial assistance he made his youth work a full-time occupation. Gruber rented offices in Plauen and built up his own administration, made contact with other nationalist groups and advertised for new members. His boys, who took the oath of loyalty to Adolf Hitler and followed the 'Führer-principle', wore swastika armbands on their brown shirts to distinguish themselves from the SA. The young Saxon was successful: in spring 1924 Adolf Lenk appointed him leader of Saxony's provincial association of the 'Greater German Youth Movement'. In July Kurt Gruber held his own first national meeting near Plauen.

> The uniform was first and foremost a symbol of belonging. And for us that was actually the most important thing. We were a community. We were a blood brotherhood and the uniform was the external symbol of this, as well as a kind of protection.
>
> *Werner Hanitzsch, born 1929*

Within a few months Gruber had gathered a following of some 2,500 youths in Saxony alone, an achievement which Hitler himself was not slow to recognise. Following his early release from Landsberg – where he had only served nine months of his five-year sentence – Hitler uttered these resounding words early in 1925: 'The dispute is now at an end. Come back now to the ranks of the old movement and leave behind you everything that belongs to yesterday.' Obediently the champions of the extreme right fell into line behind their 'Führer'. Adolf Lenk, on the other hand, fell by the wayside. Despite the re-establishing of the NSDAP he still doubted Hitler's power to hold the movement together. On his own account he founded the independent *Deutsche Wehrjugend*

(German Youth Defence). This meant the end for the brownshirt youth leader. Lenk was accused of treachery and thrown out of the party on the grounds of embezzlement and incompetence.

As Lenk's successor Hitler nominated the former army *Leutnant*, Edmund Heines. When a member of the Rossbach *Freikorps*, he had been one of the leaders of its *Schilljugend*. However Heines' new appointment caused annoyance within the Party and the National Socialist youth groups, since the *Schilljugend* was considered an elitist association made up chiefly of middle-class high-school boys. Kurt Gruber was among those who voiced their concern to Hitler. Since Gruber drew most of his membership from working-class boys in the industrial areas of Saxony and Thuringia, he expressed the fear that by linking the *Grossdeutsche Jugendbewegung* with the *Schilljugend* the recruitment base of young National Socialists would inevitably be limited to the affluent middle class. This argument was exactly the right one to use with Hitler, whose unfailing instinct for power was focused on gaining approval from the mass of the population.

> In the Hitler Youth, there may have been exceptions, but as a rule it made no difference where you came from and what your father did.
>
> *Hans-Jochen Vogel, born 1926*

In October 1925 Hitler appointed the 21-year-old Kurt Gruber as National Socialist Youth Leader in Saxony. For some time already Gruber had been enlarging his sphere of activity and was working to establish new provincial associations in Franconia, the Rhineland and the Palatinate. Admittedly, the party leadership in Munich eyed the young man's vigorous activity with some mistrust, especially as Gruber's financial support from private patrons made him largely independent. But Hitler – fully occupied with rebuilding the Party and consolidating his own leadership – could well use a man like Gruber. Ideologically the young Saxon was dependable; he, for his part, regarded Hitler as a genuine social revolutionary and obeyed his orders with alacrity. Gruber believed Hitler's notorious anti-Semitism was an unattractive but temporary symptom of the times. His keenness to serve the cause paid dividends. In order for Hitler to bring his re-formed NSDAP into line and demonstrate the unity of the movement, he called a Party Congress. On 3 and 4 July 1926 Party delegations assembled in Weimar. Thuringia, in which the city lay, was one of the few German provinces in which Hitler was permitted to speak in public. Among the youth of Thuringia, too, Gruber eagerly sought new members – to the displeasure of local National Socialists, who considered his political tendencies too left wing. They were not alone in this view, yet Hitler swept their objections aside and in his keynote speech stressed the objective of winning over the youth of Germany to the Party. At the suggestion of Julius Streicher, now Party Gauleiter of Franconia, the 'The Greater German Youth Movement' was given the name of its godfather: *Hitlerjugend – Bund Deutscher Arbeiterjugend* (Hitler Youth – Alliance of Young German Workers). Kurt Gruber was promoted to be its first *Reichsführer* or national leader and was simultaneously appointed adviser on youth affairs to the Party leadership in Munich.

> Pretty much the whole business – the kit, the excursions, the war-games, the singing – was all taken over and copied from other youth organisations.
>
> *Heinrich Fischer, born 1925*

However, the newly selected *HJ-Reichsführer* certainly did not intend to give up his position in Saxony for an office desk in the 'Capital of the Movement'. Gruber kept his distance from the 'Brown House' in Munich and built up the national headquarters of the Hitler Youth in his home town of Plauen. Soon the administration consisted of fourteen departments, dealing with, among other things, education and training, welfare, health and propaganda. Gruber published his own newspaper and ran a distribution service for 'approved' films, which were hired out to HJ groups for educational purposes. Extreme nationalist youth associations, which hitherto Gruber had courted in vain, now came to join his banner. But even in his Plauen stronghold he could not escape the increasing centralisation of the Party. The independent youth leader became a party functionary and the Hitler Youth was caught up in the machinery of the NSDAP. On 1 November 1926, when Hitler appointed *Hauptmann* Franz Felix Pfeffer von Salomon to supreme command of the SA, the former *Freikorps* leader insisted that the HJ also be placed under his jurisdiction. Hitler was happy to comply with this, as long as it meant he would have a tighter grip on his Saxon youth supervisor.

> Looking back objectively, it wasn't a patch on the Boy Scouts, in my view. In the HJ there was drill, marching, throwing grenades and so forth. But that experience of nature which the Scouts gave us, and also the comradeship – the friendships between us boys – there was nothing like that in the HJ.
>
> *Wolfgang Wüstefeld, born 1923*

Barely a month later Pfeffer von Salomon attended the first meeting of HJ leaders, which Gruber had called in Weimar. With his friendly, paternal manner the SA chief quickly succeeded in dispelling the HJ leader's initial misgivings. The two men reached agreement on common guidelines for the relationship between the HJ and the NSDAP. Members of the Hitler Youth who had reached the age of eighteen now had to join the Party. Failure to do so meant exclusion from the HJ. The Hitler Youth had to obtain the approval of the Party for all its public events. The Party also had to confirm all senior appointments in the HJ. The NSDAP thus gained control over its youth organisation, which from now on had to comply with any order from a senior Party official. Placed in such a dependent position, the Hitler Youth now differed fundamentally from other youth associations in the Weimar republic and in this respect was far more comparable with the youth wing of the German Communist Party.

However, many Party members and most of the senior SA people continued to disparage the Hitler Youth as a bunch of kids. Yet although there was often friction between the HJ and the SA,

Gruber and Pfeffer von Salomon themselves developed a cordial relationship, which was to be the basis of their collaboration over the next four years. Their first major joint demonstration attended by all the wings of the Party was a meeting of the Hitler Youth, which Gruber called at Plauen on 1 May 1927, together with members of the SA and SS. In August of that year 300 *Hitlerjungen* took part for the first time in a march-past at the first Nuremberg Party Congress. The appreciation of their 'selfless patriotism', which Hitler declared to his youthful guardsmen, was something which Gruber, as the IIJ's *Reichsführer*, could take very much as a personal compliment.

The greatest obstacle to the growth of the National Socialist youth movement, which Gruber encountered, was the lack of experienced leaders, since at the age of eighteen the *Jungen* had to join the SA. In this respect too, Pfeffer von Salomon proved open to negotiation: in October he conceded that boys who were needed as leaders in the Hitler Youth no longer had to transfer to the SA. Freed from the troublesome depletion of his ranks, the way now seemed open for Gruber to build up a self-supporting existence for young people in the NSDAP. 'At this point the sterile task of organising came to an end and the ideals began to operate', Gruber later recalled. 'Young people worked hard and succeeded in giving the Hitler Youth a face of its own. Very soon the results of this tireless and dogged labour produced signs of an independent life within the Hitler Youth. The endless marching along with the SA and the Party finally ceased. The lads began to go hiking, to hold their own social evenings – in the way they wanted to.'

Above all the HJ served as a highly effective propaganda force behind the rise of their *Übervater*, Hitler. Young activists even continued to march through the streets with the SA and SS, and swarmed out with handbills advertising public meetings and electoral events, at which they sometimes supplemented the marshals enforcing order in the hall. Admittedly, things were not going particularly well for Hitler's party. The 'brown' movement had started to falter, and by 1928 it seemed that the German people had finally made their peace with the unloved republic. It is true that Party membership had crept above 100,000 that year, but at the general election in May the NSDAP only secured twelve seats in the Reichstag. What is more, Kurt Gruber and his few thousand supporters were plagued by constant money problems. The monthly subscription of just 4 pfennig per member was no more adequate than the cash injections from the still scarce Party funds. A lucrative source of income was nonetheless found in entry charges for meetings and the official collections which accompanied the HJ's propaganda processions. In the climate of growing violence between extremists of the left and right, who were engaged in a bloody struggle for supremacy on the streets, such appearances by Hitler's junior cadre was certainly getting riskier.

> I often used to come home with two black eyes. The Hitler Youth was numerically and often also physically superior to us.
>
> *Wolfgang Wüstefeld (former Boy Scout), born 1923*

At the end of that year Hitler's youth leader was nonetheless able to present a proud record of achievement. With financial assistance from a 'benefactors' circle' established for the purpose, he enlarged his office space in Plauen. As well as a 'Reich Business Centre' he established a 'Borderland Office', which was responsible for contact with youth groups of the German minorities in the Sudeten region of Czechoslovakia and in Poland. Hitler's youth organisation had got itself noticed with mass demonstrations which had a considerable impact on the public. For the first time, on 18 November, Gruber summoned all the nation's *Hitlerjungen* simultaneously to a *Reichsappell* (national roll-call), in order to reinforce the consciousness of 'internal solidarity' and the 'feeling of belonging to the German ethnic community'. Almost the entire leadership of the HJ arrived in Plauen at the end of December, for a 'Reich Leaders' Congress'. This meeting saw the founding of what were known as *Jungmannschaften* for boys aged from ten to fourteen, which were the forerunners of the *Deutsches Jungvolk*. Girls were assembled in

*Schwesterschaften*, from which, in July 1930, the *Bund Deutscher Mädel* (BDM, League of German Lasses) emerged. Confirmed in his post of *Reichsjugendführer*, Gruber struck a note of pugnacity in his declaration of principles:

It is in the very nature of the Hitler Youth that it cannot be compared with other youth organisations, any more than our Party can be compared with other parties. The Hitler Youth is neither a political paramilitary group, nor a league of anti-Semitic Boy Scouts . . . rather is the Hitler Youth a new youth movement of social revolutionaries in the German tradition and ethnic in its nature, bound up with the destiny of the nation. It lays stress on the education and cultivation of the personality in a clear understanding of prevailing conditions and the demands they place on us. These demands are not just that we should get to know our homeland by hiking around it: we must today fight for our homeland by committing our lives to it; we must free the state and the economy from the clutches of capitalist and anti-traditional forces. From this we draw the firm determination to achieve the new socialist ethnic state of Adolf Hitler, and we know that his path can only lie over the corpse of Marxism. That is why we must not allow ourselves to be diverted and confused by secondary problems, however tempting they are. Our route has a clearly defined objective; we have a great affirmation ahead of us and within us. Through all that is crumbling, rotten and old, we make our way to the shaping of something new and better, we strive towards the Third Reich. To attain this, the *Bündische Jugend* (Youth Alliance) and equally the *Wehrjugend* (Youth Defence) are too small and inadequate a base for us. We replace the 'No' that is characteristic of all types of German youth associations, with a recognition of reality and the shaping of the new 'Yes'. There is thus maturing in us a new type of German youth: the Hitler Youth. This type, tough, fierce and sturdy, politically bound into the organisation, marches in step towards a new realistic world of National Socialism, and leaving behind the useless jumble of alliances and petty groupings, follows one man alone, their Führer, Adolf Hitler.

> For it is not a question of how many glasses of beer he is able
> to drink, but how many punches he can withstand, not on
> how many nights he can go out on the razzle, but how many
> kilometres he can march.
>
> *Adolf Hitler, 1935*

Yet the days of the 'Red-Brown' [i.e. Socialist-Fascist] leader
from Saxony were numbered. Another of Hitler's disciples was
already vying successfully for the Führer's favour. In July 1928
Baldur von Schirach had been elected leader of the NS Student
League – the first step in a meteoric career which would eventually
cost Kurt Gruber his job. For his second attempt to seize power
Hitler had – quite against his nature – adopted a prescription of
political patience and had decided to exploit the weaknesses of the
hated Weimar 'system' for his own ends, in order to gain mastery
of Germany by legal means. It was now all the more important for
the Nazi movement to gain new supporters from the affluent and
'respectable' middle class. It was mainly this milieu which rejected
the social-revolutionary slogans peddled by 'left-wing' National
Socialists. And it was particularly in the Hitler Youth that the
pseudo-socialist mindset continued to prevail, well after 1933.
Socialist ideas, blended with ethnic visions and the cranky notion
of a soldierly, 'Prussian' society, fired the enthusiasm of many
young Germans and their belief in the myth of the 'Worker' Adolf
Hitler, as the political harbinger of a classless 'ethnic community'.

> In the Hitler Youth a worker's son could be a leader, and a
> factory-owner's son could be somewhere in the rear ranks.
>
> *Hans-Jochen Vogel, born 1926*

Baldur von Schirach, the cherished son of an upper middle-class
family, would later delight in exploiting these youthful dreams in
his purple perorations: 'A single banner flutters at the head of the
HJ. The millionaire's son and the worker's son wear one and the

same uniform. For it is only the youth who are unprejudiced in this sense and capable of genuine fellowship; indeed Youth is Socialism.' Yet in reality this illusion served to bring an entire generation into line. Schirach abused the naivety of youth, its easily roused enthusiasm, its devotion and commitment to an ideology that is full of promise. As the high priest of a quasi-religious Führer-cult he turned children into the malleable disciples of a political firebrand, for the sake of whose fantasies of omnipotence thousands of *Hitlerjungen* sacrificed their lives in the very last days of the war: 'The will of the Führer is alive within them, the Führer who gave them the Word, the Führer to whom they turn: "Not for ourselves, but for Germany."' Was this 'Sorcerer's Apprentice', who idolised his master almost to the bitter end, himself a misguided idealist, a deceived disciple of Adolf Hitler?

'I brought up that generation to believe in Hitler and in loyalty to him', Schirach confessed in 1946, before the Nuremberg tribunal trying Nazi war-criminals. 'I believed I was serving a Führer who would make our people and its youth great, free and happy. Millions of young people believed this with me and saw their ideal in National Socialism. Many died for it. It is my fault that I brought up the youth for a man who was a murderer millions of times over. I believed in this man; that is all I can say in my defence.' The belated insight of a seducer. The court sentenced him to 20 years imprisonment, the whole of which he served in the Allied military gaol in the Berlin district of Spandau. Yet Schirach received this punishment not for instilling a fatally false faith but for being an accomplice in genocide: as the *Gauleiter* of Vienna he was responsible for the deportation of thousands of Jews.

Baldur von Schirach, the sophisticated offspring of a cosmopolitan, upper-class family, was not born to the career of herald to a demagogue. Emma Middleton Schirach gave birth to her second son in Berlin in 1907. She was a wealthy American from Philadelphia and was married to a Prussian officer, *Hauptmann* Carl Baily Norris von Schirach, whose forebears were also American. After leaving the army Baldur's father was appointed *Generalintendant* of the Court Theatre in Weimar. At home the parents only spoke English, and Baldur did not learn German until the age of five. Even as a child he began to write poetry and play the violin, and for a time he dreamed of becoming a musician.

The soft-featured intellectual, who later adjured the youth of Germany to soldierly discipline and selfless toughness, was himself brought up in a liberal and cosmopolitan atmosphere. At the age of ten he was sent by his parents to a 'woodland school' in the Thuringian spa town of Bad Berka, where the teaching staff were inspired by the ideas of the progressive educationalist, Hermann Lietz. In the tradition of the earlier *Wandervogel* movement, they wanted to bring up the boys to be self-sufficient and self-confident personalities, far removed from the 'corrupting influences' of the big city. According to Lietz, 'the development of body and character' was to stand 'on a par with the imparting of knowledge'. In this community pupils and teachers called each other by their first names, and the older children were expected to take responsibility for the younger ones.

It was in the aftermath of the defeat of 1918 that Baldur's carefree childhood came to an abrupt end. His brother Karl, seven years his senior, committed suicide. In the First World War he had dreamed of fighting as a Prussian officer at the front; but with the abdication of the Kaiser and the acceptance of the Versailles Treaty by the National Assembly in Weimar, his entire world collapsed. 'I do not want to outlive Germany's misfortune', wrote Karl in a farewell letter. The death of his brother intensified Baldur's hatred for a republic which was already pretty unpopular with his parents. His father resigned his post of *Intendant*, as a protest against the government. But the Schirachs were wealthy and their house in Gartenstrasse remained the glittering focus of Weimar's artistic life. Baldur returned from boarding-school and was given private tuition. While the boy grew up in the bosom of his family to be a responsible, educated citizen, battles raged on the streets between aspiring workers and nationalist irregulars. Baldur's heart throbbed for those veterans of the Front who, in armed *Freikorps* units, crushed the uprisings with bloody violence. 'All of us in Thuringia felt that a knife was being held to our throat', Schirach claimed in retrospect. 'And that if we didn't defend ourselves, we would be slaughtered by the communists.'

Filled with such militant enthusiasm, the seventeen-year-old Schirach joined the *Knappenschaft*, a nationalist paramilitary group, led by officers of the outlawed 'Black Reichswehr'. Baldur was one of the *Knappen* (meaning 'a knight's squire') who were acting as marshals at the public meeting in March 1925, where Hitler, newly released from prison, launched his election campaign in Weimar. The voice of this itinerant political preacher was alone enough to hypnotise the young man: 'It was deep and hoarse, as resonant as a cello. His accent sounded strange and simply forced one to listen to him', Schirach later recalled. He listened enthralled to the sound of the 'drummer' as he vented his hatred in tirades against the Treaty of Versailles. Before his eyes the unknown soldier from the trenches gained stature, a revolutionary who had dared to march on Munich's hallowed Feldherrnhalle and had risked his life in an attempt to save the nation. To the young man from Weimar, Hitler embodied a heroic ideal, and when the party leader was personally introduced to him after the meeting, Baldur felt as though the finger of destiny were pointing at him. Aglow with inspiration from the encounter, the admirer made a vow in the form of hymn-like verses:

> *Du gabst uns deine Hand und einen Blick,*
> *Von dem noch jetzt die jungen Herzen beben:*
> *Es wird uns dieser Stunde mächtig Leben*
> *Begleiten stets als wunderbares Glück.*

> Thou gavest us thy hand and such a gaze
> as caused e'en now our youthful hearts to quake:
> The mighty life-force of that hour doth take
> us by the hand through fortune's wondrous days.

> *Im Herzen blieb der heisse Schwur zurück:*
> *Du hast uns nicht umsonst die Hand gegeben!*
> *Wir werden unser hohes Ziel erstreben,*
> *verkettet durch des Vaterlands Geschick.*

Th'impassioned vow remains deep in our soul:
And not in vain didst Thou thy hand extend!
We strive towards our high, exalted goal,
Bound by our Fatherland, aye, to the end.

No sooner had the ardent young lyricist reached his eighteenth birthday than he joined the Party and the SA. 'Come and see me in Munich; we need people like you', Hitler advised him on one of his visits to Weimar. Party member No. 17251 obeyed the summons of his idol. After taking his *Abitur* (school-leaving examination) at a high school in Weimar, Schirach went to Munich University in 1927 to study English and German Literature and History of Art. But his studies were soon sidelined and he did not even attempt to graduate. Instead he trawled the university for new comrades-in-arms for the little group of National Socialist students, which at that time was leading a shadowy existence. Schirach showed empathy with the students who saw their privileged position under threat from the changed circumstances of the Weimar republic and could no longer hope to rise automatically to join society's ruling elite. He recruited new supporters in right-wing nationalist student societies and duelling clubs, for whose feudal *esprit de corps* this son of the aristocracy already had an affinity. Schirach sought an entrée to the Party headquarters and made contact with the Führer's secretary, Rudolf Hess, for whom he dealt with paperwork in the 'Brown House'.

One day in the autumn of 1927 Schirach met Hitler out walking in Maximilianstrasse. The Führer recognised his young admirer from Weimar and invited him back to his apartment. Eagerly Schirach proposed a big student meeting, at which Hitler would appear as the main speaker. The man whose own application to the Vienna Academy of Art had once been rejected was sceptical at first. He doubted whether he could ever win over more than 10 per cent of the student population to the Party. What is more, he was terrified of having to address a student audience. But finally Hitler gave in to Schirach's urging and promised to come, if the twenty-year-old could fill the hall of Munich's Hofbräuhaus. The young student did a good promotional job and a full hour before the event was due to begin the hall was full to capacity. Hitler arrived, made a speech and drove the students into storms of enthusiasm – a success which attracted attention even among the educated upper class. It was as Schirach had suspected: 'The undergraduates of those days wanted to be addressed by demagogues. At that time they were more susceptible than the working class to the mass hypnosis of great political gatherings. It was something which was lacking in their own experience.'

Schirach had succeeded in making the breakthrough. He had won the recognition of the Führer, who now took on the role of fatherly mentor to his young follower. Within a few months Schirach was at the head of Munich's university group which, thanks to his propaganda, had grown significantly. With Hitler's backing he put himself into contention with other internal candidates for the top position in Germany's 'brown' student movement. On 20 July 1928, aged only twenty-one, he was elected Reichsführer of the NS Student Association and a member of the executive of the NSDAP.

That summer Schirach threw away the chance of a career which would have fundamentally changed the rest of his life. While visiting relatives in the USA with his mother, his uncle Alfred Norris, a wealthy Wall Street banker living in a penthouse high above Manhattan, invited Baldur to join his firm. But since he had long ago fallen for the romantic dream of an ethnic rebirth of the German nation, Baldur politely declined, and headed 'back to Germany, back to Hitler'.

> You lads will become men, as the great war generation were. You will become brave and courageous, as your older brothers and fathers were.
>
> *Adolf Hitler, 1936*

Ceaselessly Schirach continued to plunder the universities. The niceties of college politics were of little concern to the subversive NS student leader. His objective was to bring in more members –

exactly as intended by Hitler, who stood at his protégé's side as the speaker at numerous demonstrations. There were times when it seemed that Schirach's meteoric rise had gone to his head. The well-educated, upper-class boy, who in later years was described by contemporaries as 'aloof', 'controlled' and a man with 'good manners', fancied himself in the role of brawling hooligan with a penchant for boozing and sexual escapades. Once, when very drunk at a student meeting, he drew his pistol and aimed it at a portrait of Hitler. For the Führer's favourite this indiscretion had no consequences. However, when Schirach made a grand entrance at a rally of the entire NS student membership, complete with SS escort and riding-crop, infuriated student officials demanded his dismissal. Yet his propaganda successes assured him of Hitler's goodwill: 'Party colleague Schirach has understood what it's all about: nothing else but a grand mass movement. I stand with my full authority behind Schirach.'

More and more students were joining the 'brown' ranks. The talented recruiter felt called to new tasks. He now wanted to conquer the whole of German youth for the NSDAP. On his own initiative he mounted an attack on the *HJ-Reichsführer*, Kurt Gruber: without the agreement of either Gruber or Hitler, he sent a circular to all nationalist youth associations. In response, Gruber sought feverishly to shore up his own position, visited the HJ leaders and in the spring of 1929 corralled his supporters into 32 mass meetings all over Germany. Then, at the Nuremberg Party Congress, when 2,000 *Hitlerjungen* marched past the Führer's podium amid thunderous applause, it seemed that the man from Saxony had won this trial of strength.

Yet in the continuing power-struggle with Schirach, Gruber's stamina would eventually give out. In any case, his social-revolutionary slogans were no longer appropriate at a time when Hitler was seeking political power, which could not be attained without middle-class support. Since Gruber had taken up office as *Reichsführer HJ*, the Hitler Youth had grown from just 700 members in the spring of 1930 to over 20,000, who were organised into 450 local groups. Alongside other German nationalist groups the Hitler Youth attended numerous demonstrations against America's 'Young Plan', which had been accepted by the government and which bound

Germany to reparation payments as far into the future as the 1980s. Thousands of *Hitlerjungen* campaigned in the national elections of September 1930, helping the NSDAP to achieve its electoral breakthrough. With 107 seats it was now the second largest party in the Reichstag after the Social Democrats.

> Young people don't appreciate the political background, but they like the togetherness. Being together was fun for us.
>
> *Gerhard Wilke, born 1926*

While the Nazi Party began to take off in the slipstream of the worldwide economic crisis triggered by the Wall Street Crash, Gruber was rapidly losing ground. In the struggle for supremacy within the Party the social revolutionaries around Otto Strasser had unsuccessfully attempted to stage a revolt against Hitler. Even Gruber's friend at court, the SA chief Pfeffer von Salomon, was forced to bow out following the insurrection of the SA in Berlin. Hitler now summoned Ernst Röhm to head the *Sturmabteilung*. Having returned from Bolivia, where he had spent two years as a military adviser, the newly appointed SA supremo also demanded to be given command of the HJ, whose relative independence he would no longer tolerate. On 27 April 1931 Hitler issued an instruction placing Gruber under the command of the SA's chief-of-staff. Now all HJ groups were under the orders of whoever commanded the SA. To achieve better control, the national management of the Hitler Youth was transferred from Plauen to the Party headquarters in Munich. Schirach scented his opportunity. He agitated openly against his rival: 'Gruber was absolutely the right man for the job, as long as the Hitler Youth remained a purely provincial affair. But now, at the Reich level, he shows clear signs of a lack of vision and organisational ability, and it can only be due to Gruber's pig-headedness that all nationalist youth movements are not yet united.'

In his intrigues against the Reich Youth Leader Schirach found a supporter in Ernst Röhm, with whom he cultivated a relationship that verged on friendship. Finally he revealed to Hitler his wish to lead the Party's youth wing. 'Don't be funny, Schirach', Hitler retorted. 'Do you want to waste your time on those children?' But the model pupil knew how to convince his master: 'So then I said to him: "I will build you the greatest youth movement that Germany has ever seen."' This kind of megalomania was not without effect. On 30 October 1931 Hitler appointed Baldur von Schirach, now aged twenty-four, to be *Reichsjugendführer* of the NSDAP and thus put him in control of the new generation of Party members in the NS Student Association, the Hitler Youth and the NS Schoolboy Association.

Among the Party faithful this upper-class sprig of the arty intelligentsia was not seen as the dream candidate. To the early, pioneering members of the Hitler Youth the new *Reichsjugendführer* was anything but the war-horse they had been hoping for. 'The cry went up that Baldur von Schirach was rather too much the "Baron". With the aristocratic "von" in front of his name, and his American relatives – it was really a bit much for us.' Such was the judgement of his long-time deputy, Hartmann Lauterbacher, who as a boy at high school in Austria had founded the *Deutsche Jugend*, a forerunner of the Hitler Youth. Schirach himself never matched up to the ideal of the athletic *Hitlerjunge*, full of fighting spirit, which he held up as an example to German youth. Painfully, the upper-class grandee tried to play the part of a rough, tough lad, but the impression he made was 'rather unathletic and plump'. Hitler's youth-leader was 'no back-slapper', no fighter, not someone 'you could work up a sweat with', his subordinates claimed. He was more aesthetic than ascetic, preferring hotel rooms and a cultivated lifestyle to tent camps and bean stew. There were persistent rumours about his homosexual leanings and his effeminately furnished, all-white bedroom.

> They were always saying: 'You lads are . . . The youth is . . .' And the old just don't have a clue. They don't know what's going on – they're senile. And that of course has an effect on young people. Especially when one remembers that education was not as informal as it is today, but was much more based on obedience.
>
> *Hans Müller, born 1923*

Even before their eighteenth birthday many *Hitlerjungen* were eager to join the ranks of the SA, which Ernst Röhm was shaping into a paramilitary force that had very real fire-power. The old problem of lack of leaders in the HJ once again became acute and Schirach who, with the rank of *Gruppenführer*, was subordinate to the most senior officers of the SA, demanded independence. In May 1932 Hitler fulfilled the wish of his disciple and promoted Schirach to head up a department of his own in the Reich administration of the NSDAP. He was now on an equal footing with Röhm. Henceforth he would tolerate no more 'Führers' around him – only the one above him. Hitler's youth supervisor immediately exploited his new position of power against his most serious rival, Adrian von Renteln, the interim successor to the deposed Gruber, who now commanded more than 35,000 youngsters as *Reichsführer* of the HJ and the NS Schoolboy Association. Renteln protested in vain about Schirach's intrigues and circumscribing of his authority, and finally resigned in disgust. Once again Schirach had emerged victorious in the struggle for power.

> I believe all that had a very powerful effect. Even if some people had the feeling that, well, this business isn't quite kosher, they still went along with it.
> *Imo Moskovicz, German Jew, born 1925*

In the last years of the Weimar republic the Hitler Youth contributed to the violent unrest which spread through the streets of Germany, creating conditions close to civil war. Political extremists profited from the rising unemployment and the social impoverishment of the population. With growing frequency marches by the SA and the communists ended in ugly brawls and indoor battles in meeting-halls. Bands of HJ troublemakers used stink-bombs and physical assault to break up screenings of the anti-war film *All Quiet on the Western Front*. Violence against cinema owners and audiences escalated to such a point that the film was taken out of circulation throughout the Reich.

From time to time the authorities attempted to stem the tide of youth violence with bans. In January 1930 the *Oberpräsident* of Hanover and former defence minister, Gustav Noske, banned school pupils from membership of the Hitler Youth. Other provincial governments followed his example. But Hitler's young cadres were not to be stopped by such measures – quite the reverse: the HJ exploited the image of their persecuted supporters as recruitment propaganda. Youths who were convicted as HJ activists felt themselves to be martyrs of the 'brown' movement. No sooner was an HJ group banned than it reappeared under some harmless name. They disguised themselves as 'Nature-lovers' or 'Young National Philatelists'. Their inventiveness knew no bounds: in Kiel, during a ban on the HJ uniform in 1932, a group of apprentice butchers marched through the streets in their blood-smeared working clothes. As one eye-witness recalled: 'The opposition were scared stiff of this group in particular, because they were rumoured to be carrying knives under their jackets.'

> In war-games people went for it really hard. Everyone was fired up. It was huge fun – neighbouring villages fighting each other – wooden hand-grenades, 'an eye for an eye, a tooth for a tooth'. We were playing at war.
>
> *Hermann Schild, born 1926*

Eager *Hitlerjungen* swarmed about everywhere, distributing millions of handbills and booklets, sticking up posters and painting Nazi slogans. Many parents feared for their children's safety; adolescents were at risk of life and limb in the street fighting. The former HJ activist Heinz Geese describes a typical situation: 'During the Reichstag elections in October 1932 we distributed leaflets. Our opponents, the lads from the Red Front, were making trouble for us, and whoever was outnumbered had to run for it. Sometimes they caught us and then there was a punch-up. Usually we got nothing worse than a black eye, but sometimes there were injuries which needed medical treatment.'

All too often the bloody confrontations ended fatally. From 1931 to the end of January 1933, twenty-one *Hitlerjungen* died in the performance of their 'duty' to the Führer. No-one counted the number of fighters from the Communist Party, the trade union youth groups and other 'enemy' organisations, who fell victim to the terrorism of the HJ during this period. The name of one *Hitlerjunge* from Berlin, who was murdered by youths in the 'red' district of Moabit, would soon become familiar to all younger Germans: Herbert Norkus. His father, a widower, had been forced by the economic slump to sell his little grocery shop and had joined the Nazi Party. On the morning of 24 January 1932 the fifteen-year-old Herbert was distributing leaflets with his chums when he was attacked by a gang of young communists. The *Hitlerjungen* fled, but their pursuers caught up with Herbert Norkus and felled him with several stab-wounds. The boy bled to death in the lobby of an apartment-house. His killers escaped unrecognised.

The burial of the *Hitlerjunge* at Plötzensee cemetery degenerated into a propaganda display. 'Herbert Norkus is an example to the whole youth of Germany', asserted the Revd Wenzel of the New Garrison Church. Berlin's NS *Gauleiter* Joseph Goebbels vowed vengeance: 'No-one can rob us of the hope that our day of revenge will come. Then those who now drivel on about humanity and loving thy neighbour, but fail to condemn the murder of our boy, will learn that the new Germany acts otherwise. Then may those people ask for mercy. Then there will be no second chance, for the new, young Germany demands atonement.'

Baldur von Schirach transformed the death into a martyrdom for the Hitler Youth. Every year he made a pilgrimage to the grave of Herbert Norkus and invoked the young man's 'spirit of self-sacrifice': 'What the Hitler Youth became in January 1932 it owes not least to the sacred symbol of young sacrifice and young heroism, which bears the name of Herbert Norkus.' With a cynicism that devalued their lives Schirach built up his novices' 'readiness for self-sacrifice' into a legitimation of the Nazi youth movement: 'The more who die for a movement, the more immortal it becomes. The Hitler Youth can face its critics with an historic reply: its own dead. This reply cannot be gainsaid, it is symbolic. There is no argument against a youth movement which, striding inexorably forward in unprecedented sacrifice for a moral ideal, accepts death, injury and persecution as an inevitable consequence of the struggle.'

> That principle of solidarity or loving one's neighbour just didn't exist at all. Toughness was the order of the day. Anyone who showed weakness was despised. Sympathy was taboo.
>
> *Gerhard Wilke, 1926*

The writer Karl Aloys Schenzinger took the story of the young Norkus as the basis for his novel *Der Hitlerjunge Quex* (Quex of the Hitler Youth). The hero of the book, Heini Völker, overcomes the resistance of his father, a communist, and sides with the Nazis. In this generational conflict, little Heini – nicknamed 'Quex' by his chums because he has the agility of quicksilver (*Quecksilber* in German) – stands for the 'new, young Germany' which was to arise under the sign of the swastika. In line with Nazi propaganda Schenzinger presented the murder of the boy as a 'blood sacrifice' for Hitler. In 1939 the novel was made into a film. Millions of children saw *Hitlerjunge Quex* as part of the 'youth film sessions' in the HJ. To accompany the final scene, in which Heini dies in the arms of his comrades while his face dissolves into a heaving sea of swastika banners, Schirach composed a march, which was soon being sung as a 'battle hymn' by all *Hitlerjungen* throughout the Reich:

*Unsre Fahne flattert uns voran*
*In die Zukunft ziehn wir Mann für Mann*
*Wir marschieren für Hitler durch Nacht und durch Not*
*Mit der Fahne der Jugend für Freiheit und Brot.*

Bravely flies the banner at our head.
Into the future side by side we march.
For Hitler thus we march through night and dread
With youth's flag, for liberty and bread.

*Unsre Fahne flattert uns voran.*
*Unsre Fahne ist die neue Zeit.*
*Und die Fahne führt uns in die Ewigkeit.*
*Ja, die Fahne ist mehr als der Tod!*

Bravely flies the banner at our head.
It is the flag that heralds a new age.
And leads us onward to eternity.
The banner is far greater yet than death!

To live for Hitler and be willing to die for Hitler – such became the fate of almost an entire generation, who joined in singing the heroic hymn of the 'fighting days' on their road to sacrifice for the murderous megalomania of a criminal.

> All those songs – they were about dying. Dying in the face of the enemy – dying for the Fatherland and stuff like that.
>
> *Karl-Heinz Janssen, born 1930*

There was a kind of magic in the way the HJ units with their fluttering banners, battle-hymns and slogans, brought more and more excitement-seeking youngsters under their spell. By the end of 1932 the number of members had risen beyond 100,000. But Hitler's young Nazis in the making were still only one among many youth groups, leagues and associations. Schirach wanted to prove to his Führer that he was indeed capable of mobilising the masses. He summoned the entire Hitler Youth to a 'Reich Day of Youth' in Potsdam. Once again Hitler doubted his apprentice's skills in sorcery: the risk of failure was great. Certainly the NSDAP had emerged from the Reichstag elections on 1 July as the strongest single party, Hermann Göring was now chairman, or 'Speaker' of the Reichstag, and Schirach himself had entered the national parliament as its youngest deputy. Yet Hitler was still wrestling for the chancellorship with Franz von Papen and Kurt von Schleicher. In this power-struggle everything depended on the word of the head of state, President von Hindenburg, and it was imperative that

Hitler did not make a fool of himself. Once again, he made it a condition for attending the gathering that Schirach fill the Potsdam stadium in order to be rewarded with a speech by the Führer.

This time the results of his propaganda exceeded even the extravagant hopes of the *Reichsjugendführer*. The youngsters arrived in droves from every corner of Germany; on foot and on bicycles, by truck and by train they swarmed into the little city that had been the seat of the Prussian kings. Schirach had reckoned on an attendance of around 50,000. But on 1 October 1932 over 70,000 young people crammed into the hopelessly overcrowded tent camps around Potsdam. 'This meeting was the fulfilment of a dream for the young', the former *Hitlerjunge* Werner Porsch tells us. 'Whereas previously we had been in small groups, here for the first time we got the feeling of a mass-movement, and through that, a bit of power behind our political beliefs.'

Hitler had been waiting in Goebbels' apartment while the crowds arrived, and now hurried over to the stadium. 'Your youth, *mein Führer*, has come here to provide a demonstration of their love and faith, such as no young generation has, to this day, ever shown to a living person.' With these words Schirach dedicated to his idol a stadium that was filled to bursting-point. 'There was an incredible outburst of cheering', he recalled later. 'There were tears in Hitler's eyes, so great was the effect it had on him.'

Overwhelmed by the euphoria of his young supporters, the great demagogue replied: 'I know that there are many among you whose fathers are tramping the streets without work, that many of you perhaps do not even know what fate will, in the coming days and weeks, befall your home and family.' With pseudo-socialist emotion he called on his listeners to become missionaries of the 'ethnic community':

> You youngsters should ignore professional distinctions and social barriers, ignore everything that threatens to divide you, and seek and find the German community. You must hold on to it and preserve it and let no-one rob you of it. It is never too soon to bring up the youth of Germany to feel themselves to be, above all else, German. The National Socialist education of youth shall not be for the benefit of one party but of the German people, as indeed

shall the National Socialist movement one day be Germany, and the unanimous willingness of the youth of Germany to dedicate itself to the National Socialist ideal gives clear proof of this. Let others mock and laugh; you will one day be Germany's future.

The Führer was full of praise for his leading *Hitlerjunge*. 'You have created something tremendous here', he told Schirach. 'Nothing more devastating has been done to the Schleicher government than this rally of an immense youth organisation in the immediate vicinity of Berlin.' As they returned to every part of the Reich the young people were an advertisement for the will to power of the 'national movement'.

Hitler's appointment as Reich Chancellor on 30 January 1933 and the 'Enabling Law' of 24 March dealt the death-blow to Weimar democracy. The 'fire of national revolution' unleashed a wave of persecution and arrest of communists, Social Democrats and other political opponents On the evening of 27 February the Reichstag went up in flames; the presumed arsonist, a Dutch communist, provided the new men in power with a welcome pretext for a witch-hunt. Nazi schoolboys and students burned books written by left-wing and Jewish intellectuals. Baldur von Schirach, who had immediately moved his youth headquarters to Berlin in order to remain close to his Führer, caught the fire-raising mood: 'Anyone who is against our unity must go to the stake.'

Those youth organisations which were not immediately banned and broken up, Schirach wanted to bring forcibly into his sphere of power, as part of the *Gleichschaltung*, the imposition of Nazi conformity on the nation. On the morning of 5 April 1933 fifty *Hitlerjungen* stormed the Berlin office of the 'Reich committee of the German Youth Movement'. This acted as an umbrella organisation and central point of contact between most of the youth associations and government departments of the Weimar republic, and represented more than five million young people. Under the command of 'senior regional leader' Karl Nabersberg – a close associate of Schirach – the intruders ransacked the offices. In the months that followed Schirach used the stolen documents and personnel records in the systematic elimination of all opponents of the HJ in the youth movement. Five days after the raid on the Reich committee, a mob of HJ thugs attacked the 'Reich association of German youth hostels'. The violent takeover was just what Schirach wanted in order to turn the hostels into the 'Cultural shrines of German youth'.

In the wave of enthusiasm for the 'national rising' millions of young Germans joined the Hitler Youth. 'We thought it was a good thing', Inge Scholl says of herself and her brother and sister, 'and we wanted to do whatever we could to contribute to it. But there was something else as well, which drew us in and carried us along with a mysterious power: that was the closely-packed marching columns of youth with their billowing flags, their gaze fixed ahead, the drum-beats and the singing. There was surely something overwhelming about that sense of community, wasn't there?' The Scholls' father warned his children, but in vain. Although they belonged to the Catholic youth movement, the Scholls fell prey to the enchantment of the 'Pied Piper'. Ten years later Hans and Sophie Scholl were arrested and executed as the initiators of the anti-Nazi resistance group known as the 'White Rose'.

Despite the mass recruitment into the Nazi youth organisations, at first even the most fervently nationalist youth leagues baulked at the incursions of the HJ. The non-party groups of the Youth Alliance founded the 'Greater German Alliance' under Admiral Adolf von Trotha, a friend of President Hindenburg. With indecent haste they swore an oath of allegiance to Adolf Hitler and declared their belief in the National Socialist state. Jews were excluded from membership. Yet this attempt to outflank the Hitler Youth on the right, and thus preserve their independence, failed. After Hitler's electoral victory of March 1933 and the 'Enabling Law', the coalition partners rapidly crossed over to the NSDAP and their paramilitary groups and youth organisations were incorporated into the party formations. Even the Greater German Alliance now feared dissolution. In an effort to maintain their member groups under the same leadership the Youth Alliance declared itself ready to join the HJ en bloc. But Schirach saw through this manoeuvre and turned down the offer. For the last time some 15,000 members of the non-HJ associations gathered on Lüneburg Heath in June for a Whitsun meeting. Police and SA troops encircled the camp and broke up the rally. A month later the Greater German Alliance was banned.

The break-up of the free youth alliances drove hundreds of thouands of young people into the ranks of the HJ, among them many experienced leaders who brought the customs and traditions of the youth alliances into Hitler's young brigades. Schirach needed them urgently in order to cope with the huge influx. The influence of the 'alliance' leaders had a lasting effect, most of all on the *Jungvolk*. 'A large part of the attraction of the *Jungvolk* for us came from the vigorous heritage of the Youth Alliance. Many aspects of their style, such as excursions and camping, were taken over by the HJ. The Alliance leaders brought with them the experience of how to organise that kind of thing', Count Heinrich von Einsiedel tells us. 'Without recourse to the Youth Alliance, I don't believe Schirach would ever have succeeded in gaining such an influence over German youth.' Hitler rewarded the success of his loyal vassal. In a decree of 17 June 1933 he appointed Schirach '*Jugendführer* of the German Reich', which put him at the head of all male and female youth organisations – an important step on the road to achieving totalitarian powers.

In the schools, teachers with democratic views were either suspended from duty, forced into early retirement or sidetracked into insignificant jobs. 'Old campaigners' of the Party moved into civil service posts and headmasterships. In a bid to save their professional status most of the remaining schoolteachers hastened to join the Nazi Party. Many teachers posed as zealous promoters of the Hitler Youth, ambitious headteachers competed in statistics of successful recruitment. When a school had won 90 per cent of its pupils over to the Nazi youth movement, the HJ presented it with a banner.

When the banner is no longer flying, then you will no longer exist   that was drummed into us, imprinted on our minds, and we probably believed it.

*Bernhard Mark, born 1927*

Not even young people in employment remained safe from Schirach's rigorous methods . 'The Hitler Youth won the day with strength and might; it bludgeoned its way to the top', a member of the labour youth movement recalls. 'There were more and more of them, and when we went hiking they lay in wait for us and beat us about the head with rubber truncheons.' The forcible alignment of the labour unions with the 'German Workers' Front' obliged their youth membership to join the Hitler Youth. Craft and commercial guilds decreed that 'from now on apprentices will only be taken on if they are members of the HJ or the BDM, otherwise the apprenticeship will not be recognised and penalties will ensue'. Those who refused to join the Hitler Youth were putting their professional future at risk. Sometimes HJ leaders did not shrink from blackmail. 'Why have you still not joined the ranks of the Hitler Youth?' was the question on a form which the HJ distributed in Wiesbaden in 1934. 'If you are for the Führer and thereby for the Hitler Youth, then sign the attached statement of acceptance. If, however, you do not intend to join the HJ then write to us accordingly on the enclosed declaration. . .'. The document required the signature of the father as well as the name of the employer – if the offspring was not prepared to join, the father had to face reprisals.

Once the Youth Alliance and the youth arms of the democratic political parties and labour unions of the Weimar republic had been broken up, the violence of the *Hitlerjungen* was increasingly directed against members of religious youth organisations. 'The first few times they just insulted us and tried to trip us up', recalls Wolfgang Wüstefeld, who belonged to a Catholic scout group in Frankfurt-an-der Oder. 'Later, it got steadily worse and more brutal. Once, we were coming back from a trip when the *Hitlerjungen* were waiting to ambush us on the Oder bridge. They beat us up and threw our leader off the bridge.' This was not an isolated instance. In order to escape the clutches of the HJ, many young Germans sought refuge in religious youth groups. As their membership soared, the brutality of the Hitler Youth against young Christians increased steadily. In early July 1933 Schirach himself had to call his young toughs to order: 'I hereby forbid any harassment of other youth associations by members of the Hitler

Youth. If the behaviour of other German youth associations should give cause for complaint, this is to be reported to me through official channels. . . . Specific instances will be punished.' Nevertheless, among evangelical Christians approval of the Führer-state prevailed. 'The God-given principles of home, people and state are being recognised anew. The people are arising. A movement is gathering momentum, one which promises to span class differences and long-standing conflicts', rejoiced the 'Evangelical Youth of Germany' at Hitler's seizure of power: 'Therefore the attitude of the young evangelical front at this time can be none other than a passionate involvement in the destiny of our nation and at the same time a fierce determination, as the Word of God demands.' On 19 December the Evangelical Bishop of the Reich, Ludwig Müller, a fervent supporter of National Socialism, concluded an agreement with Schirach which delivered some 700,000 young people into the hands of the HJ. The church's youth work was restricted to two afternoons a week and two Sundays a month, and from now on was only permitted to provide religious education and pastoral care. The once lively communal activities of the Evangelical Youth, which were built around excursions and camping, 'nest evenings', folk-dancing and orienteering in the style of the Youth Alliance, came to a sudden end. 'With the victory of National Socialism, the NS state has, in accordance with its obligations and its programme, taken over the task of protecting the Church', wrote Friedrich Zahn, who was appointed by Müller to the post of 'Reich Youth Chaplain': 'The Church sends its youth to march joyfully under the banners of the Third Reich.'

The Catholic Church, on the other hand, proved less susceptible to the mesmeric brownshirt creed, although few of its youth organisers saw National Socialism as an intellectual rival. 'We are determined to work together towards the great goal of a great Germany, united in social welfare and Christian culture, so that the present movement among our people grows into a genuine renewal and consensus.' While Hitler's negotiations with the Vatican ensured German Catholics the freedom to practise their faith, the dictator nonetheless treated the *Reichskonkordat* of July 1933 chiefly as a lap that he had won on the way to international recognition of his regime. In order to stem the exodus of their members into the HJ, many Catholic youth associations introduced shooting practice and paramilitary field exercises – despite the clergy's concerns over the unholy alliance between the Gospel and the Gun.

> I can remember small-bore rifle shooting, throwing Indian clubs and sports like that, which had a military character, Later we had weapon training and threw hand-grenades.
>
> *Robert Oppenländer, born 1923*

However, the declared willingness of the Catholic small-bore marksmen to cooperate was not enough to modify Schirach's claim to sole authority over the youth. Instead, the Hitler Youth intensified its recruitment campaign among young Catholics – with propaganda, moral pressure and open violence. The authorities backed Schirach in his battle with the Catholic youth movement: they were banned from public parades, their publications were confiscated and the youth groups dissolved and banned.

In the Hitler Youth belief in the Führer replaced trust in the Heavenly Father. The 'HJ year of festivals' followed the National Socialist calendar of days of celebration and remembrance. From the 'Day of Seizing Power', through 'the Führer's Birthday' to the anniversary of the failed putsch of 9 November 1923, millions of boys and girls acted as servers at the altar of a 'national religion' in the sign of a new trinity: 'Our religion: Germany! Our belief: The Führer! Our will: the holy empire of German faith!'

With endless ceremonies, calls to the flag and torchlight marches, Schirach made obeisance to his idol Adolf Hitler, who in his megalomania imagined he had been appointed by 'Providence' to be the saviour of the nation. The master of ceremonies knew exactly how to exploit the magic of ritual. At the spring and autumn equinoxes, and at harvest festivals, the children indulged with enthusiasm in mysterious customs and gave themselves up to the nocturnal fascination of fire: 'Twice a year we celebrated the equinox', Georg Beckmann remembers from those times. 'A great fire was lit. In front of the assembled Party groups, SS *Sturmbannführer* or youth leaders would make uplifting speeches about our ancestors. It all had a religious ring to it. We boys would then perform Germanic sword-dances. And when the fire had died down we revived an old Germanic custom: boys and girls held hands and jumped in pairs through the fire.'

Yet behind all this pagan hocus-pocus, the ancestor-worship and Germanic cultism, lurked the evil spirit of a horrific racial ideology, whose enforcers would end by burning human beings. 'At school templates were held up against us and our heads were measured', reports Paul Stüben. 'If someone didn't quite match the Aryan standards, they were asked: "Might your great-grandmother have been. . . ?" And then often the person would say, very tactfully: "Well, it's all so long ago; by now the healthy German blood will have conquered the Jewish." I myself had to bring my family-tree to school. Our headmaster stood up in front of us in his Party uniform and announced: "I must inform you that we have a Jewish girl in this class." We had no idea. "So you are no longer allowed to play with her, you may not do any schoolwork with her, or have anything more to do with her until other regulations are brought in." After a few days the girl disappeared. We never saw her again.'

Teachers and HJ leaders spread the social-Darwinian notion of 'natural selection' in the collective 'struggle for survival'. In their pseudo-ethnological lessons they propagated the racial image of the 'Aryan master-race', whose members had to exercise their 'right of the stronger' over those of 'inferior heredity'. Even in arithmetic tests Nazi pedagogues attempted to prove to their pupils the economic loss incurred by what they referred to as 'non-tenable lives': 'It costs 6 million Reichsmarks to build a mental asylum. How many new homes costing RM 1,500 each could be built for the same amount of money?' This insidious propaganda culminated in the persecution of the Jews who, like the gypsies, were branded as 'pests on the body of the nation'. The authoress Ilse Aichinger recalls: 'In biology we were taught that Jews and gypsies were the worst thing in the world and there was only one thing even worse: the interbreeding of Aryans and Jews, or Aryans and gypsies, because these half-breeds were either criminals or Jews, usually both.'

At an early stage the girls, especially, were familiarised with the Nazi concept of 'racial hygiene' and the requirements of their future role as mothers, which were derived from that. The Hitler Youth organised evening-classes on 'maintaining the health of the blood'. Schirach expected the female members of the HJ to develop their 'body and mind' in a way appropriate to their future role as 'mothers of new generations'. He declared the girls responsible 'for upholding the purity of their blood as part of the national bloodstock', and bound them 'so to develop their physical disposition that the heredity passed on by them enriches the nation'. In order to fulfil this task, it was their duty 'to match the beauty desired by young and adult manhood'. To meet the biological demands for 'racial renewal' through 'a hereditarily sound new generation' an HJ author wrote this about the education of girls: 'The eternal life of our people is founded on the health of our women and mothers. The educational work of the BDM includes making the entire female youth aware of the notions of breeding and selection. The archetypal German woman is complementary to the archetypal German man; their uniting signifies the rebirth of our people.' The reality, however, as a former 'lass' of the BDM found out, was that they were chiefly meant to 'produce cannon-fodder for the Führer'.

Starting with the *Jungvolk*, the well-loved tales of Germanic heroes were intended to imbue the children with a sense of identification with their forefathers. The Hitler Youth liked to explain their glorified ideals of the 'Nordic' superman and 'Aryan' conquerors of the world by their innate hardiness in battle and their soldierly endurance. Only the best were to have the duty of preserving the race. On the other hand, young people with hereditary diseases would not be permitted to bring any offspring into the world: 'For if your blood carries characteristics which bring misfortune on your children and make them a burden on the state, then it is your heroic duty to be the last of your line.'

HJ leaders systematically stirred up hatred against the Jews. At 'hostel evenings' they handed out anti-Semitic caricatures to the children as reference material. 'And then off we marched', Paul Stüben recalls of his service in the *Jungvolk*. 'We passed the municipal savings-bank where the anti-Semitic paper *Der Stürmer* was on sale. The company leader saw the news-stand and bawled: "Perish Judah!" The others took up the cry and it finally reached me. It was a matter of conscience: at first I didn't join in the shouting, just moved my lips, but then I thought: Judah's just a country somewhere thousands of miles away, and if I say "Judah, may you rot", I'm not really harming anyone personally; and so I shouted along with them.'

> It was impossible for a young person to discern the dimensions that really lay behind it all.
>
> *Imo Moskovicz, German Jew, born 1925*

The poison of persecution had its effect. When synagogues throughout Germany were burned on 9 November 1938 and the organised 'wrath of the people' was vented against Jewish citizens in the shape of marauding SA troops, *Hitlerjungen* also took part in the devastation and violence. 'In Ludwigsburg the SA people had set fire to the synagogue next to our school', the then thirteen-year-old Heinrich Kling tells us. 'Full of excitement I went off to see the fire. As I stood there, I wondered why the fire-brigade were just hosing the neighbouring houses and not the fire itself. And only then did I notice that SA men and boys from the Hitler Youth were coming out with big torah scrolls and cheering as they threw them on to the fire.' Incited by local SA and HJ leaders, or acting of their own volition, the *Hitlerjungen* roamed through the streets, smashing shop windows, and looting shops and homes. Schirach, who had not ordered the violence, was clearly appalled by the acts of terrorism. The *Reichsjugendführer* expressly forbade his charges to take part in any anti-Semitic excesses and threatened persistent offenders with expulsion from the Hitler Youth. Later, when he was *Gauleiter* of Vienna, Baldur von Schirach would display fewer scruples. In 1942, as one of Hitler's 'willing executioners', he praised the deportation of Viennese Jews as 'an active contribution to European culture'.

Many HJ members themselves felt that this violence against defenceless fellow human beings was a contradiction of their oft-invoked notion of honour and their 'chivalrous' self-image. The so-called *Reichskristallnacht* provoked revulsion and a number of *Hitlerjungen* asked themselves whether the Führer condoned such acts. 'I felt it was distasteful and repugnant – not necessarily immoral; I was unable to judge that – but repugnant', recalls one eye-witness, Horst-Werner Kunze. 'I wondered: how is this possible? And I wasn't the only one to feel that. It was really foul.' Admittedly, a critical questioning of one's own conscience was not allowed for in the HJ's timetable.

However, most young people were too dazzled by Hitler's foreign policy successes to worry. The *Anschluss* of Austria and the march into the Sudetenland were causes for rejoicing: 'From then on all the talk was of Greater Germany, and we were proud to belong to that country', Klaus Mauelshagen recounts. By then war was already in sight. In February 1937 the Supreme Command of the Wehrmacht had appointed *Oberstleutnant* Erwin Rommel to be liaison officer between the armed forces and the youth leadership. Rommel immediately proposed placing the pre-military training of boys in the hands of military officers. Schirach did not want to give up such influence. And anyway the *Reichsjugendführer* was worried that Rommel was clearly more popular with many of the young than he was himself. In the end he saw to it that the highly decorated war-hero was replaced in the post.

The Hitler Youth nevertheless remained in close touch with the military. Schirach agreed to cooperate closely with the Commander-in-Chief of the Army, Werner Fritsch, who instructed his senior officers to promote 'love and enjoyment of the soldier's profession'. HJ groups visited barracks and were invited on exercises. Officers used lectures to encourage military skills. The Wehrmacht made shooting-ranges available and advised HJ leaders on field exercises and on weapon training for their boys. Coached from childhood in the *esprit de corps* of soldiering, many *Hitlerjungen* dreamed of a career in the field-grey 'tunic of honour' – their imagination simply could not encompass the horrific reality of war. 'I was always concerned with becoming a soldier', remembers Albert Bastian, who volunteered for the *Waffen-SS* at the age of seventeen. 'I never thought about dying. I knew that in war people can lose their life, but I never thought for a moment that this applied to me.' For most of them, Schirach's speciality – the glorious sacrifice for Führer, *Volk* and Fatherland – was no more than a *frisson* that stimulated childish fantasy. 'To us, death signified something great, something sublime', says Klaus Mauelshagen. 'As the song said, "The Flag is More than Death". The man who carried the flag through the enemy lines was a hero. And mostly they died a hero's death with the flag. For us that was something special, although we had no idea what death was really like.'

> This over-emphasis on the community for which you had to make every sacrifice – this over-emphasis was taken completely for granted in the Hitler Youth.
>
> *Hans Jochen Vogel, born 1926*

Even before Hitler's invasion of Poland, Schirach had achieved his target of bringing virtually all young people into the 'state youth' of the Third Reich. With the introduction of 'compulsory youth service' on 25 March 1939, every young German was in future obliged, from the age of ten onward, to march with the Hitler Youth. On the eve of the Second World War, well over eight million children and young people wore the uniforms of the Hitler Youth. For years the *Reichsjugendführer* had drummed into Hitler's children patriotism and gallantry, obedience and self-sacrifice. At the outbreak of war more than half the HJ leaders voluntarily exchanged their brown shirts for the field-grey of the Wehrmacht. In Poland alone 314 HJ leaders died. 'We were afraid we might get there too late', recalls one of the volunteers. 'That would have been terrible. We thought the war might end first, and we might not have made it, we were that enthusiastic.' Younger lads now took over their positions. In the years that followed they reinforced the 'Home Front' in the service of the Führer. *Hitlerjungen* spent their holidays harvesting or in the Reich Labour Service. The girls helped out mothers of large families.

Whether as air-raid wardens or messengers, as anti-aircraft gunners or firemen in burning cities, Hitler's children took on tasks of 'importance to the war-effort'. In 'military fitness camps' hundreds of thousands of youngsters were given the final polish before serving in the Wehrmacht. Many of them never returned from the Front. More than one third of those born between 1921 and 1925 bled to death on the battlefields of the Second World War or died in the rain of bombs on the Home Front. From the Atlantic coast to the Black Sea, from the Arctic Circle to North Africa, and back through Königsberg and Breslau to Berlin, their graves mark the misguided route of a generation seduced, a generation whom Hitler cheated of their youth.

# CHAPTER TWO

# SUBMISSION

## KNOPP/DEICK

It is the woman's task to be *beautiful* and bring children into the world. The hen-bird preens herself for her mate and hatches the eggs for him. For his part the male provides her with food. At other times he stands guard and wards off the enemy.

*Joseph Goebbels, 1929*

In men's eyes most females obviously were stupid cows who were needed for breeding, to prevent the race from dying out. In those days mothers were expected to produce as many children as possible. Everything else was men's business.

*Gerda Zorn, born 1920*

The concept of female emancipation is merely an invention of the Jewish intellect and its substance bears the stamp of the same mind.

*Adolf Hitler, 1934*

There was absolutely no interest in women studying. They were meant to be mothers and had to look after hearth and home and enlarge the family.

*Sabine Schauer, born 1924*

We will never, on principle, make demands for the equality of the women of our nation with the men of our nation, but we will make the justifiable interests of women dependent on the overriding imperatives of our nation.

*Gertrud Scholtz-Klink,*
*Reich adviser to the NS women's movement, 1935*

I felt it was a terrible fate to have been born a girl. You see, it meant I could not place my life at the disposal of the Fatherland.

*Gudrun Pausewang, born 1928*

The National Socialist movement is by its nature a masculine movement. If we exclude womankind from the realm of public life, we do so not because we want to get on without them, but because we want to give them back their true honour. The finest and most elevated profession is still that of wife and mother.

*Joseph Goebbels, 1934*

We underwent a kind of emancipation. Even before war broke out, girls and women were given jobs that previously they would not have been thought capable of.

*Gudrun Pausewang, born 1928*

I would be ashamed to be a German male, if ever in time of war one single woman had to go to the Front.

*Adolf Hitler, 1935*

We were trained on an anti-aircraft battery by an older warden. He couldn't hide his pity for us.

*Irmgard Gaupp-Wagener, born 1926*

I call upon the young women of Germany to remember always that the woman who has the most children also gives most to the Fatherland.

*Hermann Göring, 1939*

A German girl was supposed to be blonde and blue-eyed, like they were on the propaganda posters. And have as many healthy children as possible.

*Irmgard Rogge, born 1927*

SS-Men and you, mothers of these children that Germany hopes for, show that, in your belief in the Führer and in your wish for the eternal life of our blood and nation, you are as capable of fighting bravely and dying for Germany, as you are determined to pass on your life for Germany!

*Heinrich Himmler, 1939*

I heard a girl at work say: 'If I were tall and blonde, it would be the most wonderful thing of all for me to give the Führer a child.'

*Waltraud Günther, born 1926*

When there's a war, it is the women who bear the heaviest share. They are the ones who suffer patiently in silence.

*Hermann Göring, 1939*

From the beginning of the war I was at the fountainhead, in the Transozean news agency in Berlin, where propaganda was manufactured, which was intended to turn Germans into a 'master race', young men into 'heroes ready to die for Führer and *Volk*', girls into 'women who bear children and make sacrifices', and mothers into widows who were proud of the death of their husbands, sons and brothers.

*Gerda Zorn, born 1920*

❖ ❖ ❖

From the bank of the River Oder comes the sound of jeering and catcalls. Rather annoyed, the girls in their brown jerkins launch into the next song: 'No land more beautiful. . .'. Under a leader scarcely older than themselves, the fourteen- to sixteen-year-old members of the *Bund Deutscher Mädel* (BDM, League of German

Lasses) have climbed into the Wehrmacht trenches on the west bank of the Oder in order to give some more encouragement to Hitler's last contingent.

It is the spring of 1945: poorly armed and ill-fed German soldiers are awaiting the onslaught of the Red Army. On the other side of the river two and a half million Soviet troops are preparing to deliver the *coup de grâce* to Hitler's 'Thousand Year Reich'. It is the largest army in history, with over 40,000 artillery pieces, and the Wehrmacht has scarcely anything left to put up against it. The BDM troops have been sent into their positions simply to boost morale. To sing cheerful songs before the inferno breaks out.

At the same time in the Berlin suburb of Gatow, in the guest quarters of the 'Reich Youth Leadership' a glittering party is being held. Waiters in white livery are serving champagne, cognac and cigarettes. On the dance-floor uniformed HJ leaders are dancing cheek-to-cheek with young women: a few film starlets from the Ufa studios and selected BDM lasses. The engine-noise of Allied bombers can be heard above the music. *Reichsjugendführer* Artur Axmann is fondling a blonde beauty – his artificial arm, the result of a wound on the Russian Front, is resting on the young woman's knee. Then the head of the Hitler Youth disappears upstairs with his companion. Several other gentlemen in brown uniforms follow his example.

A few weeks later on 1 May 1945 an announcer on the Reich radio reports in a trembling voice: 'We have heard from the Führer's headquarters that our Führer, Adolf Hitler, has died at his command-post in the Reich Chancellery, fighting to his last breath for Germany against Bolshevism.' It was the last lie of the regime. Hitler had used poison capsules and a pistol to remove himself from responsibility. Nevertheless, the news still aroused emotions in some people: 'I cried uncontrollably', recalls the former BDM girl Annemarie Strasosky. 'It's impossible to imagine that today. It was is if a close relative had died.' The dictator's spell continued to work from beyond the grave.

It is a phenomenon for which it is impossible to find a parallel, at least in German history: the perception of reality in large parts of the population was so distorted that not even the complete collapse of the Wehrmacht, the reduction of their homes and cities to rubble and the death of one family member or friend after another, were enough to give rise to doubt. 'For me it was really true to say that a world had collapsed', is how Doris Schmid-Gewinner, once a proud member of the BDM, describes her feelings in the hour of annihilation. Collective self-deception reached all levels of society. Girls were no exception.

A million times over, the generation who are today's grand-mothers have asked themselves, 'How could it have happened?' The attempts to give an answer are equally legion – even though for a long time the preferred reaction was silence and suppression. Yet from all the hundreds of first-person reports and interviews, one thing emerges clearly: the wide variety of experiences people had in the youth organisations of the Nazi Party. The BDM meant many different things. Orders and slogans changed from year to year. A young girl in a rural Catholic area might find 'hostel evenings', in which Hitler's career was repeated with rosary-like monotony, a welcome change from the restrictions of her parental home, while in working-class districts of Berlin, even after the introduction of compulsory membership, it was well known that girls often played truant from BDM events. While many young girls burned with irrational passions for Hitler – to the point of sending written proposals of marriage – others got away with making jokes about the dictator. But as contradictory as the reality in the BDM may have been, the years spent in Hitler's state youth have nonetheless left their traces on the consciousness of a generation. For the first time whole annual crops of young girls were (just like the boys) systematically gathered in and schooled in the mindset of a criminal system.

In the BDM we are working clearly and surely towards the final goal of giving our country a generation of lasses, who have been shaped into genuine exponents of the National Socialist world-view, and who are capable of carrying forward National Socialist ideas in generations to come.

*Trude Mohr, Reich spokesperson for the BDM, 1935*

The early beginnings were scarcely promising. Before 1933 only a tiny number of girls joined the Hitler Youth. In the *Schwestern-schaften* (sisterhoods) of the HJ they learned to blow whistles, sewed brown shirts, cared for those who were injured in meeting-hall brawls and distributed leaflets. They were a much-derided spin-off whose name was derived from their function as nursing 'sisters' tending the wounds of the brown bully-boys – at least according to the official Nazi version. What is more likely is that they were actual sisters of early members of the Hitler Youth who wanted to 'join in' as well. One of the best-known and largest of those sisterhoods, the one in Chemnitz, had just fifteen members.

Martha Assmann, the first 'league leader of sisterhoods', announced in 1930 in the Party newspaper, the *Völkischer Beobachter*, that they had been renamed 'the BDM in the HJ'. But because in-fighting between wings of the party spread to the female youth movement, it was not until 1930 that all Nazi girls' groups were brought under the roof of the *Bund Deutscher Mädel*. In the 'National Socialist Youth calendar' for 1932 the BDM is not even mentioned. At the beginning of the same year the female HJ numbered a mere 1,735 'lasses'.

Nonetheless, Hitler's pioneering band of girls attracted attention with a heated dispute over dress. The question was: blue cloth or brown? The 'Adviser for girls' matters in the HJ' defended the brown clothing by saying, 'the brown folk-costume' as worn in Schleswig-Holstein 'is not a copy of the brown shirt of the SA man. In fact we specifically want to avoid copying any male uniform. To do otherwise would surely be a visible expression of the intellectual dependence of woman on man. The lasses who want to promote and champion the ideas of Adolf Hitler, will testify to their courage and self-sacrifice proudly and with a sense of decorum in authentic German lasses' costume.' In the end, despite heartfelt appeals, it was blue skirts and white blouses that carried the day.

> Even in the *Jungmädel* we had to march – properly in step, right-turn, about-turn. I tripped over my feet and was so terrified by the bellowing of orders that I muddled up my left and my right and was almost in tears.
>
> *Ilse Burch-Lennartz, born 1929*

How should we picture the early cells of the BDM before Hitler hoodwinked his way into power? As a harassed, if fanatical, adjunct to a chauvinistic male association? As swooning groupies of the brown-shirted functionaries? The truth is less exciting – and has nothing to do with the future function of the BDM as an instrument for bringing half of Germany's youth into line with the regime. In fact the *Schwesternschaften* in some ways represented the avant-garde among the girls of the waning Weimar republic – just as other youth associations did, such as the *Wanderschwestern* (Girl Hikers) and the Girl Scouts. To go out on expeditions without one's parents, to sit around camp-fires with boys, perhaps even to dance with them in a woodland clearing on a summer evening – all that seemed like an unprecedented provocation to bourgeois society, a demonstration against the traditional moral attitudes of their parents.

In the middle-class world of Germany's first democracy, females were still widely regarded as second-class human beings. Admittedly they had had the vote since 1919, but in public life – in politics, art or science – women were seldom found in important positions. At universities women students were in a minority and were the cause of surreptitious amusement. Sport for women was regarded as obscene. Life for the mothers of most future BDM lasses was governed by the famous 'three Ks': *Kinder, Küche* and sometimes *Kirche* (Children, Cooking and Church).

The young members of the female avant-garde greedily seized every opportunity to escape these constraints. Whether as *Wandervögel* or *Schwesternschaften* – the chance to experience the 'feeling of freedom' for a few hours each week was hugely attractive to many a young girl. The urge for social liberation was the strongest card in the suit of the early BDM, even though Hitler himself did nothing to conceal his views about the role of women: 'The wife's world is her husband. Only now and then does she think about anything else.' The party mouthpiece, the *Völkischer Beobachter*, missed no opportunity to stress that women ought to be 'removed' from every sphere of public life. Thus an innate contradiction was created in the BDM from its very beginnings: on the one hand it was to be an integral component of an atavistic male society, and at the same time it wanted to pursue the goal of emancipation.

> A German girl has nationality, and only with marriage does she achieve citizenship.
>
> *Adolf Hitler,* Mein Kampf

This kind of minority existence came to an abrupt end on 30 January 1933. Because of the abolition of other youth associations hordes of girls swarmed into the BDM, which in a short time grew to be numerically the largest girls' organisation in the world. In the first year of Nazi rule the number of 'lasses' soared from 23,900 to 593,000. The younger age-group from ten to fourteen was organised in the *Jungmädelbund,* a subdivision with its own staff of leaders. The BDM itself was in turn part of the overall Hitler Youth. The Reich Adviser of the BDM remained de facto subordinate to the *Reichs-jugendführer,* Baldur von Schirach.

In the spirit of the times, the dissolution of other youth organisations only met with sporadic resistance and protest. Gertrud Hocke, who became a 'junior district leader' in the *Jungmädel* arm of the BDM, recalls: 'The name of our association was the "Young Nation Irregulars". We were all idealists and very close to nature. When all the associations were broken up, I was certainly sad, but like most people I thought: we have the makings of what is needed. I could sing well and play a musical instrument. And now I wanted to pass that on.'

The explosion of membership in the BDM was admittedly not entirely attributable to the break-up of the other youth associations. 'It was simply like a strong current', remembers Marianne Langen, born in 1917, 'a genuine mass-movement'. The joyous feeling of wanting to help build a better Germany captured the young in particular. 'The new age marches with us.' That seductive line from the old workers' song, now sung with feeling by the SA and HJ, captures perhaps better than anything the mood in the months that followed the 'seizure of power'. 'So who *wouldn't* want to join up with us then?' is the question still asked today by the former BDM leader Eva Sternheim-Peters, who experienced the pulling-power of the pioneering movement in the peaceful old town of Paderborn.

> When we sang the '*Jugendlied*' along with the Hitler Youth,
> with drums and fanfares, it was really quite an experience.
>
> *Luise Fischer, born 1920*

For most young people an added attraction was that the 'new age' meant a conscious turning-away from the world of their parents, from the republic with all its problems, and from what seemed to them the stuffy restrictions of bourgeois culture. In this respect, strangely enough, National Socialism itself has the characteristics of a youth movement. The ages of its most influential figures further bear this out. Himmler was thirty-two, Goebbels thirty-five, and Schirach a mere twenty-five when Hitler became Chancellor at the age of forty-three, making him the oldest in the top echelons of the Nazi Party.

Melitta Maschmann, whose career in the BDM reached its peak with a job as press officer in the 'Reich youth leadership', describes the effect on her of her first conscious contact with National Socialists: 'Something eerie about that night has remained with me to this day: the clatter of marching feet, the gloomy solemnity of the red and black banners, the flickering reflection of the torches on people's faces, and songs whose tunes sounded rousing and sentimental at the same time. The columns marched past for hours; among them, time and again, were groups of boys and girls who were scarcely older than ourselves. There was an earnestness in their faces and bearing which put me to shame. Who was I, who was merely allowed to stand on the kerbside and watch? I burned with such a desire to throw myself into this current, to submerge myself and be carried along by it.'

There were hundreds of thousands of others who wanted to throw themselves into this 'current', and in their recollections there is still a note of that pristine emotion: 'Everywhere torches are glowing in the gathering dusk. Slowly and deliberately I join in reciting the oath, which I have learnt by heart without really giving it much thought', is how Renate Finck remembers the moment of her acceptance into the Hitler Youth. 'We want to become *Jungmädel*. We want to have a clear eye and a capable hand. We want to be strong and proud. It is the first great rite of passage in my life. It penetrates to the depths of my heart. I am ten-and-a-half years old. I know that my life will now change.'

It is certainly true that alongside such feelings of devotion, there were those of a more profane kind: for instance the group dynamic when an entire school class voluntarily joined the BDM, or the curiosity aroused when your best friend regales you with stories of 'hostel evenings' or hiking expeditions. A woman from Regensburg, who was eleven at the time, explains the trivial reasons which made her become a *Jungmädel*: 'Some of my school friends wore blue knitted dresses which I liked very much. They belonged to an association of the Virgin Mary. I really wanted a dress like that as well (and that was my only motivation) and so my friends from primary school took me with them to their "hostel" which was in an allotment garden. On that particular afternoon it was closed. I was very upset and one of my school friends comforted me by saying that she knew a place where girls played, who wore brown dresses.'

Political motives can scarcely be discerned in such occurrences as these. The subjective experiences of young girls in the early days of the BDM only seldom have a darker side. 'I can't get the sunshine out of my memories', said one of the women we interviewed. For most of them it was still a 'lovely time' in retrospect, and quite a few talk of it as the 'loveliest time of my life'. It is only in connection with the terror and the crimes which the Hitler regime finally revealed that a mood of reflection takes over. 'All that was written on a completely different page', says Doris Schmid-Gewinner about the problems she has with her youthful memories. 'The fact that one was connected with the other is something I have never understood.'

The question nonetheless remains open as to how children dealt with the injustices which were already becoming apparent. Jewish girls were not allowed to become members of the BDM; a fact which, in the big cities at least, could hardly escape notice. Evelyn Eigermann, who is Jewish, remembers the early impact of inhumanity on her life: 'I would have liked to be a member of the BDM too. I envied all the girls who were allowed to wear the blue skirts and white blouses. It was pretty dreadful for me. Some of my classmates were sorry about it, and others were indifferent. A few said: "We belong to the BDM now. You don't, you're a dirty Jew. I've nothing against you personally, but you Jews are to blame for everything."'

The dismissal of 'undesirable' teachers as a result of the Nazification of schools was something children could witness in thousands of instances. Gerda Zorn, born in 1920, remembers the last lesson given by her favourite teacher, a man named Knief: 'He looked ill. We were wondering why he didn't sit down and begin the class. Then the door flew open. In strutted a man in SA uniform. His boots banged on the floor and he bawled "Heil Hitler". We stayed silent. "Well, Herr Knief", the man sneered, "have you said goodbye to your class? Then I must ask you to leave – I would like to begin the lesson." We clenched our fists. One word and we would have leapt from our seats. But no-one spoke up – and the door closed behind him.'

Whether it is due to perception through a child's eyes or suppression in later life, the great majority of our interviewees are unable to report many such instances of injustice. What have left their mark are the positive memories, like this typical one of a country excursion in May: 'The blouses are shining white, the eyes sparkle and faces glow in the spring breeze.' Or this confession from Eva Sternheim-Peters: 'It was the springtime of my life.'

> Of course, we were brought up to love Hitler. We knew that to us he was the Great Man, and he spoke very well. As small children we were fascinated by his personality.
>
> *Doris Brödtz, born 1924*

What was it like, this 'sunny' everyday life in the BDM, which had such a seductive effect on children? Where did its characteristic features lie? What were its methods? Wednesdays were for hostel evenings, whether in Aachen or Zwickau, in a Rhineland village or an East Prussian borough. These were usually held in a room which a group leader, scarcely older than her charges, had to 'organise' herself. 'We did a lot of singing', Gertrud Hocke tells us, 'and told each other old legends and stories.' Above all it was the words of the songs, repeated a hundred times, which sank deep into young souls – so deep that most of our interviewees could still remember at least a verse or two by heart. 'They were great', says Luise Fischer, 'sometimes I still get the urge to really shout them out once again.' How can an entire young generation be seduced? With verses full of pathos, and with tunes that are aimed at the heart. 'You actually felt a kind of intoxication', recalls the writer Gudrun Pausewang of her time in the BDM, 'when you sang one of those songs and really identified with it. Sometimes as a young girl tears came to my eyes, just because I felt I belonged to this wonderful Germany.'

Many women who sang the songs in those days have only today become aware of the deeper message in those old lines. *Wir Jungen schreiten gläubig, der Sonne zugewandt* (We young step out in faith, we turn to greet the sun); *Deutschland, du sollst leuchtend stehen, mögen wir auch untergehen* (Germany, thou shalt stand bright, though we may be destroyed); *Unsere Fahne ist mehr als der Tod* (Our flag means more than death). The words of songs were a potent weapon for turning young minds to Nazism. 'We absorbed the words without thinking about them', Ingeborg Seldte believes. 'We simply parroted back whatever nonsense was recited to us, because we thought it must be right.' The alternation of harmless folk-songs with hymns of sacrifice for the Fatherland, in the repertoire of the hostel evenings, made the whole thing easier to swallow.

> Hitler was God. I would say that if Christians have the Father, Son and Holy Ghost, then Germany's Holy Trinity was *Führer, Volk und Vaterland* – and the greatest of these, of course, was the Führer.
>
> *Sal Perel (author of* Hitlerjunge Salomon*), born 1925*

The high points in the memories of our BDM eye-witnesses are usually the excursions with the *Mädelschar*, or *Mädelschaft*, the smallest grouping in the BDM hierarchy. 'Just to get out into the countryside occasionally', goes a typical comment, 'was a terrific experience at a time when holidays and outings were almost unknown.' The usually spartan accommodation and an unvarying diet of goulash only served to heighten the romance of it all. 'There is a taste of adventure, when you come up against the changing moods of nature', explains Gudrun Pausewang. 'Excursions always have an effect on the young. It's something that touches the emotions as well as the mind. The Nazis were really very crafty in taking all that over from the Boy Scouts and youth leagues.'

The attraction of BDM events depended very much on the aptitude and enthusiasm of the leader in question, as Eva Sternheim-Peters observes. Whereas under her first group-leader she was disappointed to find a 'silly little club for girls', who were given readings from a book about Hermann Göring's late first wife. Eva was a keen and enthusiastic attender of the hostel evenings organised by the next leader to take over. This girl gave lectures about 'Heroes of the Movement' and recounted exciting tales about the 'ethnic struggle on the bloody frontiers'. With a gripping atmosphere thus established, her audience were willing to listen for the $n$th time to the – officially glorified – career of the Führer. 'I noticed time and again', adds the former BDM leader Annemarie Strasosky, 'that when only lessons were scheduled, where we had to learn the structure of the Party by heart until we dropped, and had to recite the whole of Hitler's life-story, then a lot of people stayed away. But when a jolly hostel evening was announced, with party games and songs, then we had a full house.'

> Hitler was the great solitary, who thought of nothing other than leading Germany and the German people into prosperity. People always said, he is alone; he only thinks about how Germany can be saved.
>
> *Luise Fischer, born 1920*

'Youth must be led by youth' – the maxim of the entire Hitler Youth inevitably led to a certain random quality in the experience of daily life in the BDM, but on the other hand it produced the feeling of belonging to a 'pledged community' of young people, who did not need their elders to speak for them. 'We felt we were being taken seriously', as Gudrun Pausewang puts it. 'We felt ourselves to be an equally valued part of the national community. That was a really uplifting feeling – and what also impressed the young very much was that we were thought capable of incredible achievements.' Not least of the successes that this brought was the recruitment of a sizeable corps of leadership staff. Female leaders were appointed to one of seven organisational grades, from the *Mädelschaft* of about a dozen girls, right up to one of thirty-six *Obergaue* with several tens of thousands of girls. All in all, several thousand young women were given this certainty of being part of a 'new state'. At school these new positions were of course exploited to the full. 'When you are a schoolchild', according to Sybil, Countess Schönfeldt, 'it is a fabulous feeling if you can go to the headmaster and say: "Heil Hitler, Herr Maier, Müller or Schmidt, I'm afraid I can't come to such and such a class at school. I have to do youth service!"'

'One-third ideological schooling and two-thirds physical training' – that was how, as early as 1934, Schirach outlined the work of the BDM, thus making clear the Nazi ideas on female education. A year later an adviser in the *Reichsjugendführung* gave the following definition: 'Our target is the whole person, the lass who can apply her capabilities soundly and clearly in the service of the *Volk* and the state. For this reason we are not concerned with the accumulation of any specialised knowledge, but exclusively with the community and the development of a feminine attitude.'

> Physical training was of great importance to the National Socialists. The future mothers of Germany just had to be physically fit.
>
> *Sabine Schauer, born 1924*

Indeed, physical culture formed the major part of the 'feminine attitude'. Thousands of feet of impressive propaganda film were shot showing BDM girls dancing, performing gymnastics or exercising with balls or Indian clubs. It was particularly the mass demonstrations, sometimes with more than a thousand performers, which guaranteed the 'pedagogical' background of events such as the opening of the 1936 Berlin Olympics, or at Reich party congresses. 'You are nothing, your nation is everything', the slogan from the Nazi catechism, was, for girls, nowhere more conveniently illustrated than in mass exercises like these – which had a great effect, and not only on the spectators. 'At that age, when one still hasn't really developed a personality', explains Ingeborg Seldte, who took part in the dance performances at the 1936 Olympics, 'it is a wonderful feeling to be a member of such a great mass. All thinking the same, feeling the same, doing the same.'

> The art of dance is, with music, the principal expression of our national culture. The dancers must primarily be attuned to emotion and inspiration, but not to the intellect.
>
> *Adolf Hitler, 1942*

It was in those moments that the essence of the totalitarian claim to a 'new age' was revealed most clearly: the removal of individuality in favour of a nebulous *völkisch* or ethnic identity. To quote Eva Sternheim-Peters: 'This formula – think not of what your nation can do for you, but think of what you can do for your nation – was believed in strongly by many young people at that time.' Thoughtfully she adds: 'Oh dear, the things people call idealism.' At party congresses and mass parades this form of programmed devotion was given reality in the stage management of uniformed cohorts. Whole football stadiums were filled with the brown of the HJ and blue-and-white of the BDM. No doubt among all those cheering girls there were many who laid their enthusiasm on a bit heavily, as per instructions. Hanne Baer-Page remembers Hitler's arrival at huge events like these: 'The whole time that the men were driving past down below, which must have been half an hour, we had to keep our arms raised. At both ends of each rank there was someone who walked to the centre of the rank and back, and whenever an arm started to droop, he would fling it up again.' Fascination and violence, the two keys to understanding National Socialism, are relevant to all the massed parades and gymnastic exercises by the girls of the regime.

The somewhat older performers in the gymnastic displays, those aged eighteen to twenty-one, found a place in a branch of the BDM known as 'Faith and Beauty'. Membership was voluntary in the thirty or more 'working groups' which offered subjects ranging from dance and fashion to bringing up children. In complete contrast to the rather juvenile and austere younger echelons of the BDM, femininity and especially preparation for motherhood were emphasised here. Annemarie Strasosky: 'I was in "Faith and Beauty" as well. People still talk about it in glowing terms. It was an aesthetic pleasure to see several hundred girls dressed in short gym-tunics, which were quite daring in those days but also very feminine, all doing the same movements simultaneously. I mean, what was so terribly wrong with that?'

In saying this, she makes an observation which applies to many people's youthful memories. The description of isolated and in themselves harmless experiences serves to explain one's own powerlessness. Of course, neither gymnastic exercises with hoops nor dances performed on a green meadow, are 'wrong'. What was wrong was simply the purpose which lay behind all the efforts of the regime, 'to seize the hearts of youth', as Goebbels had demanded.

> There is surely nothing finer than to educate a young thing for oneself: a lass of eighteen or twenty years old is as pliable as wax. It must be possible for a man to impose his stamp on any girl. Indeed, a woman wants nothing else.
>
> *Adolf Hitler, 1942*

Less often filmed, but as much part of daily life in the BDM as graceful club-swinging, was marching. Night marches, orienteering marches, training marches – the girls, too, were kept permanently on the go. Many of our eye-witnesses were able to tell us in detail about the strain of these forced marches, the blisters on the feet and the chafed ankles. In addition there were aptitude tests and trials of courage – all conducted on the strict principle that performance was everything. Anyone who did not meet the physical demands was branded a 'failure'. 'It was sheer torture for them', as Doris Schmid-Gewinner well remembers. 'If a girl said she couldn't swim, she was simply chucked into the water. It was brutal, absolutely brutal, when I think back on it today.'

The requirement to 'continually prove yourself' was characteristic of the work done with 'Hitler's children', whether on marches or in the hobby room, drawing or singing, acting in plays or reciting poetry. The best were showered with praise and awards, and even recommended for leadership posts. Hitler's Reich was a tough, performance-based society, even for the girls. 'Every morning we had roll-call', Maria Eisenecker tells of a BDM camp. 'After breakfast we were told, today there's a bed inspection. The next morning there was shoe inspection, then hand inspection, ear inspection, you always had to have everything clean and tidy, just like the army.' Over everything stood the *leitmotiv* of negation of one's own identity. 'It is not necessary for you to live', went one slogan from the manual *Education of Youth*, but it *is* necessary that you fulfil your duty towards your *Volk*.'

In 'Faith and Beauty', the dance group, we wore white dresses and coloured bodices, and we danced, threw up our arms, bent over from side to side. Some were more talented than others. We called it 'Faith *in* Beauty', not 'Faith *and* Beauty'.

*Gerda von Irmer, born 1929*

On the other hand, the merciless way in which the Nazi state dealt with those who could not, or would not, fulfil their 'duty', seems strangely to have been erased from most memories. The daily teasing of girls who flunked the tests of courage, the discrimination against 'non-Aryans', right up to the programme of compulsory euthanasia for the handicapped – only when questioned did some of the former BDM 'lasses' admit to having been marginally aware of such things. Nonetheless, the girls were thoroughly involved in the mechanics of ostracism. Ceija Stoika, who, as a member of a Romany community, narrowly escaped death in a concentration camp, describes a typical scene with BDM girls of her own age: 'They had already guessed from my brightly coloured skirt that I was a gypsy kid. I was obviously scared. They spat in my direction, right in my face even, and shouted: "Gypsy riff-raff!"'

Children could become messengers of terror even towards their own parents. Particularly tragic were the cases of denunciation within a family. Usually the father or mother had let slip some derogatory remark about Hitler or had listened in to the banned BBC during the war. 'The children were of course educated outside the parental home, and to a massive extent', explains Gertraude Wortmann, 'so much so that quite a number spied on their own parents. Not out of malice, but because they believed – in their naivety – that otherwise they were doing wrong to the Führer.' Annemarie Strasosky, who caught her mother listening in to 'enemy broadcasts', but did not report her, describes how deeply torn she felt: 'When I came home from BDM service, pumped full of slogans, and my mother was sitting by the wireless-set listening to British broadcasts – that really made me terribly unhappy.'

Doris Schmid-Gewinner saw a case of denunciation in her family: 'My sister was going to be made a group-leader and needed my mother's permission. My father was away fighting. So then my mother said in a loud, clear voice: "My daughters are not going to be officers' mattresses." A few days later she was taken away and put on to compulsory labour. Someone had reported her. And from that day on the grown-ups spoke only French at home, because it *must* have been someone in the family.'

Even within the BDM the terror extended well beyond 'racial' theory and political indoctrination. Disruptive behaviour and lack of interest were punished. Anyone who did not toe the line had her 'knot' taken away, the kerchief which formed part of the uniform. 'If a girl behaved badly', the former BDM leader Margarete Kassen remembers, 'she had to come to BDM meetings in ordinary clothes, or else got bawled out by the assembled team.' Several witnesses even told us about hours of 'punishment exercises' as a penance for what was usually a harmless misdemeanour. Once membership of the state youth organisation had been made obligatory by the 'Law on the Hitler Youth' of 1936 and a supplementary 'implementation ordinance' in 1939, even police methods were used. 'If they were absent for too long without an explanation', says Annemarie Strasosky, ' a lot of girls were dragged along to BDM service.'

Such indications of the need for disciplinary measures reveal that the Hitler Youth was far from being able to rely on 100 per cent enthusiasm from the boys and girls. In contrast to the way it is presented in propaganda writings of the time and not a few self-justifying 'youthful recollections', tacit objection to youth service was common and massively widespread. 'All those roll-calls', one interviewee tells us, 'the compulsion for everything to be totally organised, that was what I really disliked. I usually tried to bunk off the big parades. Those massed processions meant nothing to me. I once told the group-leader: "I'm seeing spots before my eyes." Then I was actually allowed to sit down and was given some lemon tea.'

The motives of all those youngsters, who of course were put down as slackers or party-poopers by their more zealous comrades, ranged from plain boredom to a deeply felt desire not to be even a small cog in the machinery of injustice. Anyone who, perhaps from firm religious conviction or influenced by critical parents, harboured reservations towards the 'new age', was obliged to develop camouflage strategies. 'Well, you know', Elisabeth Zimmerer explains her non-cooperation. 'I listened to it all, the shouting and always the same slogans and thought-processes. Then I simply sat down and did absolutely nothing. I just squatted there like a block of wood.'

As women, we never suffered from feelings of inferiority. We did not think we were worth less than the boys, nor were we ever treated as such.

*Elisabeth Zimmerer, born 1928*

Even in the Führer-state, which one would imagine to have been comprehensively permeated by terror, it was possible for niches to survive, in which people could withdraw with impunity from the uniformity of society. A woman who was a sixteen-year-old high-school pupil at the time confirms this: 'We made a request to the district office of the BDM, the *Untergau*, for permission to set up a music study-group instead of doing BDM service. One of our teachers had said he was willing to help us with this. After three weeks we told him we could manage on our own, and then we just gave the whole thing up. No more BDM service, no study-group – and nobody missed us.'

Are such experiences merely rare exceptions to the rule? Tiny islands of resistance in the broad current of submission? Or do they prove that a large number of girls really did persist in widespread silent opposition? It is impossible to divide the youth of those days numerically into enthusiasts, lukewarm supporters, objectors and active resisters. Even historians have considerable difficulty in making an empirical assessment of the realities of German society in the Nazi period. With the truth buried by postwar suppression and clouded by censorship or the official massaging of contemporary source material, a quantifiable judgement on our grandmothers' (and grandfathers') generation must remain in the realms of wishful thinking. The degree of consent to the regime, and the point in time when it was given, were in any case dependent on age and social milieu, on regional origins and family background – and, in the latter half of the dictatorship, not least on the war situation.

Nevertheless, we were struck by the frankness with which many of the women we interviewed admitted to their own enthusiasm. Gertraude Wortmann is still surprised at it today: 'We laughed. We sang. We even tied garlands in our hair. We celebrated the harvest thanksgiving, because we all had full stomachs.' The 'achievements' of the regime in the 1930s – full employment, the abandonment of the Versailles Treaty, seen as the 'shameful peace' – were all that was needed to convince the young of the advantages of the 'new age'. The fact that the cure for unemployment turned out to have been achieved at the cost of a horrendous national debt, and that the Versailles reparations terms had already been *de facto* significantly mitigated by the Weimar government – these were things which most people never found out in the sterile media environment of Nazi Germany. This news manipulation proved so successful that even today many a discussion comes up against objections like: 'Yes, but what about the autobahns?' or 'At least it was safe to walk around the streets at night!'

Is there any point in comparing like with unlike? The majority of our 'old girls' attempt to draw parallels with 'the youth of today'. Time and again we heard it suggested that the hysteria which greeted Hitler's appearances was 'just the same as for Michael Jackson'. Another refrain is that a lot of the 'values' of that era are completely absent in the youth of today. The answers to the question as to what 'good things' have remained from the BDM years, come like shots from a pistol: 'Comradeship', 'doing one's duty', or 'discipline' – all drawn from the catalogue of minor German virtues. But the negative side is not totally ignored. 'We were not asked our own opinion', one interviewee admits. 'Criticism or even discussion was frowned upon. There was nothing but orders and obedience.'

> We were the better members of the human race, we were the more competent, we were the more beautiful. And the Jews were the opposite – that was how it was presented to us.
>
> *Irmgard Rogge, born 1927*

How can adolescents be made to toe the line? A key element in all the youthful memories that we collected are the countless ceremonies which were part of the BDM's normal routine. Flag parades, dedications and emotional speeches were all intended to forge individuals into the 'pledged community'. The annual HJ calendar was simply packed with festivals and commemorations for the 'Movement'. It began with the 'Memorial Day of the Martyrs of the HJ' on 24 January, reached its first climax only six days later on the anniversary of the 'Seizure of Power', and continued in the following months through the 'Führer's Birthday' on 20 April,

Labour Day on 1 May, then Mother's Day and the Summer Solstice, and reached its eerie and blood-chilling climax on 9 November, the day of Hitler's failed *coup d'état* in Munich in 1923. At the time, people were already aware how closely this string of 'festivals' was related to the landmarks of the Church's year. In this, the pseudo-religious character of National Socialism was recognisably attacking the roots of Christianity. Neither Hitler's concordat with the Pope nor all the congratulatory messages to the new Führer from the German bishops did anything to alter that, and the dictator revealed more than once to his most intimate circle that, after the war was won, 'accounts must finally be settled' with the churches.

An emotional high-spot among all the festivals was the induction of a new year's crop of youngsters, a spectacle which was simultaneously reminiscent of prehistoric initiation rites and ecclesiastical ceremonies. From 1936 onward these festivals of commitment took place at a single location, Marienburg Castle near Danzig, the ancient seat of the Grand Master of the Order of Teutonic Knights. By the light of burning torches, deep within the venerable walls, hymns were sung, promises made and oaths sworn, with all the emotionalism which that era could offer. The performance was broadcast by radio throughout the Reich, where, in innumerable little swearing-in ceremonies, the same oath was taken: 'I vow to serve the Führer Adolf Hitler loyally and selflessly in the Hitler Youth. I vow obedience to the *Reichsjugendführer* and to all leaders of the HJ. I vow by our sacred banner that I will always try to be worthy of it, so help me God!'

---

If I'd been a boy, I would have wanted to go off to war as well.
*Irmgard Rogge, born 1927*

---

The fact that the nationwide oath was always sworn on the evening of 19 April, that is to say on the day before Hitler's birthday, was of course deliberate: a whole year's crop of youth as a birthday present! The black scarf of the BDM, which on those evenings was tied for the first time 'solemnly, like a military decoration', as our informants tell us, seems in retrospect to symbolise a taking into possession. A bond was being sealed – and most of the girls consented with enthusiasm.

Some of the sound recordings of these ceremonies have survived in their entirety, lasting as long as several hours. To listeners today these certainly do not sound enthralling; at best they seem weird. Shrill female voices in formulaic chants such as 'flames to heaven'; speakers praising the Führer in a liturgical monotone and with endless repetition; choirs singing such phrases as 'holy grace gave us the Führer' – the impact of these live nocturnal transmissions does not reach as far as our own time.

Admittedly, for the girls and boys who had been awaiting with feverish excitement the great moment when they would be allowed to 'belong", the words from the ether acted like a demonic spell. When emotions are deliberately released in order to distort the intelligence, children are easy prey. Eye-witnesses still find difficulty today in explaining this effect. 'Today it is impossible to comprehend', says Gertraude Wortmann.

It is a fact that most young people found themselves in a veritable frenzy, a collective delirium. And if the adults were also so susceptible to this, can one reproach the young for it? '*Wir gehören Dir*' (We are yours) – the three words spelled out, letter by letter, by tens of thousands of BDM girls in Berlin's Olympic stadium, were not just taken from the propaganda grab-bag. 'I'm glad young people can laugh about it now', says Gudrun Pausewang, 'but we took it dead seriously.'

> I felt really good in the BDM. It was a terrific community and it gave us companionship, friendship and a sense of togetherness. It was something which they could get young people excited about.
>
> *Luise Fischer, born 1920*

This emotional pull reached its greatest strength in the years just before the war. After an unprecedented propaganda campaign, those girls born in 1926 joined the BDM as *Jungmädel* virtually *en bloc* in 1936. In the following year there were as many as 2.8 million 'lasses' in the female Hitler Youth. But not only was the induction of *Jungmädel* carried out with extravagant ritual. Whether it was the swearing-in of new group-leaders or the promotion of a year of *Jungmädel* to the 'proper' BDM, the HJ's master of ceremonies exploited every opportunity to renew the emotional spell which guaranteed compliance and at the same time conveyed the feeling of being important. This bond was underpinned by various proofs of performance which had to be furnished beforehand. In the *Obergau* of Munich, for example, the girls had to pass examinations before being taken on in the BDM. One of the subjects was 'ideological' knowledge with questions such as: 'In which city are the Reich party congresses held?' or 'When and where was our Führer born?' Then they had to recite the words of songs. At least one verse from the 'Horst Wessel Song' was compulsory – but after four years with the *Jungmädel* this was generally no problem. The test concluded with 'order exercises' such as marching in the prescribed manner and putting on a little play with parts given to each girl. 'At 2 p.m. you will report for acting', is the relevant instruction from the Gau leadership.

> In its nobility the human body is freed from its violation and decline. A new world of beauty is heralded.
>
> *Adolf Hitler, 1934*

Now that party and state were penetrating so deep into public life, the visual environment was also changing. In the rare film footage from those years which was *not* shot for propaganda purposes, the omnipresence of the symbols of the regime is obvious. As well as the swastika flags and brown uniforms, the white blouses and blue skirts of the BDM are particularly noticeable. When not 'on duty' the uniform was admittedly not compulsory, but many girls apparently enjoyed wearing their 'kit' as often as possible. 'You were always properly dressed, no matter whether it was for a christening, a wedding or funeral', was the excuse often given to us; and another eye-witness adds: 'We had a teacher who beat us with a cane. We soon discovered that if a boy wore his HJ uniform or a girl her blue and white rig-out, there were no beatings. Because then he would have been beating the new state.'

True, fear of the teacher's cane may have carried less weight than the pride in wearing the girls' uniform with its insignia of the 'new age'. All the same, the 'kit' was anything but practical – too hot in summer, too cold in winter. 'One was always freezing in the nether regions', Eva Sternheim-Peters recalls with a rueful smile. Not that this deterred the keenest ones, even in the depths of winter, from trying to live up to the BDM imperative to be 'tough'. 'So we always took pride in wearing white knee-stockings, even in winter if possible', Christine Schemman relates. 'Our mothers were of course pretty horrified. So then we put on long stockings at home, only to take them off again in the hallway and put on our knee-stockings.'

For the endless physical training exercises a short sports-dress could be worn in summer. 'A strapless, ribbed, cotton chemise with the HJ insignia, and with it black satin elasticated shorts', as Eva Sternheim Peters describes it. 'It looked quite chic and was forbidden at the convent school I went to.' In fact, in many remote parishes priests tried, to the general displeasure of the girls in question, to ensure that for PT the body should be covered more adequately than by the scanty, officially sanctioned garments. Even so, the saucy little shorts had little to do with permissiveness in the modern sense. As regards physical love, the BDM carried on the old bourgeois traditions without a break. 'Sexual self-discipline' was the watch-word. Girls should be like 'fresh, clear, clean German air'. 'A saying that was drummed into us', Margarethe Kassen tells us, ran: 'Keep your blood pure, it is not yours alone. It comes from afar and flows far onward. All the future lies in it. Keep clean the cloak of your immortality. That was very clear!'

> In the BDM, lasses are being brought up to be carriers of the National Socialist ideology.
>
> *Baldur von Schirach*

Needless to say, despite such injunctions to self-control, the sight of hordes of uniformed BDM gymnasts suggested quite different ideas to their male contemporaries. A whole series of corruptions of the initials BDM clearly betrayed their ulterior motives: '*Bubi drück mich*' (Squeeze me, babe), '*Bald deutsche Mutter*' (Soon a German mother), or '*Bedarfsartikel deutscher Männer*' (Requisites for German men). Yet the reality was overwhelmingly chaste. 'I can remember,' says Doris Schmidt-Gewinner, 'how proud we were when an HJ leader was crazy about one of us. But then one just shrugged and said "I'm a good German girl". A German girl is chaste and demure, and doesn't have a baby until she is married. But then she has one straight away.' Eva Sternheim-Peters confirms this: 'Young people then were of course completely different from today, when the average age for first having sex is fifteen. In our day, it was at least twenty, if not later.'

If the urges became too strong for the regulations, then the threat of punishment loomed. 'With girls aged between sixteen and eighteen you can't stop it happening', says the former BDM leader Margarete Kassen, 'and if there were girls who were running around like wild things, they were given a serious warning that they had to behave decently.' But if all warnings fell on deaf ears and a 'lass' got pregnant, then – with very few exceptions – her membership of the BDM was immediately terminated.

For the great majority the consequence of these moral strictures was that their first love remained a matter of unfulfilled longings. The chastity demanded as an ideological ideal found expression in an almost clinical cleanliness. One interviewee described how girls with dirty blouses were sent home. Any form of make-up and the wearing of jewellery were also considered disreputable – 'except for a wrist-watch'. Smoking in uniform was forbidden as well. The correct appearance of a 'German lass' was completed with an approved hairstyle. Long plaits or, after the 1936 Olympic Games, the 'Olympic curl', were what the party line dictated.

> It was wonderful: the lasses in their white blouses, in the beautiful and harmonious movements of the dance under the brilliant sunshine of a September day! It was praise and recognition enough when the Führer said that the sight had made him forget everything else!
>
> *Gertrud Herr, born 1910, BDM leader in 1938*

The dictator liked to surround himself with uniformed girls turned out in this style. Whole railway coaches full of BDM cheerleaders were despatched to Berchtesgaden, where they were permitted to complete their pilgrimage on foot to the Berghof. Up in his mountain retreat Hitler was waiting with his entourage, so that the newsreel cameras could capture his familiar performance as the 'lovable Führer'. The images so created fit perfectly into a *galère* of bloodthirsty twentieth-century tyrants, from Stalin to Ceausescu, all of whom liked to be photographed beside their fresh-faced young subjects.

This was certainly not the first time Hitler had shown a partiality for adolescents. In his *Mein Kampf*, the manifesto he wrote while in prison, he devoted many awkwardly formulated paragraphs to the theme of youth and demanded the 'rearing of thoroughly healthy bodies', as a guarantee of the survival of the 'Germanic race'. The man who never fathered any children himself assigned girls and women the principal role of childbearers. 'The woman, too, has her battlefield', was how he praised the part played by the *Frauenschaft*, or women's delegation, at the party congress in Nuremberg. 'With every child she brings into the world for our nation, she is fighting this battle. But it is *her* battle, and the man has his own battle. The man stands up for his nation, just as the woman stands up for her family. The man stands up for the entire national community, just as the woman stands up for the children to whom she has given the gift of life.' On a recording of this speech preserved in the German Radio Archive thunderous applause can be heard from the largely female audience.

> To me, a female who gets involved in political affairs is a horror.
> *Adolf Hitler, 1942*

One of the riddles of the Nazi period is why so many girls, who had actually set themselves the goal of breaking out of the straitjacket of bourgeois morality, accepted without complaint the stereotyping which turned out to be just as traditional as that of their parents – namely the widespread reduction of the tasks of women to those of maintaining a home and raising a family. 'You see, all that lay so far in the future for us', we were told by our respondents – and also that anyway the girls 'silently' opposed the role imposed upon them 'from above'.

Proof of any open rebellion against male domination in Hitler's Reich is not to be found, either in the BDM or in the NS *Frauenschaft*. They accepted without any noteworthy objection the official denunciation of moves towards 'female emancipation' as 'an invention of the Jews', and they accepted the fact that as far back as 1921 women had been excluded from the executive of the NSDAP, and that all senior positions in the party were reserved for men. It is significant that scarcely half our respondents could name even one *Reichsreferentin* (female national adviser) of the BDM – for instance the scheming Jutta Rüdiger, who after the war published numerous articles in defence of the BDM – whereas the names of the two male *Reichsjugendführer*, Schirach and Axmann, were familiar to all.

One explanation of this acceptance of a highly conservative image of women may lie in the ability of the BDM to suggest precisely the opposite. Subjectively, the younger children in particular felt that joining the state youth organisation was a step to freedom, because the image projected by propaganda turned away from the 'romance-mad middle-class teenager' towards a girl who was both physically fit and beautiful, and who would mature into a 'courageous' woman. 'Strong, self-confident and independent', is how Eva Sternheim-Peters remembers her vision of the future, 'and if a husband came along, I would be his equal as a partner and companion in battle, like the women in the Icelandic sagas.' Gudrun Pausewang also had the feeling that she was following a new ideal in the BDM; 'She had to be healthy, she had to be capable, and she had to be a colleague to her man. That was a tremendous turnaround from the First World War period, when she wasn't a colleague, she was still just a spouse, who looked up to her husband – but definitely from several steps below him.'

*Straff aber nicht stramm, herb aber nicht derb* (upright but not rigid, tough but not coarse) – that was how the *Reichsjugendführung* liked to picture their girls. And this image was in fact well received, particularly by the *Jungmädel* and the junior years of the 'real' BDM. Slogans about 'Motherhood as the highest fulfilment' were only a very distant murmur and many of them had not even reached puberty. Not until the onset of womanhood did their interests begin to shift. It was only when girls began to think about their future working life that the vague notions of their youth proved to be an illusion. 'Higher tasks' remained the preserve of the boys. By 1933 a quota system had been introduced in higher education, limiting the proportion of female students to 10 per cent.

Consistent with this, it was stated in the written policy of the Hitler Youth: 'A limit must be set on too great an accumulation of knowledge, to permit the healthy development of the girls.' And elsewhere: 'We want lasses who believe unquestioningly in Germany and the Führer, and who in time will implant this belief in the hearts of their children; then will National Socialism and thereby Germany last for ever.'

A life's task of producing children to meet the specifications of the system – this was the future for *Mädel* planned by Hitler's henchmen in the *Reichsjugendführung*. But not a word was said now about heroines in the mould of Nordic deities. It was becoming painfully clear to many once-enthusiastic girls that under Hitler's rule women were second-class human beings: 'I felt it was a dreadful fate to have been born a girl, a woman', Gudrun Pausewang confesses. 'You see, it meant I could not place my life at the disposal of the Fatherland.'

Hitler himself countered any accusations that his regime was hostile to women, with biting derision. 'Then along comes foreign opinion', he joked in another speech to the *Frauenschaft*, 'and says, look, old man! The outlook for women in your country isn't too good; they are oppressed, muzzled and enslaved. You're turning women into nothing but domestic animals. You won't give them any freedom, any equality. Well, I say that what is a yoke for one person is seen as a blessing by another. What seems like heaven for one person, is hell for the other, and vice versa, of course.' Indeed, the dictator did not have to worry about any possible demands for emancipation on the part of his female 'compatriots'. 'After the war', says Annemarie Strasosky, 'we were told that we had been deprived of our freedom all those years. For me that was a completely new point of view. I hadn't even noticed that we *weren't* free, because the concept of freedom, as it was now explained to me, had been quite unknown to me.'

> The most important thing for the future is that we have masses of children! The general rule must be that a family is not guaranteed until it has at least four children; they should in fact be four sons!
>
> *Adolf Hitler, 1941*

A further explanation for the apparently willing subordination of a whole generation of young women in an atavistic stereotype can be found in their 'relationship' with Hitler. Many of our witnesses confirm that this man – who seen through today's eyes is anything but attractive – exuded a powerful magnetism which had nothing to do with his politics. A considerable number of former *Mädels* today admit a kind of emotional attachment to the dictator. Here is a sample from our interviews: 'He was the Supreme Father. I know it's incomprehensible today, but that's how it was.' 'It really was a deep, intense love. I can't put it any other way.' 'Exactly the same as God. I felt about him exactly the same way I felt about God.'

Eva Sternheim-Peters describes how the manipulative teaching at school and in the BDM had coloured her image of Hitler: 'His coming was an incredible stroke of historical luck; that sounds grotesque today, but that's what it was to me and to many others. It was something almost mystical. I suppose it was rather like the legend of the emperor Barbarossa in the Kyffhäuser cave, or something of that kind – anyway, we felt fortunate to be allowed to live in the very time when this unique man, Hitler, existed.'

When one watches the most extravagant scenes of jubilation from the Nazi period, such as Hitler's appearance at the 'German Gymnastics Festival' in Breslau in 1938, at the entry of German troops into the Sudetenland in the same year or during the 'victory celebrations' after the campaign in France, it is noticeable that the cameras capture the strongest emotions among girls and women. Many of the pictures show such ecstatic excitement that one cannot but assume that there was a physical element in it.

Hitler an object of erotic fantasies? Understandably we found no proof of this in our interviews, but there is another source, left behind by some of his most ardent admirers: love-letters to the dictator. The fact that these have been preserved for posterity we owe to the illegal collecting obsession of a former German communist named Willy Eucker, who returned to Germany in 1945 in an American uniform. Having changed his name to W.C. Emker, he worked for the US military authorities in Berlin. 'Of course we went to see Hitler's Reich Chancellery', he told us. 'We walked through the rooms with huge bomb-holes in all the ceilings and mountains of paper scattered everywhere. I picked a few letters from a pile. They were addressed to "Our beloved Führer". We shoved some of the letters in a bag before leaving the building.'

After that Emker sneaked through a side entrance into the ruins of the Reich Chancellery several dozen times and put into his bag things that the Soviets obviously had no interest in. That was how several thousand letters from the 'private correspondence' of the 'Führer and Reich Chancellor' reached the United States, where extracts were only briefly made accessible: petitions, requests for autographs and mail from female admirers. Even though these presumably represent only a fraction of Hitler's fan-mail, these often yellowing letters do allow us to look into the depths of German souls during those benighted years.

The love-letters from women and girls fill a whole filing cabinet. They range from the ardent assurance of 'true love', through offers of marriage, to the wish of 'a woman from the Saxon lands' to conceive a child by Hitler – the reason being: 'The mere thought that you should have no children gives me no peace.' It is highly probably that Hitler never personally held any of these missives in his hand, though they were addressed to 'my dear heart-throb', to 'the sweetest and best love of my heart', or to 'dearest, madly desired Wolfie'. As a rule the Chancellor's office replied with standard letters ('Please accept our warm thanks . . .'). Admittedly, if a female admirer was particularly persistent and wrote again and again, the local police would certainly be informed. Quite a number were then declared 'mentally disturbed' and packed off to so-called 'clinical institutions'.

These women and their letters are certainly extreme exceptions – but they give an example of what a powerful attraction Hitler exercised on women in particular. It is, however, a matter of record that every woman who actually got close to him came to an unhappy end. His niece, Geli Raubal, worshipped him and finally killed herself because he did not give her the attention she demanded. Eva Braun suffered for many years in the enforced role of a secret mistress, attempted suicide several times and only on the day before her death in the bunker did she have the dubious honour of being allowed to call herself 'Frau Hitler'. The upper-class Englishwoman, Unity Mitford, was the most persistent of all his fans and even though successful enough to be invited to dine at the dictator's table, was so unhappy that she shot herself in the head in Munich's Englischer Garten. Love for Hitler invariably proved to be a fatal trap.

On a much smaller scale, our witnesses hint at how they fell under the spell of this man. 'Hitler looked into my eyes and stroked my cheek', Lore Schaaf of Hamburg tells us, 'and that was an indescribable experience for me. I thought it was fantastic and never wanted to wash again. My mother said: "You're crazy", and I probably was.' Ilse Holl took part in a mass dance display by BDM 'lasses' at a Reich party rally and describes how she heard about Hitler's reaction: 'Apparently he sat up very straight and said: "My word, when I see those girls of mine like that, all my worries could melt away." And what did we do? We hugged each other and wept with joy. We'd been dancing for the Führer himself. Frightful, wasn't it?'

Annemarie Aumüller tells of a visit by Hitler to Königsberg, which ended in the evening with a long, standing ovation by a group of HJ and BDM members: 'We kept on shouting in unison: "Lieber Führer, sei so nett, zeig dich mal am Fensterbrett" (Dear Führer, won't you please show yourself at the window). And when we had shouted long enough he appeared again and we began frantically shouting "Heil Hitler" again. It went on like that, back and forth, for hours, so that at school the next morning we were, in the truest sense of the word, speechless, and those of us who weren't made an effort to seem genuinely speechless.'

When you looked at him you saw only the eyes. Then came the voice with its particular quality, revealing his thoughts. Poets and writers have tried to capture these impressions. They have never quite succeeded.

*Gertrud Herr, born 1910, BDM group-leader*

What made Hitler as a man so attractive to women at the time? Probably the most important factor was that in all the propaganda media he presented himself as the unattainable loner. The Führer's private life remained completely hidden from the public. The Germans did not hear about Eva Braun until after the war. No 'average German' knew that Hitler liked to stay in bed until about midday, and that he preferred lazing around the Berghof to getting down to his paperwork. The images released to the newsreels, by contrast, led people to believe in a Führer who in reality never existed – a man obsessed by duty who appeared to spend every free moment in the service of his people.

What is more, when seen from an unreal distance, surrounded by massed cohorts, illuminated by domes of light, this artificial figure aroused the deepest feminine yearnings: the desire to help, support and admire. In the love-letters as well as in the statements of our respondents we clearly detect emotions which have their origins in the role of both mistress and mother. The desire to summon him back from his almost mythical remoteness into their home, hearth and bed – therein lies, no doubt, the essence of Hitler's mysterious attraction to girls and women. 'What a pity he doesn't have a wife, we always said to each other', is how Hildegard Schindler sums it up. 'A nice man like that really ought to have a wife. Then perhaps everything would be much better for him.'

It can be argued that the description of Hitler's 'relationship' to the girls of those times comes close to a viewpoint which perceives the dictator as the active party and the girls merely as 'objects' of seduction. This would certainly be in line with one prevailing view: whereas the men, as perpetrators of the criminal purposes of the regime, stood and still stand at the heart of the historical debate about guilt and involvement, posterity has been happy to assign to women the role of mere supporters, who grieved over their menfolk, trembled for their own lives in air-raid shelters and ultimately, as *Trümmerfrauen* (the women who cleared up the rubble), had to cope with the reconstruction of Germany.

> Men who didn't belong to the Party were jerks. Only someone who was a good National Socialist was a real man.
> *Elisabeth Zimmerer, born 1928*

It seems that women may have been treated too leniently in all this. For of course they voted, joined in, or looked the other way, just as much as the men did and perhaps cheered 'Heil Hitler' just as often. That said, in a historical assessment allowances have to be made on the grounds of youth for the generation of *Jungmädel*, as much as for their male counterparts, the *Pimpfe*, just as today's legal code permits the plea of 'diminished responsibility' in the case of juvenile offenders. 'As children we were simply abused', recalls Gudrun Pausewang. 'We believed in the truth of what we were conditioned to believe in.'

For girls, as for everyone else, the essential message of this 'creed' was of course 'racial' teaching – the mania about 'good' and 'bad' blood. The superiority of the 'Aryan' race in general – and in particular over the Jews – was conveyed in the BDM's teaching materials just as it was in schools. The seeds of injustice were sown even in infants' primers. Our respondents often quoted from a pamphlet entitled *The Poisonous Mushroom*. Here is a sample: 'There are good mushrooms and there are bad mushrooms. There are good human beings and bad human beings. The bad ones are the Jews. But it is often very hard to tell the good human beings from the bad ones.' Gudrun Pausewang recalls another chapter from this infamous smear-sheet. 'There was a story in *The Poisonous Mushroom* which I could not get out of my mind all through my childhood. A girl is sent by her mother to the dentist; she sits in the waiting-room with another girl, who is the first to be called in by the dentist. He of course has a Jewish face, with a hooked nose, protruding lips and bags under his eyes. So now the first girl is sitting alone in the waiting-room and she hears a scream from the surgery: "Oh no, Doctor, please don't, Doctor!" Then silence. Then the dentist comes out and tries to beckon her in. At this point she runs away. And as a child I was left wondering what on earth the Jew was doing to the girl in his room? Naturally that aroused my fantasies enormously.'

> If we succeed in re-establishing this Nordic race in and around Germany, and if we induce them to become farmers and produce from this seed-bed a people of 200 million, then the world will belong to us.
>
> *Heinrich Himmler, 1929*

True, only about half of our interviewees thought they could remember any incitement to anti-Semitism at all, either in the BDM or at school. Regional particularities may play a part in this, as may the mechanism of suppression that is part of the human mind. Those who can still remember the manipulation are very clear about its effectiveness. As Irmgard Rogge puts it: 'There's this saying: steady dripping hollows the stone. And we were like a stone on to which things were slowly dripped, until we believed that it was all perfectly all right.' Margarete Kassen even admits: 'Race was the most important word in our lives.'

The other aspect of this calumny – what might be called the deceptive attraction of racial obsession – was the idealisation of typical 'Germanic' attributes. The ideal Nordic woman should of course be blonde, blue-eyed, tall and fair-skinned. Those who could, gave nature a helping hand. 'I bought a big bottle of hydrogen peroxide', Ursula Sempf from Berlin tells us, 'and washed my hair with it, then rinsed and dried it. When my mother saw it, of course she boxed both my ears. "What *have* you done to your hair?" she scolded. But by then it was too late. All of a sudden I was very Nordic and blonde, white-blonde in fact. Incidentally, that was just before I went on work service, where I was very popular with the leaders because I was so lovely and blonde.' The ideal of beauty, whether male of female, was omnipresent.

Maria Eisenecker argues that children and young people could scarcely defend themselves against the poison of brainwashing: 'We were never questioned on these subjects. We could only repeat to show we had understood. Our own opinions were not asked for.' All the same, one may speculate about what inner conflicts were triggered when socialising with a Jewish school friend was suddenly forbidden, or when in 1941, as one witness tells us, her mother cut her Jewish friends out of the school photographs. Before the physical annihilation started, liquidation began with the faces.

> I had this one Jewish friend, and she asked me: 'Why can't I be in the BDM?' I didn't know what to say.
>
> *Irmgard Gaupp-Wagener, born 1926*

Nonetheless, dealing with injustice took many very different routes. The most terrible must be that taken by the women and girls who volunteered to perform their 'service to the Fatherland' as wardresses in concentration camps. The most honourable was that chosen by those who engaged in open conflict with the regime. Inge Scholl, the sister of Sophie, who was executed after the arrest of the 'White Rose' group, tells this anecdote: 'I remember going on a cycling tour. One evening a fifteen-year-old girl suddenly said: "It would all be so lovely, if it weren't for this business about the Jews." In Sophie's class at school there were two girls who were Jewish: Luise Nathan and Anneliese Wallersteiner. Sophie was very upset about that.'

'What I want is a violent, dominating, unafraid and cruel youth. The young must be all of these things. They must endure pain. There can be nothing weak or soft about them.' This demand by Hitler was increasingly put to the test, when the murderous activities of the regime could no longer be ignored. The majority of our respondents thought they had known about the burning of synagogues and the deportations by the time the war had started. On the other hand, most had no idea about the mass murder which was taking place behind the front line and in the camps. Barbara Röper from Koblenz says: 'Well, I had certainly *heard* of Dachau, but not of course any details of what went on there. But people would sometimes say to me: "Shut up, or you'll go to Dachau."'

The pogrom on the night of 9 November 1938 left particularly deep marks on the memory of our witnesses. It was officially justified as the 'soul of the people' boiling over, though this was disproved if only by the fact that in countless districts it was several days before the local Party officials took any action. 'They dragged an old woman downstairs by her hair'; today Gertraude Wortmann still shudders at the memory, 'and I stood there and thought: what are they doing, what are they up to, what is this? But in the end I thought: she must have done something wrong, she must be a criminal. Then I vomited.' Gudrun Pausewang, who in 1938 was living in a little village in Silesia, also tells of the great emotional difficulty she had in trying to reconcile the emerging terror with her child's image of the world: 'Outside the shattered window of a little haberdashery shop the old Jewish owner was sweeping up the broken glass, and a semi-circle of people had gathered round the shop to stare. What struck me very much was how quiet it was. An extraordinary silence. No-one shouted: "Dirty Jew!" because they knew the man and I don't suppose he had ever done any harm to anyone. Then something happened which still disturbs me to this day. As a ten-year-old I felt a deep sympathy for this man, who was being pilloried and was, as it were, sweeping up the shattered pieces of his life. And I thought: For heaven's sake, I'm not supposed to feel sorry for a Jew. That inner tension was incredibly strong.'

Even BDM girls shared the classic dilemma of the German population during the Nazi period: anyone who knew Jews personally, still more if they were friends, had to try to resolve the contradiction between the propaganda of hate and their sympathy for individuals. The possibilities open to them were certainly limited. Either you made up your mind to reject the propaganda and help the victim, or you turned your back on your Jewish acquaintance. There was seldom any compromise. The thousands of 'U-boats', the Jews who were successfully hidden in Germany from Eichmann's bloodhounds, are proof of the fact that some people did choose the first option – even if it put their own lives at risk.

However, as soon as one joined the BDM, influence in the other direction began. Melitta Maschmann tells of a favourite exercise of her *Untergauführerin* or district leader. 'Sometimes she would make us march three abreast along the Kurfürstendamm in Berlin, and jog part of the way at the double. Then we had to make us much noise as possible with our feet. "This is where the rich Jews live", she said, "so it doesn't matter if their afternoon nap is disturbed a bit."'

Annemarie Strasosky, who worked at a branch office of the BDM, came into contact with the machinery of terror simply because of the location of her office: 'Directly below us was the SD department, the security service. It was the only department that was protected by a security door, so that, unlike on our floor, you couldn't just walk into the offices. From time to time we heard screams coming from there. That had a tremendous effect on us and made me very scared.'

When the deportations started and in the east the darkest chapter in German history began to take its course, a vague feeling spread through the population that something monstrous and unspeakable was going on. It was true that the extermination camps were a 'secret Reich matter', but tales told by ordinary soldiers on home leave about mass shootings behind the front lines, and the uncertainty about what was happening to the Jews who were being deported eastwards, aroused the worst fears. Doris Schmid-Gewinner, who was in the BDM during the war, thinks that even then she must have 'known all about lampshades made from human skin' and 'gold teeth being ripped out' – she may be an isolated case, certainly, but also an example of striking frankness compared to the many who must then have known enough to know that they did not want to know any more.

We learned that 'KZ' stood for Konzentrationslager
(concentration camp). That's where people who were against
the government were kept, and they had to be re-educated
and had to concentrate on Hitler.

*Luise Fischer, born 1920*

We have no reason to disbelieve all those witnesses who tell us
they knew nothing about the Holocaust until the end of the war.
Anyone who had a particularly protected childhood or who grew
up in a remote area could have remained entirely spared any
knowledge of the crime. How else can we explain the violent
reactions in Germany when the victorious Allies showed films of
the concentration camps? True, the reticence on the question of
guilty knowledge gets rather clouded by the human capacity to
forget things which ought not to be true. Lore Walb, who was also
once a member of the BDM, tackles the problem of the Nazi
period in a very penetrating way in her diaries and in so doing uses
her own example to shed light on the phenomenon of suppression.
'I am nailed by the verifiable facts', she writes self-critically. 'The
excuse of "forgetting" doesn't hold up. The fact that I can no
longer remember, and merely keep the defensive feeling of "don't
look!" in my memory, proves that I had an awareness of wrong
and a fear of seeing wrong being done. If I had paid attention to
the terror and the inhumanity, my whole framework of values
would have collapsed.'

Some of our witnesses contribute concrete experiences to the
discussion, which shed light on how widespread the terror was.
Barbara Röper, for example, did 'auxiliary war service' in 1943–4 as
a tram conductress in Koblenz. "Once we had a special trip along
the far bank of the Rhine', she recalls, 'and we were told, this time
you don't have to take the fares in these two cars, they're only going
as far as the railway station.' She no longer remembers the precise
circumstances, but at the time she certainly realised the purpose of
the journey. 'They probably took the people somewhere to be
killed. That would certainly have dawned on us, perhaps it did dawn
on me.' Just like Barbara Röper, hundreds of thousands must have

come into contact with the unimaginable – whether as policemen or railway employees, as notaries or merely as chance eye-witnesses.

But what was the effect of the terror on children who were not yet capable of grasping the horrific reality? Waltraud Günther is still deeply moved as she tells how she watched aghast and uncomprehending as her schoolgirl friend was deported: 'I went to pick her up on the way to school one morning – well, we were still not even ten years old. A truck was parked in front of her house and furniture was being thrown on to it. For me, as a child, it was terribly distressing. I thought: how mean of her, she didn't even tell me she was moving.' Only later, Waltraud Günther says, did she understand what had really happened to her friend.

> When I was twelve years old, my father told me about the concentration camps. He also told me straight out that if I were ever to speak about them, not only would he be demoted, but we would all get to know one of these establishments from the inside.
>
> *Gerda von Irmer, born 1929*

The central questions still have to be put to a whole generation: What did you know? What did you do? Needless to say, the answers can only be individual ones. Yet there were widely available models for how to deal with the internal conflicts. From today's standpoint one of the oddest was to seek the guilty men among those in the immediate circle of the 'beloved Führer'. Gerda von Irmer tells us: 'People always used to say – "if only the Führer knew about that". Whenever there was talk about someone being in a KZ or something awful happening, people would say: "If only the Führer knew, but all that is kept from him."' The notion of the Great Criminal himself as the victim of evil men behind the scenes was as widespread as it was outlandish, yet it explains why, after the attempt on his life on 20 July 1944, so many Germans were relieved that Hitler had survived.

At the same time the dictator and his henchmen were hardly reticent when it came to announcing their murderous plans: take

Hitler's outburst in 1939 when he said a war would result in the 'annihilation of the Jewish race in Europe', or Goebbels' slip of the tongue in the *Volkspalast* speech when he briefly revealed the truth with the word 'extermination'; or Göring's notorious speech after the Stalingrad debacle, when he threatened dire consequences if 'the Jew were to take revenge on German women and children' – revenge for what?

Indeed, as the fortunes of war turned against Germany, the propaganda hinted more and more clearly at the true dimensions of the 'Final Solution', in order to make the Germans accomplices who would have to remain bound to the swastika, for better or worse. Many of our interviewees can still remember clearly how, when the victors marched in, they feared a final court of criminal justice: 'We thought we'd all end up in a Siberian labour-camp.'

> Rumours went round that in the concentration camps people were tortured to death. But you were never allowed to talk about it or you would end up there. When I did my service it was as if the fear was blown away, and was replaced by a deep feeling of community. I did not associate the two extremes: on one side KZs and fear, on the other cooperation and happiness – they simply *couldn't* come from a single source . . .
>
> *Doris Schmid-Gewinner, born 1930*

In the conversations with girls of the Hitler period it became clear to us how traumatised many members of that generation are and will probably remain for ever. Usually it was in comfortable living-rooms, radiating the charm of middle-class affluence, that stories of human tragedy came to light. The most disturbing of them come from the victimised races. Ceija Stoika, who is proud to be called a gypsy, had to live through great pain: from the moment when she received an urn by post from the concentration camp, containing her father's ashes – to her own odyssey through the world of the camps, from Ravensbrück to Auschwitz. Especially vivid in her mind are the wardresses in the Ravensbrück women's camp: 'Those women with their boots and their riding-whips – if one of them said "shut yer mouth" and then hit you, obviously she would draw blood. You were beaten on the head, over and over again. It's a dreadful humiliation, having that done to you by a woman.'

When the war ended the Ravensbrück wardresses were put on trial. It can be seen from the court records that the younger wardresses often started with a 'career' in the BDM. The most brutal of them were executed, such as the notorious Dorothea Binz, who took a perverse pleasure in tormenting the inmates. Yet even when assessing these hangman's assistants, it is necessary to make a distinction: two of the wardresses had smuggled letters from their charges to the outside world and for that they became prisoners themselves. Irritating as it may seem, humanity could occasionally survive, even in an SS uniform, especially since in the final years of the war more and more wardresses were recruited compulsorily. What this could mean for a young woman is indicated by Evelis Heinzerling who, as leader of an anti-aircraft battery, had a new girl assigned to her from the Reich Labour Service: 'She had previously been a wardress at Ravensbrück and merely said that her father had got her out of there because she couldn't stand it any longer. I was sorry for her. She was very wrapped up in herself and didn't tell us a word about the camp.'

> The Ravensbrück concentration camp was run by women, who were worse than Satan, worse than the men in Auschwitz. They were indescribable.
>
> *Ceija Stoika, born 1934, former KZ inmate*

Girls like that, detailed off to be part of the machinery of murder, show what became of the enormous initial enthusiasm during the war years. The voluntary spirit had become service, service had become duty, and duty had finally become compulsion. Millions of girls had to work in agriculture and industry to replace the men who had been drafted. For whole age-groups, what had looked like play-acting in the pre-war years, now became deadly serious. All the collecting, from old clothes, through Colorado beetles to herbs for making tea, the annual summons to the 'Winter Aid Campaign', the 'stew-pot Sundays' and farm duties, were now replaced by sober work in arms and munitions factories. Nearly all our respondents had to do compulsory service in the war years and most of them now realise that their efforts made it possible for Germany to continue the war. Naturally, the threat of punishment hung over anyone who refused. 'Mother always told us', Doris Schmid-Gewinner recalls, 'do what they ask, otherwise you'll end up in a concentration camp. Any mistake can be fatal.'

Most of all it was being assigned to farms that evokes the most positive memories among many 'labour-maids'. For girls from the big cities, farm service provided the first intensive contact with nature. The extent to which young people were involved in agriculture is shown clearly by the harvest in the autumn of 1942, praised in the propaganda as the 'Battle of the Producers', in which over two million BDM 'lasses' and *Hitlerjungen* took part. Gisela Maschmann describes how this kind of work led to a new awareness: 'In those weeks I experienced something wonderful: physical exhaustion. It transformed itself into an irrepressible joy in achievement. When the temptation to fall in a heap got too great, there was one last remedy: to look over at the camp flag.'

The illusion of belonging to a 'national community' fighting for its survival released enormous energy for work. Even the younger ones felt under an obligation to prepare the ground for the 'Final Victory'. 'In the hostel evenings we did everything we could for the soldiers', Doris Schmid-Gewinner remembers. 'We knitted for them, we wrote letters to them. It was simply a matter of: they're fighting for us, we must do something for *them*!' Irmgard Rogge illustrates the extent to which the girls, too, were gripped by the obsession with a heroic death as the supreme sacrifice for the Fatherland: 'I can remember how as a young girl I sometimes stood in front of the mirror in a heroic pose and imagined I could now lay down my life for *Führer, Volk und Vaterland*, and then everyone else could live in peace. Those were the weird sort of moods I had.'

'For us it will be a sacred duty to protect and perfect our Fatherland, since our traditional enemies, who are encamped around us, try again and again to make our blooms wilt.' That's the sort of rubbish we wrote in essays in those days; that was how we were educated, Nazi-style.

*Erika Augustin, born 1921*

In 1944, when the battle-fronts were creeping ever closer to the borders of the Reich, 'moods' like that could turn into sad reality. Up to that point Hitler himself had resisted all the urging of his paladins to draft women into the Wehrmacht. The background to this was his reactionary chauvinist's perception of gender roles. 'I would be ashamed to be a German male', he had declared before the war, 'if, in the event of war, a single woman should ever have to go to the front. If men become so pitiful and cowardly that they excuse such conduct by calling it equality for women – then no, that is not equality, because nature has not created women for that. Woman was created to tend the wounds of the man; that is her task.' However, the need for more 'human material' for a war that had already long been lost, caused the dictator to break even this promise.

Yet even in wartime a limit must be placed on women's work at the point where it would be a threat to the nation's lifeblood.

*Guidelines issued on 19 October 1938*

From 1943 onward women and girls were drafted for office jobs in the Luftwaffe and the intelligence services, and from 1944 they were officially called up for service with anti-aircraft batteries, in other words for combat duties – and 'preferably as volunteers', as an official document noted. 'I did actually sign up voluntarily, in order to help win the war', says Ingeborg Seldte, 'because I just thought it had to be done, and I had to help.' About 50,000 *Soldatinnen*, as the female soldiers were called, were indeed sent into action by the end of war, and a good many of them lost their lives. There are no statistics to show how many women operating searchlights and anti-aircraft guns died in the night air-raids, or how many Wehrmacht auxiliaries fell victim to Allied dive-bombers. Evelis Heinzerling, who led a battery of the Reich Labour Service and had over a hundred 'maids' under her command, remembers the fear that gripped them when things got serious: 'In one group we had three dead and seventeen wounded after a low-level air-attack, and the girls were so terrified that they refused to go on. They just said, we're not going out there again.' Elisabeth Zimmerer also observed, on flak duty, how girls were unable to withstand the nervous strain – with disastrous results. 'Once there was a heavy attack on the searchlight base next to ours. And the girls who were manning it ran for cover, there were so many bombs falling. Later they were shot for cowardice in the face of the enemy.'

Yet it was not only the fear of being killed that weighed on the young women – it was also the scruples about killing. 'It was terrible. I remember one situation when I actually had an enemy in my sights', Elisabeth Zimmerer tells us. 'If I had followed the orders we had been given, I should have pressed the trigger. But I didn't do it. I *couldn't* do it.'

> I couldn't press the trigger. I would rather have got myself shot than be responsible for the death of another human being.
>
> *Elisabeth Zimmerer, born 1928*

If the awareness of war for most women and girls had consisted, in the early years, of Wehrmacht bulletins, casualty statistics and food rationing, now they were engulfed in the brutal reality. Serving in field-hospitals was probably where this came home to them in the worst way of all. Maria Eisenecker, who worked as a nurse, tells us: 'It was certainly very stressful and I was particularly affected by seeing young men lying there with their legs blown off, who couldn't live but couldn't die. For many, the pain was so great that they lay awake all night, and not even strong medication like morphine was any help.' Faced with such reality, propaganda in *Junge Welt*, the 'Reich newspaper of the HJ', seemed like hollow mockery: 'The finest thing and that which most closely matches girls' sensibilities is service with the Red Cross in the field-hospitals. It is here that the girls of the BDM have found their finest task and truly become the "helping mothers of the homeland."'

Any remaining illusions of the once enthusiastic 'lasses' finally vanished in the night bombing-raids on the big cities. Confronted by rows of corpses and whole residential districts reduced to rubble, very few went on believing in a 'new age'. Instead, many were overcome by impotent rage. Doris Schmid-Gewinner, who as a fourteen-year-old in Stuttgart had to put identity-tags on dead bomb victims, and in 1945 was trained to use a *Panzerfaust* grenade-launcher, describes her feelings: 'I don't believe I thought: I'm going to die for Hitler. No, just that we must go for the people who are hurting us so much. If you can imagine how much I hated the bombers in those days – now just let them come for Stuttgart, I thought. Then I would have fired off all my *Panzerfaust* grenades at them.'

> This period gave us our independence – there was a war on – and we had to stand up for ourselves. We were equal to almost any situation.
>
> *Waltraud Günther, born 1926*

In every dictatorship, fanaticism resulting from a lack of information is one of the strongest pillars that support the regime. Yet seldom does the contradiction between reality and an illusory world seem to have been greater than in Germany in the last months of the war, in 1944–5. Bearing in mind the hopelessness of the military situation, it is puzzling and depressing to learn how astonishingly widespread was the willingness, if necessary, to make the supreme sacrifice for *Führer, Volk und Vaterland*. But looked at objectively, the fact that this enabled the regime to carry on with its genocide makes the blind dedication of a large part of the population a terrible indictment of twentieth-century Germany. 'Doubts about the rightness of it all never entered our heads', is how Irmgard Rogge explains her determination to hold out to the bitter end. 'You see, our ideas were so coloured by what we heard from our soldiers, from the armed services, and by the air-raids, that we scarcely thought about anything – except what the enemy were doing to us. And how that had to be avenged.'

> It was quite obvious to us that women had to replace the men who were fighting on the front line. We couldn't choose what we wanted to do; that was dictated to us from above. And we obeyed these orders without hesitation.
>
> *Irmgard Rogge, born 1927*

Much of what was true of the BDM in the pre-war period seemed in the war years like a distant memory. In the minds of our witnesses these were 'bleak', 'depressing', even 'dark' years, in stark contrast to the 'sunny' days before the outbreak of war. There are no more descriptions of euphoric country rambles – instead only the daily horror of war. Even the strict morality of the early years became lax. The new direction, chiefly dictated by the SS boss, Himmler, and the shadowy figure at Hitler's side, Martin Bormann, was: to have children at almost any cost, in order one day to replace the millions who were dying or being taken prisoner. Married SS men were given a salary bonus for every new child. The so-called 'national emergency marriages' were intended to bring together single women or service widows with 'battle-hardened and genetically healthy' men; and in the *Lebensborn* (Fount of Life), a registered association run by the SS, unmarried mothers were given the opportunity of bringing their children into the world anonymously, in order to combat the number of abortions.

> No matter how widely the field of women's activity may be drawn, in the end the ultimate goal of a truly organic and logical development must lie, and continue to lie, in the bringing up of a family.
>
> *Adolf Hitler, 1932*

The almost total secrecy of the new *Lebensborn* homes, combined with 'revelations' published after the war, has led to the association being regarded, right up to the present day, as a kind of 'brothel for breeding Aryans', a view which does not stand up to examination. In the *Lebensborn*, babies were *born*, not conceived. The children given away for adoption by their mothers were to be brought up by SS staff and later handed over to loyal Nazi foster-parents. What did in fact turn the *Lebensborn* into a criminal enterprise were the 'baby-raids' carried out by the SS in the occupied countries. Tens of thousands of often blond children of Polish, French or Norwegian mothers were dragged off to the Reich for the purpose of 'nordifying' the German people. A considerable number of these children never found their way back to their parents again.

In the BDM, too, the demand of the regime for more 'children for the Führer' left its mark. Ilse Burch-Lennartz tells us: 'My sister was put into a camp for girls, and right beside it there was a men's camp. Then one night, after the girls had gone to sleep, the commandants of both camps opened the doors and windows and sent the lads over to the girls' camp. Needless to say, they leapt on the girls. My sister fled in tears.'

---

The end of the war was a catastrophe. It was the destruction of everything we believed in.

*Gudrun Pausewang, born 1928*

---

Finally, as the war was raging on German soil, hundreds of thousands of women and girls became prey to the victors, both in the east and the west: the rapes were an outpouring of the hatred which had grown up in the years of German campaigns of destruction. Nearly all our respondents tell of the profound fear that seized them as the Allies marched in, of attempts to make themselves as unattractive as possible by wearing old clothes and smearing dirt on their faces. 'I went around like that for months on end, you've no idea', says Gertraude Wortmann. 'They hunted us like hares. They came round night after night. They smashed our doors in. I can still to this day hear the screams of the women. But they never got *me*.' For all those who were less fortunate, the spiritual wounds from this abuse will probably never fully heal.

It is perhaps part of human nature, that personal experience of suffering is what our memory can retain most clearly. The descriptions of those days of violence and violation are among the most forceful passages in our interviews with eye-witnesses. The trauma of total defeat – combined with the recognition of having been misused by a totalitarian regime – is still a vivid memory for the former 'lasses' of the BDM. As Gudrun Pausewang puts it: 'Having to admit to oneself that one had believed in a false ideal, that the whole thing was a lie and that one had been abused – that hurt terribly.'

Certainly not all of them have succeeded in reconciling what had seemed to them the 'lovely time' of the BDM years with the shadows of Auschwitz. 'I can't sort it out in my mind', Evelis Heinzerling tells us; 'it is beyond my powers of comprehension. If I were to really think it through, it would probably drive me to despair.' Eva Sternheim-Peters, who has movingly captured her process of self-knowledge in literary form, says this: 'Probably all I have in common with the person I once was is my name. I might even ask myself: is that really me, or is it someone else?' Gertraude Wortmann is equally hard in taking herself to task: 'That someone can be as dazzled as I was, and as credulous, must have a lot to do with one's personality.'

> We were cheated of our youth.
>
> *Hilde Seffert, born 1930*

Today Hitler's 'lasses' are grandmothers, quite a few are even great-grandmothers. After the war they made a fresh start and in both Germanies, east and west, they helped to build from the rubble the country they now live in. They are often reproached with having remained all too silent. The women we spoke to did not. On the contrary, most answered our often uncomfortable questions with astonishing frankness. Perhaps the time has finally come for that. Nearly all of them claim to have belonged to a generation who were politically abused – and yet for most of them their own youth remains just a bit of a mystery. 'Today, when I meet children and young people, aged roughly fourteen to sixteen', says Gertrud Hocke, 'I'm amazed how totally different they are. I mean, I feel as if we had been asleep in those days, as if it had been a bad dream.'

# CHAPTER 3

# BLOODSTOCK

## KNOPP/MÜLLNER

In the light of this theory, the ethnic state must focus its entire educational effort not principally on pumping in mere knowledge, but on the rearing of thoroughly healthy bodies. Only in second place comes the training of mental faculties. But here again pride of place goes to character development, especially the promotion of will-power and decisiveness, combined with an eagerness to take responsibility, and only then comes academic schooling.

*Adolf Hitler*, Mein Kampf

It is our aim to arouse the fighting spirit in you lads and to keep it alive. You must strive for and achieve those things which the Führer has in mind for the building of Germany. As a symbol of this the banner of the future is raised here, the banner for which the SA suffered and bled, the banner for which the best went to their death.

*Ernst Röhm, chief-of-staff of the SA*

Through the exaggerated importance placed on physical education the Adolf Hitler Schools fulfilled the expectation which the regime placed in them: to produce combat-ready, performance-minded managers of power, but ones who would still follow instructions in times of conflict!

*Harald Scholtz, born 1930, former Adolf Hitler School pupil*

The job waiting for us was simply to be a *Gauleiter* in Siberia. That was drummed into us.

*Klaus Geue, born 1931, former Adolf Hitler School pupil*

The first thing we had to learn was obedience. The thought behind this was: only someone who has learnt to obey orders knows how to give them.

*Uwe Lamprecht, born 1929, former pupil of the*
*Napola school, Plön*

We kept seeing these photos showing Hitler bending over a little *Pimpf*, the great man stroking the boy's cheek or putting a hand on his shoulder. We wanted him to do that to us. After all, we were boys of the Adolf Hitler School. We bore his name.

*Theo Sommer, born 1930, former Adolf Hitler*
*School boy*

By the end of the war I had learned how to die for my Fatherland, but not how to live for it. Our thinking was totally shaped in one direction: You are nothing, your *Volk* is everything. Germany must live, even if we have to die. '*Deutschland*, thou shalt stand and shine, though we may be destroyed.'

*Hans Buchholz, born 1927, former pupil of the*
*Napola school, Naumburg*

In political life, being a genius is, on its own, as good as worthless if you don't possess character. In a political leader character is more important than the so-called quality of genius, courage more important than wisdom or insight. What matters is that we build up an organisation of men who safeguard the nation's interests with persistence, tenacity and, if necessary, with ruthlessness. That is what matters.

*Adolf Hitler*

I am ashamed how little we knew about German poets and men of letters – from Thomas Mann to Gottfried Benn; how scanty our knowledge of mathematics was. So in the intellectual area our qualifications were pretty miserable.

*Harald Grundmann, born 1927, former Adolf Hitler School boy*

Anything that is weak and not strong enough is choked off and dies. It is killed, mercilessly and pitilessly, and that is the best thing for it. That is how the good Lord has arranged Nature.

*Heinrich Himmler, 1944*

If anyone showed weakness he was considered a wet, a weakling, a coward, a disgrace to the whole platoon or the whole company.

*Hans Müncheberg, born 1929, former pupil of the Napola school, Potsdam*

The fact that physical exercise is given the highest priority needs no explanation. The fine and healthy bodies of the Nordic race and its steel-hard will are the model we aspire to.

*Bernhard Rust, Reich Minister of Education, 1935*

❖ ❖ ❖

The men in white surgical coats were sitting in the gymnasium. In front of them was a long table on which lay folders, documents – and strange metal objects. For example, a longish measuring instrument reminiscent of the antennae of a giant insect. Next to it a small black box containing glass eyes which stared dead and empty from their mounts. Each eye-colour had been assigned a number. The men called it an 'eye-colour table'. There was also a strip of wood from which samples of hair – smooth, wavy, frizzy, brown, black, fair – hung ready for use. The men looked around sternly, like judges in pursuit of the truth. They were searching for something they called 'racial truth'.

The boys stood stripped to the waist and clad only in shorts, rather intimidated by this row of strange men. They had an idea of what was going to be done to them. They had heard about it in biology class and in 'racial theory', as the subject was called, in which the teachers sold them anti-Semitism as though it were a science. Their craniums would be measured and they themselves examined for 'good racial qualities'. Only 'racially pure boys', they had learnt, measured up to the standards of the new German *Herrenmensch*, and would be members of the 'master-race', which is what they were to be brought up to be. They were elite pupils of the *Nationalpolitische Erziehungsanstalt*, or Institution for National Political Education (*Napola* for short). Scarcely older than twelve, still children in fact, they nevertheless had the prospect of one day being the 'new generation of leaders' who would rule the 'Thousand Year Reich', perhaps as a *Gauleiter* in Kiev or Minsk, an army commander in the Urals, or a governor in India or any other country where the swastika might soon proclaim the sovereignty of the 'Greater German Reich'. But it would be impossible for any of them to become a 'leader' in the German empire without a 'Green Card' pronouncing them racially fit for service. That is precisely why the men in white coats had come to Naumburg. They were employed by the SS's Central Office for Race and Colonisation, and their job was to certify the 'racial quality' of the *Jungmannen*, as the pupils were called.

It was the day of reckoning in Naumburg, not least for *Jungmann* Hans-Georg Bartholomäi. He stepped on to the scales, had his height measured, and then one of the men snapped open a long calliper-like measuring apparatus which felt cold against Bartholomäi's cheekbone. Did he have the 'right' kind of cranium? Did he fit the template? Pupils of this elite school must be 'predominantly Nordic', the instructions to the doctors stated, but 'Falic' or 'West Germanic' were acceptable. And what about *Jungmann* Bartholomäi?

One of the doctors produced a mysterious combination of letters and numbers. Everything appeared to be in order. After giving Bartholomäi a final, searching look, the men were apparently satisfied. 'Like most of us, I got away with having a "well-balanced racial mix",' as Bartholomäi remembers the day he was 'racially defined'. He gives a rueful smile at the thought, so absurd today, of judging a person by their supposed 'racial character'. 'I was Aryan second class', laughs Hans Müncheberg, who was then a pupil at the *Napola* in Potsdam. 'My best friend, on the other hand, whose head was shaped like old Hindenburg's, was classed as "Falic". That's how we were graded: either as Nordic, Falic, Dinaric, West Germanic or Balto-Slavic.'

It was time for our injections. We had to line up, stripped to the waist, in gym-shorts. Along came the doctor. The hypodermic was jabbed into one's chest and then the tip of the needle was broken off. It was now stuck in one's chest. Then a little nurse came along and with trembling hands used tweezers to pull the needles out again. They had been deliberately broken off in each boy's chest.

*Klaus Geue, born 1921, former Adolf Hitler School boy*

In the crazy theories of race and 'blood-based affinity' the ideal was the Nordic *Herrenmensch*. All the leaders of the future were actually supposed to meet the very highest criteria. But in fact this was true of only a few. When Hans-Georg Bartholomäi looked around at his fellow-pupils, scarcely any of them lived up to the desired image. 'Out of more than 400 boys in the school, only eight were accepted as "Nordic-Falic". They were tall, fair-haired, and blue-eyed, with nose and forehead running in a straight line.' The rest of the 'hand-picked' group were, like himself, a 'racial mishmash', a fact which as a rule had no serious consequences. Only one of Naumburg's elite pupils had to leave following the doctors' visit. Their findings sounded like the verdict on a serious crime. This *Jungmann*, so it was said, had a 'round, Balto-Slavic skull'. 'I'd rather not tell you his name', says Hans-Georg Bartholomäi, and it almost sounds as though the verdict might still have importance today. 'He had to leave the school. He was pure Balto-Slav.'

In addition to academic qualifications, political attitude and personal capacity for achievement, it was criteria of physical heredity that decided who, in the Third Reich, would benefit from an education which promised a great future. As in Britain's exclusive Eton College, the Nazi schools were where the select few would be educated as leaders of a German empire, a new aristocracy who would command with toughness and even brutality, but who would also master the modern technology of power. But from the outset the schools contained inherent contradictions: they were intended to turn children into critical, well-educated and cosmopolitan leaders, who nevertheless had to swear unquestioning obedience, sacrifice and loyalty to Hitler unto death. Nazis with a critical faculty? 'We were supposed to be loyal followers of the Führer and convinced National Socialists', says Hans-Günther Zempelin, once a pupil at the Oranienstein *Napola*. 'We were expected to be capable of independent thought, to have a will of our own, to command respect and be able to make decisions for ourselves. The two things clearly didn't go together. You cannot be a convinced National Socialist, loyal to the Führer, *and* think critically.'

Contradictions were part of everyday life in Hitler's elite schools for breeding the new kind of German. They were intended to be the German equivalent of Harvard or Cambridge, yet they were never more than indoctrination centres for political hard-liners: swastika cadets with dreams of great careers – as *Gauleiter*, Party leaders or army commanders. They were to embody Hitler's ideal of a ruthlessly aggressive young generation, of whom the world would go in mortal fear: dominating, pitiless and filled with hate for anything that was not considered German. 'What we trainers of young leaders want to see', said an SS officer in 1937 at the *Ordensburg* (SS college) in Vogelsang, 'is a modern form of government modelled on the ancient Greek city-state. The best 5 to 10 per cent of the population are selected to rule, and the rest have to work and obey. Only in this way are those peaks of achievement possible, which we must demand of ourselves and of the German people.'

Had Hitler's Reich lasted only a few years longer, the first of these elite graduates would have reached positions of power – men who from boyhood upwards had known only one thing: how to serve their Führer and annihilate his enemies. 'After one generation at the most', said Albert Speer after the war, 'the old stratum of leaders would have been replaced by a type of man who had been educated according to new principles, at the Adolf Hitler

Schools and the *Ordensburgen*, and who even in Party circles would at times be regarded as *too* ruthless and arrogant.'

> That the Jew is evil, was to us the most obvious thing in the world. It came up again and again, and we didn't think about it. It was a history-lesson that we had to learn.
>
> *Hans Nagel, born 1927*

In *Mein Kampf* Hitler had already laid down the cornerstones of a militaristic and militant form of education which, after the Nazis seized power, became the norm for all German schools. 'The *völkisch* (ethnic) state', Hitler wrote, had to 'focus its entire educational effort not principally on pumping in mere knowledge, but on the rearing of thoroughly healthy bodies. Only in second place comes the training of mental faculties.' In sport, which 'trained the body and the will', Hitler's children were intended to develop 'war-worthy qualities of character'. The schools were there to impart not so much knowledge as hateful images of the Jews or the fatal teaching of the 'right of the stronger', and the ideal of the battled-hardened *Herrenmensch* with virtues claimed as specifically Germanic: loyalty, courage, endurance, obedience and willing self-sacrifice.

Myths and legends carried more weight than insight and knowledge. This was how Hitler would create a 'new breed': a tough, savage, pitiless youth, a generation of 'ringleaders'. Once Hitler was in power, school textbooks and timetables changed accordingly. 'Racial and *völkisch* viewpoints' were stressed. Nazi ideology invaded the classroom and swept aside all modern and forward-looking pedagogical concepts. The school system had made itself totally subordinate. Any teacher who refused to recognise the signs of the 'new age' had to leave his or her job. Now it was a matter of 'physical and ideological schooling', for the teachers as well. In 'pedagogical academies' and 'teacher training establishments' they were to be brought into line so that they could realise the 'battle-aim of Germany's schools' on the educational front line: the moulding of a 'political man' 'committed to service and self-sacrifice for his people', and 'well-versed in racial theory'. As the author Ludwig Harig, an alumnus of the Idstein teacher-training college, recalls: 'Teachers had to prepare children for the fact that one day they would go to war, fight the enemy and show selfless courage, so as eventually to bestride Europe and the world as a *Herrenmensch*.' The phrase 'sacred wrath' was used. 'A wrath which, as a German, you had to feel against anything and anyone who was not German.'

Whether someone was German or not was decided by their 'racial origin'. If you did not fit into the pattern of a wrong-headed racial theory, you were not even allowed to be a hanger-on, and even before joining the HJ, children were taught by people whose first duty was to imprint the correct 'racial feeling' on their young charges. As Hitler had ordained: 'No boy or girl should leave school without having been led to a complete understanding of the necessity and nature of blood-purity.' How the teachers were to proceed, how they were to convince and manipulate their pupils, was presented to them in an easily digestible form – in booklets like *The Jewish Question in the Classroom* in which it was stated unambiguously: 'The racial and Jewish question is the central problem of National Socialist ideology. The solution of this problem ensures the existence of National Socialism and thereby the existence of our people for all eternity.'

Above all the 'new German' had to be Aryan. That was without doubt the prime consideration. And he certainly had to be an advocate of National Socialism, in order to be able to spread this idea everywhere.
　　*Peter Zollenkopf, born 1934, alumnus of the Putbus Napola*

But how was the 'Jewish Question' to be brought alive to children? The pamphlet proposed: 'The more natural and unforced the manner of its presentation, the more lasting is its effect. The appropriate subject for this natural and at first quite unobtrusive introduction is nature study.' Aids to putting the case then follow. In the animal world creatures keep to their own species, a herd of chamois never allows itself to be led by a deer, and a cock starling only mates with a hen starling. 'Each species only feels attracted to its own kind and in turn reproduces its own kind.' Only when man intervenes and produces 'artificial cross-breeds', so the teacher was told to argue, 'do unnatural hybrids and mongrels appear', which 'combine in themselves only the worst qualities'. Examples such as these were meant to lead on to the 'racial and Jewish questions'. This kind of recommendation was followed widely – for example in the Hamburg school attended by Rudolf Banuscher. His memory of the humiliating charade he had to endure there is still painful to him today. A teacher singled him out in class, Banuscher relates, 'then he said: "Do you all know what a hybrid is?"' The class was silent. Every one of the children had heard of hybrids in biology lessons. After a short pause the teacher pointed his finger at Rudolf Banuscher and said: 'Here's one. The mother's a Jewess. Need I say more?'

At that moment, Banuscher says, he felt as though he were in a bad dream. He stood in front of the class, branded as a pariah. How would his classmates behave towards him? Even today Rudolf Banuscher is surprised at what happened next. 'There was no particular reaction from them at all.' Many of the boys came from better families, generally conservative ones, who clearly knew how to protect their children against the 'new spirit' in the schools. However, most children had no defence when exposed to the hatred which leapt out at them from their books. The very youngest were handed poison in the children's books published by Julius Streicher, the *Gauleiter* of Nuremberg, whose venomous rag, *Der Stürmer*, provided a forum for anti-Semitism of the crudest kind. The books, with titles like *The Poison Mushroom* or *Trau keinem Fuchs auf grüner Heid und keinem Jud bei seinem Eid* (Never trust a fox on the heath or a Jew on his oath) were cunningly tailored to young minds – and they flooded and contaminated the country from end to end. Hans Negel, who went to school in Nuremberg, recalls that the content of those books 'became the quintessential truth for us. It was obvious to us that Jews were evil.' 'Jews were always described as Germany's misfortune', says Günter Glowka, in those days a schoolboy in Magdeburg. 'All the caricatures and articles in the papers had an effect on us. And the school really had nothing against us boys being anti-Jewish either.' Gerhard Wilke, who went to school in Berlin, reports that the teachers 'were always actively anti-Jewish. In subjects like racial science we were taught that the Germanic race was the superior and leading race.'

Wilke's teacher had followed precisely the guidelines from the Ministry of Education. In 1935 the minister, Bernhard Rust, laid down the law to the teaching profession: 'In discussing the European races and especially the ethnology of the German people, the predominantly Nordic racial blend of modern Germans must be highlighted, in contrast to other, ethnically alien groups, which in particular means the Jews . . . The dangers of mixing racially with alien groups are to be emphasised, since peoples and cultures can only do justice to their mission if they fulfil the historical task assigned to them by virtue of their race.' Nor did Rust have any doubts about the overriding importance given to sport: 'The fine and healthy bodies of the Nordic race and its steel-hard will are the model we aspire to.' Sports such as boxing were intended to increase self-confidence to the point of arrogance. The first steps on the road to a future of war were already taken at school.

The defining factor in the young generation who would have to shape this militaristic future was, for Hitler, the 'racial quality of the human material available'. It was the task of the state, he said, to 'pick out from the entire number of *Volksgenossen* (compatriots) the most able individuals and raise them to office and honours'. Only in this way could innovation be achieved. As Hitler wrote in 1925, in *Mein Kampf*, 'Education must find its culmination in burning into the hearts and minds of the youth in its charge, a sense and feeling of race that is both instinctive and rational.' Upon these pillars of an inhuman educational philosophy were constructed a series of selective schools in which Hitler's mania about breeding a new German *Herrenmensch* was to be put into practice. These included the 'Institutions of National Political Education' (*Napolas*), the Adolf Hitler Schools and also the Reich School of the NSDAP, at Feldafing on Lake Starnberg, near Munich. By the end of the war there were 37 *Napolas*, in addition to the Adolf Hitler Schools and the Reich School.

What they instilled into us in those days are things which democracy has surely benefited from. We were not wasting our time.

*Ernst Esser, born 1926, former pupil of the Reich School of the NSDAP, Feldafing*

More than 17,000 boys attended these schools. The first generation of a new 'political aristocracy' was ready to take power. Sifting and selection went on at all levels in the Reich, in the Wehrmacht as much as in the civil service, but these measures can be seen as particularly pernicious in the case of 'Hitler's children' who were defenceless dupes of the seduction techniques of the regime. They were full of enthusiasm and easy to control. The regime exploited all this, most of all in the schools for future leaders.

'Into these schools', Hitler told an audience of arms workers in Berlin on 10 December 1940, 'we are bringing talented youngsters, the children of the broad mass of our population. Workers' sons, farmers' sons, whose parents could never afford to put their children through higher education . . . Later on, they will join the Party, they will attend an *Ordensburg*, they will occupy the highest positions. We have a goal which may seem fantastic. We envisage a state in which each post will be held by the ablest son of our people, regardless of where he comes from. A state in which birth means nothing (*sic*!) but performance and ability mean everything.' This was the only time that Hitler mentioned his elite schools in a speech.

Nonetheless, the most widespread type of elite school was a birthday present to him. On 20 April 1933 a man who had hitherto been largely unknown decreed that 'the three former cadet schools in Plön, Köslin and Potsdam should be converted, while preserving their traditions, into institutions of national political education in the spirit of the national revolution'. Where once Prussian cadets had learned their military skills and where in the 1920s 'state educational institutions' trained their pupils, now novices of a coming elite were to be schooled, and turned into uncompromising servants of the Führer, the people and the Nazi state in all its aspects – efficient leaders for a modern tyranny.

This man's name was Bernhard Rust. He had been a high-school teacher and, since 1928, *Gauleiter* of the South Hanover–Brunswick region. In Hitler's wake he rose to be 'Reich Commissioner' in the Prussian Ministry of Culture, and with the founding of these 'pilot institutions' he intended to make his own contribution to the 'National Socialist revolution'. Rust ingratiated himself with President Hindenburg in order to be nominated minister. He knew that the venerable Field-Marshal had once been a cadet in Wahlstatt and would certainly welcome the disguised revival of the military cadet schools that had been banned under the Treaty of Versailles. Immediately after 'Potsdam Day', 21 March 1933, when Hitler demonstratively stood shoulder to shoulder with the conservative elite in Potsdam's garrison church, Rust judged it the right moment to take charge of the 'new' cadet establishments. The plan worked: on 20 April 1933 Rust, newly appointed as Prussian Minister of Science, Art and Education, set about educating Germany to be a 'national state'.

The *Napolas* were to be his chief weapon in the struggle towards the goal of building 'a kind of modern Sparta' in Germany, to which everyone who wished to remain a German citizen had to sign up. The pupils of the *Napolas* were to make themselves useful in all spheres of Hitler's state, as an ideologically reliable, militaristically drilled ruling class. Schooled academically and militarily, they were intended to be the ideal of the 'globally effective German'. The *Napolas* placed a correspondingly high value on imparting the skills needed for warfare. Cross-country sports were considered 'fundamental' and essential for the 'moulding of a new youth'. Thus, in the first year of their existence, the *Napolas* went on 'manoeuvres'. What the boys learned in the process was presented in Plön on 28 October 1933, among others to the Chief-of-Staff of the SA, Ernst Röhm. Two hundred schoolboys played soldiers in front of him. Röhm was so impressed that he had himself made patron and lent his name to the Plön *Napola*.

> Except in the classroom, everything was done on word of command and by numbers.
>
> *Hardy Krüger, born 1928, former pupil of the*
> *Adolf Hitler School, Sonthofen*

The regular army also showed an interest in the schools that were drilling children to be little soldiers. In the summer of 1934 *Jungmannen* from various establishments gave the War Minister, Werner von Blomberg, a taste of their military ability. 'In the displays of cross-country sports, 72 *Jungmannen* in uniform jumped into the river Weser and swam across in close-packed groups. As soon as they got to the other bank they coolly began to perform field exercises', wrote one observer. 'The visitors felt that a new spirit had made its appearance here.' A proper man, Blomberg declared in praise of the *Napolas* style of education, could only be one who as a boy knew how to be a real boy.

Yet another eminent visitor had been struck by the 'new spirit'. After taking a look, Heinrich Himmler, the *Reichsführer-SS*, asked Rust if he could take over three of the establishments as preparatory schools for the SS. Before very long, Himmler wanted to incorporate all the *Napolas* into the SS. His influence on the schools grew steadily – to the point where Minister Rust only had a formal say in their running. In 1936 the SS appointed *Gruppenführer* August Heissmeyer, head of the Central Office of the SS, to be Inspector of the *Napolas*. The SS paid for the uniforms of the *Jungmannen*, and from 1941 also supervised the 'racial selection'. In the end, almost nothing happened in the *Napolas* without consultation with the SS. Although the purpose of the *Napolas* was not specifically to produce young recruits for the SS, Himmler was able to insist on almost complete authority over them. Though not for this reason, many pupils opted for a career in Himmler's 'Black Order': *Napola* graduates were not expected to feel bound by any moral principles, but exclusively by the will of the Führer. They were to be preachers of the ideology, ambassadors and disseminators, whose task was to be the cement binding the people and the dictatorship into a single 'national community'. In 1933 the newly appointed head of a *Napola* was given a send-off by Rust, with the words: 'Turn the lads into National Socialists!'

Individual personality no longer counted. All that mattered
was the community, which marched according to
standardised guidelines.

*Rolf Diercks, born 1915, alumnus of the Plön Napola*

The same applied to the pupils of another type of selective
school. In 1937, Robert Ley, the Nazi Party's head of
organisation, and the youth leader Baldur von Schirach, founded
the Adolf Hitler Schools. Both of them mistrusted the *Napolas*,
over which they had no influence. In the Adolf Hitler Schools,
however, everything would be different. They were under Party
supervision, were intended to bring on political leaders and
were seen as preparatory schools for the *Ordensburgen*, the
establishments for training future dictators. Every *Gau* would have
its own Adolf Hitler School, though this remained a pipe-dream,
since there was not enough money for that. In those days no-one
talked about schools for the elite. If you meant 'elite' you used
words like 'selection' or 'continuous selection' – a process in
which every pupil had repeatedly to prove himself and hold his
own. Thus, all but the strongest would be 'sifted out'. In the
'Thousand Year Reich' that had just begun, Ley declared with
conviction, the governing group would only include those who
had proved themselves through performance in a continuous
process of selection: 'The Adolf Hitler Schools are establishments
for the political education of a chosen few young Germans.
Anyone who has completed this training is a politically moulded
and unquestioning fighter for National Socialism. Fanatically
imbued with faith in the idea, he must be an example of National
Socialist life to the entire people, a solid guidepost for all waverers,
and an enemy to all who infest the nation. The young pupil will
not be the beneficiary of a Party institution, but its representative,
a bearer of the ideas which have been implanted in him there.'
The Adolf Hitler Schools would be the forges of brownshirted
cadres, who were promised fast-track careers.

For the 'pick of German youth', who would apparently gather
in these schools, 'every career in the Party and in government'

would be open. But before being appointed *Gauleiter* or governor of some remote region in the conquered east, a hard road had to be trodden: five years at an Adolf Hitler School, then military or labour service, and, after a further selection process, acceptance as a *Führerjunker*, in the *Ordensburgen* in Sonthofen, in Bavaria's Allgäu district, Vogelsang in the Eifel mountains and Crössinsee in Pomerania, where aspiring leaders, as 'torchbearers of the nation', would have to be given an ideological 'finish' and more military discipline. Everything was laid down on paper: in the first year, schooling in the 'racial philosophy of the New Order' in Vogelsang, in the second year, 'character-building' in Crössinsee, and in the third year, lessons in 'administrative and military duties and diplomacy' in Sonthofen.

'We want to know,' said Robert Ley at the topping-out ceremony at Sonthofen in 1935, 'whether these men carry in themselves the will to lead, to be masters, in a word: to rule. The NSDAP and its leaders must want to rule . . . We want to rule, we take delight in ruling, not in order to be a despot or to revel in sadistic tyranny, but because it is our unshakeable belief that in all situations only one person can lead and only one person can take responsibility. Power rests with this one person. Thus, these men will for example learn to ride, not so as to enjoy a social advantage, no, they will learn to ride in order to have the feeling of absolute domination over a living creature. The rider must be able to master the horse, not with his spurs but with his will.'

---

We were meant to appear sophisticated, and be able to speak several languages. I remember a teacher once saying: 'You're nothing until you can speak ten Arabic dialects without a trace of a German accent.'

*Hans-Günther Zempelin, born 1926, alumnus of the Oranienstein Napola*

---

The *Junker* training ceased with the outbreak of war. Furthermore, the Party's establishment of higher education, the so-called 'University of the NSDAP', which was to be attended after the three *Ordensburg* years, remained a fantasy of the selection fanatics. It was never built.

The only establishments to be completed and put into commission were the three *Ordensburgen*, Sonthofen, Vogelsang and Crössinsee. Initially these provided accommodation for the Adolf Hitler Schools, but this was a temporary solution, due to Ley's insistence that the pupils who bore Hitler's name should only be taught in 'National Socialist premises'. New educational institutions had no business being in 'buildings of the past'. The *Ordensburgen* served as emergency quarters until new homes were built in the *Gaue* for the Adolf Hitler Schools. Sites had already been earmarked and plans drawn up: Potsdam on Lake Templin (*Gau* Kurmark), Waldbröl (Cologne-Aachen), Asterstein near Koblenz (Koblenz-Trier), the Goethe Park in Weimar (Thuringia), the Schlossberg in Tilsit (*Gau* East Prussia), Hesselberg (Franconia), Mittenwald (Munich-Upper Bavaria), the Bismarckhöhe in Landstuhl (Westmark) and in the Gespensterwald near Heiligendamm (Mecklenburg).

While the Party looked for funds for these expensive prestige buildings, Sonthofen became the centre for all the Adolf Hitler Schools. As many as 1,700 pupils from ten schools were crammed into classrooms and halls behind the rough-hewn walls. One of those boys, Joachim Baumann, remembers: 'We were so full of enthusiasm that it was important to us not to fall by the wayside during these long years of training, but to put all our strength into preparing for the day when death would compel the Führer to lay aside his invisible sceptre, when we would be called upon to secure his dream of the Thousand Year Reich and carry it forward into the next decade and the one after that.'

I am sure my classmates did just what I did: they absorbed this ideology totally. So totally that there was absolutely no alternative to it.

*Ludwig Harig, born 1927, alumnus of the Idstein Teacher Training College*

Self-confidence was certainly not lacking in these future leaders. They considered themselves the 'best of the best'. Even during their schooldays, they became intoxicated with ideas of a great future, which they believed they would be able to shape. 'In our class the target was: *Gauleiter* in Siberia', says Klaus Geue, a former Adolf Hitler School boy. His fellow-pupil Baumann adds, 'I knew it would be like being in the Jesuits; they don't ask either, where they're going to be sent. I was prepared for that.' Sworn as in a knightly order, they were united by the feeling of embodying a 'new age'. 'What we felt was: "We are the young generation. We are the chosen"', says Adolf Hitler alumnus Harald Scholtz. 'We are the ones who will bring change to Europe, and everything will have to follow.'

This kind of arrogance was nourished day after day. 'They continually wanted to build us up', recalls Heinz Giebeler, a former Adolf Hitler pupil at Sonthofen. 'You boys are the best, you are our great hope.' The massive school buildings themselves gave the pupils the sense of being an elect. Magnificent palaces like those of Bensberg or Oranienstein served as residences for the *Napolas*. The impression made by the *Ordensburg* at Sonthofen on new arrivals was thoroughly overpowering. With its mighty castle as the central feature, the complex in the tranquil Allgäu resort was more reminiscent of a gigantic fortified romanesque church. 'Intimidating and oppressive', was how young Harald Grundmann saw it when he first arrived. 'But the next morning it looked like a holiday paradise to me.' The other buildings, including the so-called *Schöner Hof* (Beautiful Court) with its parklike lawns, looked to many like a resort or a comfortable hotel – from the outside at least. Of his first day at Sonthofen, Baumann can still say now: 'I felt like a prince.'

The teaching was relaxed and more like a lecture. We called the staff by their first names. During classes they would leave the room and trusted us not to copy from each other.
*Hardy Krüger, born 1928, alumnus of the Adolf Hitler*
*School, Sonthofen*

Pride filled the hearts of the 'elect'. Yet none of the Nazis' selective schools succeeded in establishing such an intense emotional bond with their pupils as did the Reich School of the NSDAP at Feldafing, on Lake Starnberg in southern Bavaria. Even today, more than half a century after the last class was held there, the 'Feldafingers', as they call themselves, go into raptures when they tell stories about 'their school'. Indeed, no school in the Reich could compete when it came to lavish equipment and surroundings. The slogan 'If you want to seduce, you must offer something seductive', was put into practice in full. The scholars learned to play golf on one of Germany's finest courses. They sailed across the lake in the new Olympic-class dinghies. Twenty-five cars and motorcycles were available for motor sport. Even the accommodation was luxurious and exclusive. Forty grand country houses served as halls of residence. Martin Bormann Jr, son of one of the most powerful figures in the Third Reich, and a student at Feldafing, describes large mansions whose owners, after the boycott of Jewish businesses on 1 April 1933, 'either sold up because they saw no future in Germany, or had simply made their getaway without selling'.

The rulers of the future were to want for nothing, and the training of the next generation of leaders would cost the regime a pretty penny. If an Adolf Hitler pupil broke one of his skis, he was immediately given a new pair. Sports instruction covered sailing, fencing, riding, rowing, gliding and, for the senior classes, even driving and motorbike-riding – leading to a driving licence for those who would soon be at the controls of the nation. Even the uniform reinforced the feeling of belonging to a sworn confraternity. 'All the external trappings singled us out as being something special', recalls Hans-Georg Batholomäi ( *Napola,* Naumburg). 'There was a wide range of travel and "manoeuvres", as we used to call them. We could go skiing and gliding. We went to the Alps, we went to the lakes. That was pretty unusual for any boy in those days. We were even graced with visits by the *Reichsführer-SS*, Heinrich Himmler, the Reich Minister of Education, Rust, and others. People made a fuss of us. And of course we picked up on that.'

We always used to say: *Napolas*, huh! Adolf Hitler Schools,
huh! In comparison to us they were the underdogs. We felt
ourselves superior to the other Party schools.
*Otto Schuster, born 1925, alumnus of the Reich School of the*
*NSDAP, Feldafing*

The educators had their hands full keeping their charges under
control and admonishing them to behave with decorum. The
'elect' were permitted to be high-spirited but not high-handed. But
a boy aged twelve, who boarded as one of the select few in
*Ordensburgen* and castles, did not always find it easy to keep his feet
on the ground. Joachim Baumann remembers how heartily they
laughed when one of his classmates said: 'Listen, if the Nordic race
is the best, and if the Germans are the best of the Nordic race, and
if we are the best of the Germans, then we must be the best in the
entire world.'

The obsession with defining abstruse 'racial criteria' had completely
taken hold of many a pupil even before the first classroom lesson. It
started with the entrance examination. The club for future rulers
only admitted those who fulfilled the most important condition –
'Aryan antecedents'. Every elite pupil had to show evidence of
'racial purity' and 'healthy heredity in the family tree', in order even
to reach the final stages of selection. As a boy Theo Sommer,
latterly editor of the newspaper *Die Zeit*, was determined to get
into an Adolf Hitler School. 'In my case there was a major
problem', he recounts. 'Sometime back in the early nineteenth
century some parish ledgers had been burnt. There were gaps in
my family tree. It was a shock for me not to be accepted straight
away.' Theo Sommer had himself photographed from every angle.
The photos were sent to Berlin where they were examined by
'racial specialists'. After several months he was immensely relieved
to get the news: 'You're Aryan. You'll do.'
      Joachim Baumann had no such anxieties. He was lying ill in bed
at home – it must have been early in 1937 – when his mother
came into the bedroom with a newspaper in her hand. 'Just listen

to this, young lad! The Führer's setting up a new school, and the type they're looking for fits you perfectly: your parents are National Socialists, you're bright at school *and* you've done well in the HJ, what with all those pennants and badges! And it's all for free. Well, what d'you think?'

Baumann's father was anything but happy to see his son go off to a 'cadet college or some such thing'. However, his mother wanted her son to make something of himself, not just go to elementary school and then get an apprenticeship somewhere, but to have the best chances in life. It would cost them nothing and would be 'an honour'; that was how his mother talked his father into it, so Baumann believes today. His father finally gave in. For his son Joachim was also dead set on becoming an Adolf Hitler School student, and bearing the name of the man who, soon afterwards in the *Ordensburg* of Sonthofen, seemed 'almost Christlike' to him.

Baumann fulfilled all the criteria. His family tree had no gaps in it, his parents were 'politically reliable', and because he had 'proved' himself in the *Jungvolk* and the HJ, he was recommended to the Adolf Hitler School by the local Party executive, which was the only way to get into one of these exclusive establishments. It was impossible to make an independent application, for Adolf Hitler pupils were 'summoned' – by 'those with authority in the Party'. Firstly, however, each hopeful had to prove himself in the 'selection camp'. Baumann attended a course at HJ-*Bann* (Company) No. 152 (Marienburg-Stuhm). Out of sixty boys ten went on to the field selection course in Marienwerder. Baumann was one of those to pass this hurdle. Now he would be tested on his 'leadership qualities', his 'instinct' for controlling others, his 'strength of character, toughness and decency'. In the selection camp the programme was: fourteen days of war-games, gymnastics on apparatus, combat-style night operations, night marches, tests of courage, as well as arithmetic, reading and essay-writing. In the boxing-ring they had to show 'who's aggressive and goes for it', as Baldur von Schirach had demanded. 'The best things about the selection course were the war-games at night', wrote one Adolf Hitler student. 'We stormed an enemy defensive position in the forest. We all had to keep a good lookout, in case an enemy

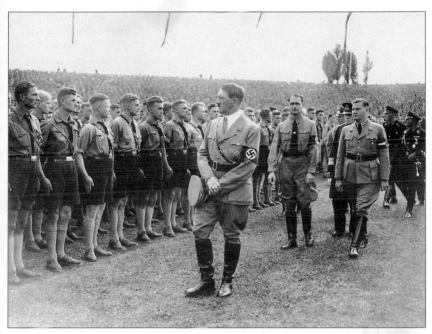

1. 'One will commands, which the rest must obey . . .' Adolf Hitler, Rudolf Hess and Baldur von Schirach (far right) at the Reich Party Rally in Nuremberg, 1936

2. 'In uniform you felt you were taken more seriously, You were now one of the big boys . . .' Corps of trumpeters of the Jungvolk

3. Going on trips was something most children had never known . . .' HJ expeditions offered adventure and a change of scene

4. 'The stars above us . . .' The HJ fell back on the proven traditions of the Youth Alliance – the romance of the camp-fire

5. 'The rearing of fighting fit bodies . . .' Boxing training in an HJ camp

wir sind
zum Sterben für deutschland
geboren

HORST WESSEL

DEUTSCHLAND

ERWACHE

6. 'We were born to die for Germany': memorial at an ancient Germanic site in Murnau, Upper Bavaria

7. *Young women attending the* Deutsches Turnfest *in Breslau greet Adolf Hitler,*
*31 July 1938*

8. 'Be faithful and good, as a German lass should . . .' Even the kindergarten was commandeered for the acclamation of the Führer

9. 'To think that you should have found me . . .' The cult of the Führer led to extravagant fantasies

10. *'There must be no weakness or tenderness in the young . . .' Hitler in a typical gesture for the camera*

11. 'We could see that we were needed . . .' Setting off for harvest duties

12. 'I would be ashamed if one single woman had to go to the Front . . .' Women Luftwaffe auxiliaries in 1944

13. 'For a long time I believed in our victory . . .' Wehrmacht girl auxiliary taken prisoner in 1945

14. 'We immediately felt rather superior . . .' Pupils at the Reich School of the NSDAP at Feldafing on Lake Starnberg

15. 'Educate the children to a healthy hatred . . .' Not all teachers heeded Julius Streicher's watchword, yet every school had its 'ethnic instruction'. The writing on the back wall reads: All calamities come from the Jews

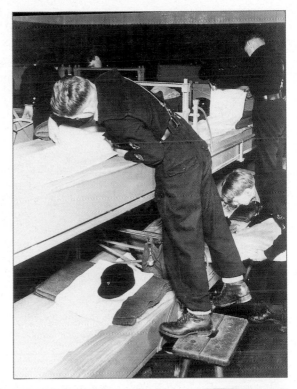

16. 'We even had to sleep by numbers . . .' Bed-making at an elite boarding-school

17. 'Youth will be led by youth . . .' In Hitler's schools the boys were to learn how to command others

18. *'That would be just right for you, my lad, with all your badges and things . . .'*
*Gliding was one of the wide range of leisure activities that attracted many into the HJ*

19. *'He who shoots first lives longer . . .' Demonstration for education minister Rust*

20. '. . . I learned to die for my fatherland, but not to live for it . . .' The future elite were given military training by highly decorated soldiers

21. 'Open your wallet, or you'll stop a bullet . . .' Hitlerjungen *collecting scrap metal for the war effort*

22. 'The battle is ours, count not the dead . . .' Hitler's children were to learn how to wage war

23. 'The "in" phrase is "hang loose" . . .' Hamburg 'Swing Kids', a protest against conformity

24. 'All I kept thinking was: I don't want to die . . .' Young German soldiers at Stalingrad

25. *'We must fight the fight to the end . . .'* Generaloberst *Heinz Guderian (centre) addressing the HJ on trench-digging duty. On the right,* Reichsjugendführer *Artur Axmann*

26. *'Germany possesses a secret weapon: its youth . . .' Boys of the SS-Panzer Division 'Hitler-Jugend' in France*

27. *'Because they didn't think about what could happen to them . . .' A soldier of the Panzer Division 'Hitler-Jugend', killed in Normandy*

28. '. . . to receive such a decoration for my relatively modest service as a messenger!'
Joseph Goebbels congratulates Wilhelm Hübner in front of newsreel cameras

29. 'I was a child. I had no insight
whatsoever, no overview of events, no
understanding and no experience . . .'
A boy-soldier being frisked by an
American GI

30. 'I learned to cry . . .' A young
airman after being taken prisoner

attacked from behind. We had to fight hand-to-hand as well. Then we chased some partisans, We were the attackers.'

> Our education was tough, and it was authoritarian, completely undemocratic and scarcely imaginable these days.
> *Hans-Georg Bartholomäi, born 1924, alumnus of the Naumburg Napola*

War-games and sport counted just as much as scholarly achievement. Physical strength seemed even more important than reading and writing. Another boy hoping for a place in the Adolf Hitler School, Harald Grundmann, also found that out: 'In route-marches with full packs and in war-games it was all a matter of physical stamina. In my time at the school I was never overstretched mentally. But I certainly was physically.'

There was method behind all this. 'The man who wants to live asserts himself', Hitler declared, 'and a man who cannot assert himself does not deserve a life; he will disappear. The earth is not there for cowardly nations, nor for lazy or weak ones; the earth is there for those who take it. The earth is a challenge cup, which is always awarded to the nations who earn it, nations who show themselves strong enough in the struggle for existence to secure the foundation of their own survival.'

Hitler's students were to live up to this claim and more. They were to be executors of the faith – Hitler's heirs. This was another reason why Joachim Baumann had to prove he had 'guts'. He climbed into the boxing-ring. When he saw his opponent, he realised that somehow he had to survive the next few minutes. The other boy was taller, heavier, stronger. It seemed as though the three rounds would never end. Blow followed blow. Then the *Gauleiter* of East Prussia, Erich Koch, entered the room. The fight was interrupted while an HJ leader gave him a report. Then more blows rained down on Joachim Baumann. By the end of the third round his defeat was confirmed. Baumann pulled off his left glove. The thumb was red with blood, but not from boxing. Three weeks earlier, while building a model aircraft, he had caught it on a circular saw and the wound had opened up again. When Koch saw the thumb he must have thought he had before him a particularly fine example of youthful courage and imperviousness to pain. He turned to his adjutant and said, 'He's our man!' Anyone able to ignore a wound like that without complaint seemed the right kind. Joachim Baumann was now an Adolf Hitler student. He felt as though the sword of knighthood had touched his shoulder.

Simply passing the selection process gave him the proud feeling of having achieved something, of being better than his contemporaries, of belonging to an elite. 'I was immensely proud', recalls Heinz Giebeler of his acceptance into the Adolf Hitler School. 'It was something I could go back and tell my old schoolmates about. I was glad because my parents were glad and I was enormously happy.'

> We bear the Führer's name with pride; we want to be his best.
> And no-one asks where you're from; it's what you are that
>    counts.
> We do nothing by halves. We sing and we march.
> We march along in step.
>
> *Song of the Adolf Hitler School*

With each week of lessons that passed in the formidable *Ordensburg* of Sonthofen, the future for Joachim Baumann took on a more tangible form: 'We were to be the future political leaders of Germany. We were to be exemplars and educators for the entire nation, and also to encourage the ones who didn't really want to be part of it. We would have to talk them into it.' In principle, the choice of career was open, but Baumann knew what the Party expected of him as an Adolf Hitler School alumnus. Many of his friends wanted to become officers, but Baumann's aim was to be a political leader. Today he can only look back on that with amazement.

Many youngsters dreamed of such careers in those days, and their parents even more so. In the case of the *Napolas*, parents could enter their sons for the entrance examination after their third or fourth year in elementary school. Admittedly school fees had to be paid here, between 10 and 120 Reichsmarks according to income. Attendance at other elite boarding-schools was free of charge.

However, other children went on to a *Napola* because they had been noticed by their elementary-school teachers and were considered 'worthy'. The *Napolas* imposed strict selection criteria. For example the head of the Potsdam *Napola* issued the following guidelines: 'Delicate children with physical defects, with hereditary illnesses (cardiac or ocular defects) are completely unsuitable.' Rejection of 'a capable and racially unexceptionable boy with such a defect' was indeed 'a matter of personal regret, but humanitarian feelings are not admissible. The common good of the healthy does not permit us to pay regard in any way whatever to the sick or those who have any form of weakness.' Even wearing glasses was enough to guarantee rejection by a *Napola*. And pulling strings did not always do any good. Thus, many offspring of the families of Nazi bigwigs fell at the selection hurdle. At Bensberg a nephew of Robert Ley, the head of Reich organisation, and the son of the district head of the HJ, were both rejected on account of 'physical and intellectual shortcomings'.

But a boy who made it, who was athletically above average, who passed the essential test of courage and got through eight probationary days, became a *Jungmann* in what the education minister, Rust, called ' a model institution of National Socialist group education'. The novices were just ten years old when their life as elite pupils started. They had been snatched from their familiar surroundings, far from parents and friends, and were helplessly exposed to the total domination of the institution – easy prey for the Nazi system. The school was to be their new family. 'At the National Socialist educational establishments', it was stated in the entrance conditions of the Bensberg *Napola*, 'the *Jungmannen* are on duty and in uniform every minute for nine years. Only those boys are accepted who are so dedicated to National Socialism that they give up all their schoolboy attitudes and pranks and are willing to live a new kind of life.'

This new life was precisely like that in an army barracks. 'I came straight from home into a military environment', says Hans-Georg Bartholomäi about his first days at the Naumburg Napola. It came as a shock to many of the new boys. Everything was alien. The tone of voice used by the staff was harsh; cupboards were called 'lockers', classes were 'platoons'; the new clothing was a uniform. Only in the holidays could they return home and see their parents. From the first day they were ordered around in a military manner and did everything by numbers. They all had to grasp one simple proposition: 'You are nothing, your *Volk* is everything.'

Day in, day out, the timetable was strictly regulated. Nothing was left to chance. 'We were marched around from early morning until the evening', says Hans-Georg Bartholomäi. 'After being woken we had to parade in the quadrangle, then we had early morning sports. After breakfast it was back to the bunkroom, then another parade, and we were marched to our classrooms.' Every morning there was a bed inspection, which meant trouble for bed-wetters! Then there was a check in the washrooms and probing looks to see whether neck and ears were clean. Anyone who was 'picked up' could expect a punishment, such as extra parades or press-ups. 'We had to learn obedience, the idea being that only when you know how to obey orders are you able to give them', says Uwe Lamprecht, a former pupil of the Plön *Napola*.

'Quick change' – that was a favourite amusement of our instructors. And one man who really took it to excess was a platoon leader, who we had for a long time . . . It was all about getting into one outfit or another in the shortest possible time. Then changing into the next lot of gear: sports kit or best suit – it was one thing after another. Finally – and this was the really mean bit – when our lockers were in a complete shambles, there would be a locker inspection.
    *Peter Zollenkopf, born 1934, alumnus of the Putbus Napola*

That was the purpose of the dormitory inspection, clothing inspection, full kit inspection, standing to attention, flag parades and at noon every day a new slogan which the entire community had to follow: 'Those fear death the least whose life is worth the most.' – 'He who wants to live, let him fight, and whoever will not fight in this world of eternal struggle, does not deserve his life.' – 'Our lives are worth nothing if they are not dedicated to Führer and nation.' Even the works of Goethe had to be pressed into service: *Habt endlich Courage, euch erheben zu lassen, ja euch belehren und zu etwas Grossem entflammen and ermutigen zu lassen.* (Finally have the courage to let yourselves be elevated, be taught, aroused and encouraged to be something great.). There would be a roll of drums. The pupils stood to attention and from time to time a blood-chilling chorus would ring out: 'Sacred Fatherland in peril, ere the enemy robs you of your crown, Germany, we will fall one by one.'

It was not long before every one of them had absorbed the lesson: anyone who disregarded or broke the rules and laws was ostracised – with all that entailed. 'You wanted to avoid attracting attention, so as to escape punishment', Gerd-Ekkchard Lorenz recalls from his days at the Potsdam *Napola*. 'At the same time there was a kind of pecking order. Someone who was often caught for misdemeanours was known as a "whistle", a "fiasco" or just a "no-hoper". The names of those in trouble were announced at the parades before mealtimes.' Those who did not toe the line were pilloried. Someone who was not a 'good chap' had nothing to laugh about. He was 'cut dead'. 'This meant that for quite a time the platoon didn't speak to him, he was completely ignored', explains Peter Zollenkopf, once a pupil at the *Napola* in Putbus, on the Baltic island of Rügen. 'That was punishment enough. And if the offence was something more serious, then there was a further stage, known as the "Holy Ghost". Then boys would creep up on him in bed at night and smear shoe-polish all over his backside. If he still refused to learn his lesson, he got a beating – this was known as a "platoon thrashing" or a "belt drubbing". Our education required a certain physical and spiritual robustness', says Harry Bölte, of the Ifeld *Napola*, 'which decent but sensitive boys often couldn't handle. We were often intolerant towards individualists and the more sensitive types. Anyone who diverged from the norm was beaten into shape.'

'At this school a National Socialist attitude to life has to be the governing principle', a newspaper article about the Plön *Napola* declared. 'Here the strictest intolerance must prevail against all those forces which run counter to National Socialism.'

What forces these were, within the youthful community, was decided as much by the pupils as by the staff. According to the principle 'educate yourselves' the boys were allowed to take their turn in exercising the power of command. In the *Napolas* each 'platoon' was commanded by a *Jungmann*, who had in this way to show proof of his capacity to give orders to a unit. In the Adolf Hitler Schools even twelve-year-olds, as 'duty *Pimpfe*', were responsible for the entire progress of the working day: getting up on time, parading for classes and meals, for orderly bed-making and clean finger-nails. 'That way he learns to give orders and gains the subconscious strength of self-confidence which is necessary in order to command obedience', a staff member wrote enthusiastically in the Nazi press. 'The following week another *Pimpf* takes over from him: and so he then learns to obey again. In this way the platoon of newly admitted *Pimpfe* gradually becomes a team.' For Heinz Giebeler, a former Adolf Hitler student, the principle of 'educate yourselves' brings back less happy memories. 'What it produced was more or less a rule of force among the boys. And it was the smaller and weaker ones who suffered under it.' The platoon leaders, who were two or three years older, were endowed with a kind of unlimited authority. They had total control over the pupils, had to settle disputes, were allowed to hand out punishments and order beatings. They had the power to make life hell for their classmates. 'Our schooling was tough, authoritarian and completely undemocratic', is the verdict of Hans-Georg Bartholomäi.

The 'communal education' at Hitler's boarding-schools was indeed rough and merciless. Any boy arriving fresh to the school was first of all 'inducted' into the hierarchy by staff and older pupils – which certainly included beatings for anyone who did not adapt swiftly. The first months at the bottom of the pecking order were the toughest for many pupils. But as soon as another intake arrived, as some alumni recall today, 'you were no longer the lowest piece of dirt, you were the second lowest'. Everyone had to get through this penance. 'Only the weak give up', was the cry. Being forced to make one's presence felt and hold one's own in a group of boys left its mark on quite a few postwar careers. The list of names of those with a background of Nazi elite schooling, who subsequently achieved something in democratic Germany, is a long one: the banker Alfred Herrhausen (Feldafing), Count Maynhardt Nayhauss, the *Bild* newspaper columnist ( *Napola*, Spandau) the film actor Hardy Krüger (Adolf Hitler student), the former East German politician Werner Lambertz (Adolf Hitler student), the former ambassador and spokesman for Willi Brandt, Rüdiger von Wechmar ( *Napola*, Spandau), the former Austrian Minister of Justice, Harald Ofner ( *Napola*, Traiskirchen), the journalist Hellmuth Karasek ( *Napola*, Annaberg), the artist and designer Horst Janssen ( *Napola*, Haselünne) and the former editor of *Die Zeit*, Adolf Hitler student Theo Sommer. All of them had learned to be tough – tough on themselves and, if need be, on their fellow-pupils as well.

'Once we were ordered to hand out a punishment', recalls Heinz Giebeler. 'One of the pupils, who was actually one of the weaker ones, had been guilty of some trivial offence against school property. And we were ordered, or at least it was "suggested" to us, to give the boy a flogging. So we did, and I still remember seeing the red weals on his back, where we beat him with leather straps.'

Punishments were also given directly by the staff, who were predominantly drawn from the Hitler Youth, the SA or the SS. It was they who really ran the institutions, even though they wore the same uniform as the pupils. According to Harry Bolte ( *Napola*, Ifeldt), 'this was intended to show that older and younger colleagues were living cheek-by-jowl, as a conscious rejection of the traditional teacher–pupil relationship in the average high school. The relationship between the *Jungmannen* and those educating them was meant to be one of comradeship.' In 1940, the head of the *Napola* in Potsdam issued these instructions: 'Staff and *Jungmannen* form a solid confraternity, one which is permeated by discipline and order, to live under the law of authority and to master all the tasks they are set.'

The staff, known as *Erzieher* (educators), were usually aged under thirty. The boys could never escape them. They slept in the same dormitories, gave the lessons, supervised their homework and issued orders when on manoeuvres, in camps or on parade, morning, noon and night. The *Erzieherkorps* had to dedicate themselves 'fanatically and selflessly to the cause' as demanded by *SS-Gruppenführer* August Heissmeyer, who from 1936 onward was Inspector of the *Napolas*. 'Only high-grade individuals can be educators at a *Napola*, men who are mentally, physically and characterwise quite outstanding.'

There was no shortage of such 'educators'. Even today, many of them feel a bond of friendship with their elite pupils from those years. Hans-Günther Zempelin, who was a pupil at the Oranienstein *Napola*, says: 'All our teachers I would classify as above average today, and some of them were professionally very good. They were without exception strongly committed to teaching and most of them had a motivating influence on the pupils. All were unambiguous supporters of National Socialism, some were just sympathisers, many were convinced idealists. Fanatics were the exception.' Yet they all laid great emphasis on minor virtues such as discipline and order. And at every institution there were slave-drivers who put the fear of God into the boys, abused their power with senseless drill and took the motto 'praise be to that which toughens' as a licence for unrestricted harassment. In the process, they tried out various methods not only for disciplining the future leaders, but also for making them feel small, to show them their own powerlessness, to break them in order to build a new kind of man out of the wreckage, one who would assiduously carry out even the most senseless order.

---

It was obvious to me that the educators we had, those who had been recruited from the HJ, were admittedly good mates and wanted the best for us. But they just didn't know enough. The result was that, looked at from today's standpoint, we were a bit provincial in our intellectual development.

*Harald Grundmann, born 1927,*
*former Adolf Hitler School pupil*

The quick-change routine, jokingly called 'masked ball' or 'fancy-dress party', was one of the forms of harassment most favoured by the staff of the *Napolas* and the Adolf Hitler Schools. The choice of name alone shows what a despicable game it was intended to be. With ever decreasing time allowed, the pupils had to switch from one uniform or outfit to another, at random. 'It began with simple impositions', as Hans Müncheberg (*Napola*, Potsdam) describes it in his autobiographical novel *Gelobt sei, was hart macht* (Praise be to that which toughens), which is based closely on fact. 'In five minutes get into your best uniform with overcoat and képi!' 'In four minutes, fatigues and full pack!' 'In three minutes, track-suits!'

Then came the 'amusing' variants: 'In four minutes, ski-pants, summer shirt and trainers!' – 'In three minutes, winter jerkin, shorts and lace-up shoes!' – 'In four minutes, fatigue jacket, swimming-trunks, slippers, groundsheet round your neck and toothbrush in your left hand!'

At the bunkroom door stood an *Erzieher* with a stop-watch in his hand, announcing how much time had already elapsed. Anyone who couldn't keep up had his name taken, and was considered 'conspicuous'. When every member of Müncheberg's platoon was on the 'conspicuous' list, the educator confined them to barracks and ordered a locker inspection. It was no wonder that after a 'fancy-dress' session, chaos reigned in the bunk-rooms. Free time was cancelled, to be replaced by hours spent cleaning up and mending clothes. Finally, it was the boot-room and a shoe inspection, followed by a washroom inspection.

The next morning began with another bunk-room inspection. An educator named Erkenbrecher took his time over it, looked for and found everywhere the pretexts he needed for handing out further punishments. 'OK, so you still won't do what you're told?' he bawled. 'That's fine by me. After breakfast, parade in your winter kit – and that means all of you!' 'It was a baking hot day in the summer of 1940', Hans Müncheberg tells us. 'We had to shove all our schoolbooks into our back-packs, and then came the order: "Parade in marching uniform!" Erkenbrecher insisted on us marching in step, keeping strictly to our rank and file and singing "How often have we marched along the narrow jungle path. . .".'

Erkenbrecher still wasn't satisfied. The singing sounded like a lot of parrots screeching, he said. 'You miserable bunch of layabouts. Let's see you jog! At the double!' Carrying the heavy packs, the smaller boys like Müncheberg couldn't keep up. 'I see you gentlemen are taking your time', sneered Erkenbrecher and barked out a stream of orders: 'Caps off! – Ear-flaps down! – Caps on! – Packs off! – Packs to the front! – Knees bend! – Bounce! Bounce! Bounce!'

Müncheberg, exhausted, stumbled and fell. 'I didn't say anything about lying down! Geddup and keep going!'

Müncheberg was on the point of collapse. 'Then I heard: "Stand to attention, you wimp! C'mon! Hold your pack in front of you!"'

Müncheberg tried to lift the pack full of books. He couldn't budge it. 'I could hardly breathe. The heat seemed to have dropped an airtight lid on me.'

Erkenbrecher didn't let up. 'What's this, then? Refusing to obey an order?' *Jungmann* Müncheberg reeled to one side.

Erkenbrecher screamed at him: 'Jerks like you louse up the whole squad! Go on, geddout!'

Müncheberg fell forward on to the clinker, made burning hot by the sun.

Almost all the alumni of the 'elite schools' can tell similar stories about drill and hard grind, and about *Erzieher* who took out their aggression on them. 'One time', Hans Günther Zempelin of the Oranienstein *Napola* remembers, 'an *Erzieher* was standing on the sports-field and he deliberately blew his whistle very softly. At the first whistle, we had to run up a small hill and wait at the top. Then he blew again and we had to run back down. He did that to us ten times. If he'd shouted at us, it wouldn't have been half so bad. But the mean thing was, he blew the whistle so softly that we had to keep our ears pinned back in order to hear the command. It was humiliating.'

Yet persecution creates solidarity, it provokes a defiant reaction among the boys, who ally themselves against their 'slave-drivers' and feel themselves to be a 'confraternity'. Gerd-Ekkehard Lorenz, then a pupil at the Potsdam *Napola*, recalls 'punishment exercises' in free time: 'At first everything went as normal. March

training, then the dreaded command: "On to the running-track –
go, go go! On the ground, down! – Up! – Down! Crawl forward
slowly!" Soon after that it was the "duck-walk" with packs held in
front of us. The boys in front stayed lying on the ground, then
struggled to their feet. When we were back on the march again,
we got the order: "Gas-masks on!" In no time at all, the eye-
glasses were misted up. Then: "Let's hear a song." We sang, not a
marching-song, but an old "up yours" kind of song: "We ain't got
pie-eyed yet, we ain't got pie-eyed yet, not like we're gonna get!"
When we had repeated the refrain three times, the order came:
"Cease singing! – Gas-masks off!" A little while later: "Section,
halt! Left turn!" We were standing as solid as a wall. Defiant – and
with smiles on our faces. The *Erzieher* allowed us to dismiss. The
square-bashing had come to an abrupt end. We had put up a
challenge, and we had won. For us, there was something
fascinating in all this.'

The concept was a success: when tough demands are made on
someone, he feels special. The pupils had to be pushed to the limit
of their capabilities. They had to learn to overcome their fear. This
was the reason why tests of courage were part of the daily routine,
aimed at creating an appetite for the 'hard and dangerous life'. So
the boys of the Adolf Hitler School at Sonthofen had to jump
from a squatting position over the parapet of the upper storey of
their dormitory building – without knowing whether a safety-net
was waiting below to catch them. The same thing happened at the
*Napolas*. 'We got the order: "Jump"', says Uwe Lamprecht, of the
Plön *Napola*, 'and there are two things to realise here: firstly I had
to have the courage to jump into the unknown, but secondly I
had to trust the person giving the order not to make me jump to
my death, unless it was absolutely necessary. If I had been a soldier
later on, it could well be that he would have had to send me to my
death, but I was to have the courage to carry out this order, and I
had to trust my commanding officer not to give an unjust order.'
   Thus it was that the 'elect' in all the schools had to show
courage when ordered to do so. In the open-air swimming-pool
non-swimmers had to let themselves fall backwards into the water
from a 10 foot high diving-board, and they were not pulled out

until they surfaced for the third time. Hardy Krüger, the film actor, who attended the Adolf Hitler School, Sonthofen, describes how he and two other boys had to hack two holes in the thick ice on a frozen lake. The holes were 10 yards apart and, one after the another, they had to climb into one hole and swim under the ice to the other.

> One of the principal goals of that education was to cultivate in us an unquestioning punctuality, unquestioning discipline, unquestioning obedience. As teachers we of course had to convey this to our pupils.
>
> *Ludwig Harig, born 1927, graduate of the*
> *Teacher Training College, Idstein*

'One objective was to make you overcome your weaker self, the coward in all of us', says Theo Sommer. 'We had to jump into the swimming-pool from the 10-metre board wearing full equipment, with back-pack and steel helmet.' The helmets were firmly fastened with a chin-strap. 'When you hit the water, it almost tore your head off.' Tests of courage were set even in the admission examinations. Anyone who refused was immediately rejected. Hans Müncheberg (*Napola*, Potsdam) sums it up: 'If you displayed any weakness, you were just a washout, a weakling, a coward, a disgrace to the whole platoon or the whole company. For us the First Commandment was to prove your manliness, not show any womanish weakness. To be able to stand pain.'

Because toughness was the prime requirement, there were swimming contests at Plön in water that was only a little above freezing-point. There were cross-country runs through ice and snow, barefoot and stripped to the waist. Everyone had to try to keep up. 'To give up was just considered a disgrace', says Theo Sommer. 'Our physical stamina was driven to the limit.' And Klaus Geue remembers from his time at the Adolf Hitler School: 'When we were boxing, boys from older platoons were often brought in, and we were given a helluva beating.'

> . . . There is no sport which promotes the spirit of aggression to the same degree as boxing, which requires lightning decisions, and which develops steely suppleness in the body. If two youngsters settle a dispute with a fist-fight, it is no rougher than if they did so with a piece of polished steel . . .
>
> *Adolf Hitler*, Mein Kampf

In this way sport was intended to develop the boys beyond their limitations. They were pushed to the point of total exhaustion, to the point where conscious intelligence cuts out, all fear of death evaporates and identification with everything which the system stands for is total. 'We were meant to find that precise point beyond which, if need be, we would give our all for *Volk* and Führer', as Uwe Lamprecht puts it. Once you get past that point, they said, you grow out of your old self. After all, it was Germany's youth, steel-hardened through sport, who would carry out Hitler's planned conquests. The *Festschrift* for the tenth anniversary of the *Napolas* proclaimed: 'One of the most essential means of education in a school run in the spirit of National Socialism are the physical exercises . . . It is of little importance whether one *Jungmann* or another comes in first place. What is important and character-forming is the experience of being superior to others . . . If two boys fight bravely in the boxing-ring, then afterwards both are filled with the gratifying feeling of achievement.' And the curriculum of the Adolf Hitler Schools laid down that 'the aim of physical education is the recognition that fighting is the expression of the elemental will to live, both of the individual and the community. It is living ideology.' What this meant in terms of day-to-day reality was summed up by an *Erzieher* in his report on 'a mountain trip in the Allgäu'. Excursions of this kind, he wrote, 'demand the most complete commitment, the most solid comradeship and the highest courage. Here we sometimes deliberately face the challenge of danger, in order to look it clearly in the eye and to recognise ourselves in it. A long, cross-country ski hike, with food-intake deliberately kept to a minimum, sorts out the "weaker brethren", and here I was especially pleased that none of the boys flaked out or even pulled a face. In the triumph over the "weaker self" I see a fine example of the will to self-sacrifice that is necessary for ultimate commitment.'

By the 'ultimate commitment' was meant war, and even skiing served as a preparation for this. Baldur von Schirach's pronouncement that the Adolf Hitler Schools 'really had nothing to do with schooling in the traditional sense', was being proved true. The pupils were intended, as he put it, 'to learn to believe in the impossible.' And – through war-games and manoeuvres – they were to learn what was feasible in war.

At elite schools such as the *Napolas* the year's programme contained several weeks of manoeuvres and field exercises. Here the *Jungmannen* marched out in columns and camped in tents, in order to play at war. They were still throwing clubs, but when war came it would be hand-grenades. They learned how to camouflage themselves, how to make use of ground cover, how to read maps and orientate by compass, how to issue orders and follow them. They had to give first aid to the 'wounded', as they might later at the Front. They had to overcome and 'kill' the enemy. Every *Jungmann* wore a woollen 'life-ribbon' on his arm. If it was torn off, the wearer was counted as dead.

Each school conducted its own spring manoeuvres. However the summer manoeuvres brought all the schools together in one 'theatre of war'. There would then be a large-scale simulation of the 'real thing' – on Lüneberg Heath, on the flat Darss peninsula on the Baltic or beside Lake Faak in southern Austria. The schools travelled there in special trains, were divided into 'red' or 'blue' teams and marched towards each other. As in a real war they had reconnaissance troops and advance motorised units to probe the territory ahead. 'Combat units' waited in readiness as the two 'armies' approached each other. The climax of every manoeuvre was the 'final battle'. Hans-Georg Bartholomäi describes the scene: 'As in the age of Frederick the Great, the two armies marched towards each other on a broad front, with standard-bearers, attack-buglers and marching bands in the vanguard. The newsreel cameras had been set up, and Heinrich Himmler, or Rust, the education minister, would be in position with their staff.

Then a great free-for-all would break out. You had to tear as many blue or red ribbons as possible off the wrists of the "enemy". Afterwards we proudly wore the ribbons in the buttonhole of our tunics.' In wartime the ribbons were replaced by Iron Crosses. 'With boys having been prepared in this way, it is hoped that the army will have an easier job training them up to be first-class soldiers', wrote the head of a *Napola* in 1938, on the subject of military games and manoeuvres.

The war was still only a game. The 'dead' got to their feet again. The *Jungmannen* still had no real weapons, only 'weapons of honour' such as a dagger, on which was engraved the motto of all *Napolaner*: 'Be more than you seem' – a permanent injunction to prove themselves anew every day. At every *Napola* the awarding of the 'Dagger of Honour' to pupils of the 6th Platoon turned into a pseudo-sacred ceremony of dedication. The solemn act was considered a high-point in the life of a *Jungmann*. Henceforth he had the right to bear the weapon as a 'symbol of honour'. He was now seen as capable of defending himself. With his 'side-arm' as the dagger was known, he was able to defend his 'honour'.

'Only death or your disloyalty can release you from your obligation' were the words with which the head of the Plön *Napola* sent the *Jungmannen* on their way. 'Keep your body and soul as pure as this steel and be as hard as the steel of your weapon of honour!' Then the *Jungmannen* had to vow comradeship unto death. 'If one of us two falls, the other shall stand for both.'

Like a talisman the dagger was intended to keep burning the flame of faith in the struggle for a supposedly 'sacred cause'. 'Even the ancient Teutons had their sword of initiation and the medieval knights their accolade', wrote a fourteen-year-old *Napola* boy in his school magazine in 1941. 'In these ceremonies the youths laid aside all childish things and had a sword placed in their hand, so that they could fight for their people alongside the older men and keep their honour pure.' So far did the cult of the dagger go that it was only permitted to be drawn for cleaning. According to Uwe Lamprecht, the *Jungmannen* of Plön were adjured 'only to re-sheath it when blood was upon it, the blood of the enemy against whom we had to defend ourselves, if he attacked us'. 'We were proud to be given this dagger', Hans-Günther Zempelin (*Napola*,

Oranienstein) says today. 'It was a male rite of passage, like those in primitive societies. But it worked.'

The portentous words with which the school heads accompanied the awards also had their effect. 'Thousands of *Jungmannen* in all the National Socialist education establishments have received this weapon before you and borne it with honour', declared the head of the Naumburg *Napola* to his *Jungmannen* on 9 November 1944. 'Hundreds of them have fallen, as old comrades loyal to their vow to Führer and *Volk*. Let only death wrest this weapon from your hand.'

The cult-like elevation of concepts like honour, loyalty and death claimed its victims even in the early *Napola* years. One evening a *Jungmann* at Plön, who felt excluded from the group, took his dagger of honour into the grounds of Plön castle. He was a 'gifted individualist' as his fellow-pupil Rolf Diercks describes him. 'Right there in the castle gardens, he stabbed himself through the heart with his dagger.'

For many, the pressure of having to live in a community of fighters, of never showing weakness and of withstanding military discipline, just became too great. Homesickness, fear of the *Erzieher*, non-stop competition with one's room-mate, who was perhaps tougher, who could put up with more or could hand more out, led many to the limits of their psychological and physical powers of endurance. Even so, the number who would give up and ask their parents to take them away from the school was very small indeed. The belief that they were among the best, their pride in being one of the 'elect', gave them the strength to hold out. 'You must prove yourself!' was the motto of the elite pupils. When Hans-Günther Zempelin, as a *Jungmann* at the Oranienstein *Napola*, lay exhausted on his bed at night, he thought to himself: 'God, do I always have to stand to attention, always have to obey orders?' The answer was always the same: '*Jawohl*, you *must* do it. You owe it to your education, to your Führer and to your *Volk*.'

Klaus Geue, who spent a few months at the Adolf Hitler School in the *Ordensburg* at Sonthofen, asked himself the same question, but the answer was a different one. He urged his parents to rescue him from the *Ordensburg*, to spare him the drill and the beatings. Geue's parents allowed themselves to be persuaded. Their son was released – but with a crushing verdict which applied to the parents as well. They had 'let the boy's distress make them respond sympathetically to his importuning, which merely further reinforced his anti-school attitude', wrote the head of the Adolf Hitler School in East Prussia, *Oberbannführer* Ludwig Magsam. The judgement on Klaus Geue was that he was admittedly 'gifted and intellectually fully up to our requirements'. However, the reason for his 'failure' lay in his 'traits of character'. He was, Magsam said, 'an individualist with particular expectations from life' who saw the communal schooling as an 'intolerable restriction on his personal freedom. What made things harder for him was that he is highly sensitive and took to heart every trivial insult and criticism from his superiors. His obsession with the idea that he had to get away from the Adolf Hitler School at all costs led to a nervous condition which, according to the school doctor, was of a completely psychosomatic nature.' The report ended with the words: 'His departure is no loss either for the school itself or for the future corps of leaders.'

Klaus Geue went back to attending a 'normal' school and found there were gaps in his knowledge. Was this the fault of his *Erzieher*? At the Adolf Hitler Schools the average age of the teaching staff was twenty-seven, and most were former HJ leaders. When the *Napolas* first started many of the staff were highly qualified, but the standard dropped as more and more teachers were drafted into the Wehrmacht. At all the elite schools the curriculum was equivalent to that of a good high school, but the interpretation of it varied widely. The *Napolas* were those in the best position to give their pupils a comprehensive education. However, the Adolf Hitler Schools were there for one overriding purpose: to be Party seminaries delivering more ideology than knowledge. Here, especially, Hitler's words pointed the way: 'It is not our professors and scholars, not our poets and philosophers, who have dragged our nation back from the abyss. It is exclusively the political soldiery of our Party.'

Such words did not fail to influence the teaching in Hitler's schools. In subjects like 'ethnology' things were taught 'which prove the correctness of our ideological position': 'ancient and modern history, geography, racial theory, the German language, cultural history, economic and social theory, philosophy etc.' The American correspondent Howard K. Smith, who in 1941 was reporting from Nazi Germany for CBS Radio and the *New York Times*, among others, wrote about the Adolf Hitler Schools: 'Their curriculum is amazing. Besides studies in doctored German history and the three 'R's, the boys are taught to mine coal, build bridges, and are made to undergo physical tests which put the training of Spartan youth in the shade'. Smith concludes that 'the strain of the underlying education is warping. They are taught to believe in German superiority to all other peoples, they are rigorously indoctrinated with the racial ideal, taught to hate Christianity, both as a religion and as a norm of values, and to believe in the divinity of the Führer. They come out of the Adolf Hitler schools, technically capable, strong, clean and alert, but with a sense of values not much higher than that of an orangoutang. . . . Their allegiance is to the Führer alone. The highest goal any of them can attain is to die in battle for the Führer.'

'The special feature of our training was of course the shaping of our awareness', admits Hans-Georg Bartholomäi ( *Napola*, Naumburg). 'Not only did we have to live up to the Führer's demands, that the youth of Germany should be "as fleet as greyhounds, as tough as leather and as hard as Krupp steel". Within ourselves we had to be "real guys" and dedicated followers of his ideal. That's why, in addition to the normal classes we had two hours a week of "political education", in which we dealt with *Mein Kampf* and Alfred Rosenberg's *Myth of the 20th Century*.' Ideology had a special place in the timetable. In subjects like 'NSDAP', 'A world survey' or 'nationalist policy' the discussion was mainly about ideological questions, Hitler's rise to power and the teaching of hate for 'differently created' and 'inferior' people. One of the most important topics in history teaching at the select schools was the Treaty of Versailles: 'We were constantly reminded of this so-called "shameful peace", to the end that we must at all costs win back the territories lost in 1918–19, and that it was indeed our duty to make sure this came about', recalls Rolf

Diercks, who was then at the Plön *Napola*. Every day *Jungmann* Diercks had this 'shame' thrust in front of him. In the Knights' Hall of the Plön academy there was a 'black window', also called the 'Versailles niche' – in which the text of the Treaty of Versailles lay on a pedestal swathed in black velvet. It was pierced by a dagger and surrounded by chains. On the day the school was inaugurated, 28 June 1933, the anniversary of the signing of the Versailles treaty, the head of the Plön academy uttered this call to arms: 'My young comrades! Our lives are dedicated to Germany. The consequences of the dictatorship of shame confront us every day. We are oppressed in every sphere. Germany is not free. You shall not rest until the treaty has been abolished. Germany must be freed, even if it costs us our lives.'

No subject was more suited to indoctrination than the teaching of history. 'We were taught that some of our emperors had looked too much to the south, and too little to the east', Theo Sommer remembers from his time in Sonthofen. 'In history lessons, colonisation of the east was, as it were, presented to us as the duty of every German.' Even lessons in the German language had to serve as a platform for all kinds of propaganda, as the topics of many a school essay show: 'In Germany dictatorship and tyranny prevail! Germany is arming for war! German culture is being trampled on! What is your answer to these vicious foreign headlines?' Assignments like this gave teachers the opportunity to check on how closely their pupils were following the party line. In the Nazi academies ideology was not only taught, it was also examined.

The textbooks did the rest. They were chosen by the *Napolas* according to their 'value for race, nation and current situation'. They had to cover: '1. Teutonic culture and history. 2. The evolution and destiny of the Teutonic and German ethos in the confrontation between the Teutonic world on the one hand, and Christendom and the classical world on the other. 3. The forces of the present.' Thus teachers of German culture dealt by choice with ancient Germanic poetry, Icelandic sagas, or the early medieval German Song of the Nibelungs. The leaders of tomorrow read passages from the works of Nietzsche, such as *The Will to Power*. The canon of literature also included works of pure propaganda, such as Paul de Lagarde's *Belief in Germany* or Hans Grimm's *People without Space*, as well as war literature by Ernst Jünger (*Combat as Inner Experience*) or Werner Beumelburg (*Seventeen Years Old at Verdun*). Every subject was ideologically tainted, even language teaching. In Latin the teachers and pupils devoted themselves to such absurd topics as 'Roman authors and the Jewish Question'. In ancient Greek, Plato's texts had to provide a philosophical gloss to a 'criticism of democracy'. Above all, it was in German 'nationalist policy' and biology that classroom work most often served an ideological purpose.

In the final examinations for 1937–8, the *Jungmannen* had to answer the following question in the maths paper: 'An aircraft drops a bomb from a height of 2,000 metres at a speed of 108 km per hour. After what lapse of time and at what location does the projectile hit the ground?' In biology, one of the questions was; 'What facts prompt the racial researcher to seek the future of the German people in the destiny of the Nordic race?' In 'nationalist policy' the question was asked: 'What foundation did the Führer give to the National Socialist movement, in order to lead it to victory?'

Not surprisingly, in most subjects the pupils of supposedly 'elite' schools lagged behind those in normal high schools. The emphasis was on sport, war-games and manoeuvres, although one or two establishments were able to retain the last vestiges of the ideal of a humanistic education. In no leadership school was the Nazi educational dogma taken to such extremes as in the '*Reichschule* of the NSDAP' in Feldafing. It had actually been set up by the SA. However, after the SA leadership had been liquidated in the 'Röhm Putsch' of 1934, the Party seized absolute control. Powerful paladins such as Rudolf Hess, and later Martin Bormann, took on the role of patron of the school, which was less than demanding in its selection procedure. Sporting performance, health, a good appearance and character and a good family background were sufficient. The teaching in Feldafing was restricted to 'the things which the future citizen will find necessary for his career and his fighting contribution to the building of National Socialism'. The main subjects on the curriculum were German language, history, geography and instruction in National Socialism. The key role, however, was given to sport, to which 14 hours a week were devoted. For the leaving examination all that was required was an oral test and an essay on a topic chosen by the examinee, such as 'From tribesman to compatriot', 'Every revolution aims to recreate mankind', 'War as creator of a new order in the inner life of the nation', or 'May the spirit of Germany bring about a healthier world'. No 'Feldafinger' ever failed his final examinations. Did any ever have to stay back and re-take them? A member of the master race could hardly be asked to do that.

Those graduating from Feldafing had the same experience as one *Jungmann* from the Plön *Napola*, who, ten months after taking his final examination in 1938, came to the sobering conclusion that 'we are adept both physically and mentally; we may be quicker but we are certainly more superficial . . . Our superiority is in the area of ideology . . . We have been dealing with these questions, though often in an unhealthily superficial way, so that such opinions as we hold often become dogmatic, and we tended to dismiss the hardest and most important problems in a few sentences. Many who listen to us, struck dumb by our certainty, tacitly accept our assertions; others draw our attention, succinctly but painfully, to the hollowness and superficiality we display in these matters.'

Very soon the word got around among German parents how undistinguished the education in the so-called elite schools really was. The *Napolas* had an image problem. They were said to 'turn out stereotyped people', and gave preference to 'bird-brained athletes'. Rather unsuccessfully the *Napolas* attempted to rectify this image in an article in the *Völkischer Beobachter* in May 1944: 'We are certainly *not* a community of dunces! . . . Any boy who has a gift for singing, drawing or mathematics . . . is not forced into the Party mould but is encouraged and thus runs no risk of being alienated from the rest of the school, but nor does he, as one *Erzieher* puts it, "adopt the fancy frills of virtuosity".' Former *Napola* pupils like Falk Knoblau know how much credence to give to such words. When he transferred to an ordinary school, Knoblau needed special tuition in order to catch up with the syllabus at the junior high school in Görlitz. Today he says: 'It was depressing, the fact that this had to happen to me, coming from an elite school. It was shame-making.'

Men make history. And we make the men.
*August Heissmeyer, SS Obergruppenführer and*
*Inspector of Napolas*

At the end of their school career the pupils were seldom over-burdened with knowledge. 'Your academic knowledge is sufficient for you to fulfil your duty as soldiers', the commandant of the fourth year of the Adolf Hitler School told his charges as he sent them on their way. 'What you lack and what we could not give you, the hard school of war will make up for in its wealth of life experiences.'

And what *did* they lack? Harald Grundmann, an Adolf Hitler School pupil, says: 'I am ashamed to think how little we knew about German poets and men of letters – from Thomas Mann to Gottfried Benn; how scanty our knowledge of mathematics was. So in the intellectual field our qualifications were pretty miserable.' And from Harry Bölte, *Napola* Ifeldt: 'To my mind, the gravest disadvantage was that we grew up in a religious vacuum.'

Where faith in Hitler was preached there was no room for other religions. Initially the *Napolas* placed restrictions on religious instruction; then they abolished it altogether. At Naumburg the *Jungmannen* asked their supervisor: 'Do National Socialism and Christianity go together at all? The Church receives a subsidy of 200 million marks from the state. Is that justified? Why do we have to learn the Jewish Ten Commandments? Why did the Church refuse a burial-service for an SA man?' After 1938 there was no longer any confessional religious teaching in the Napolas. In 'questions of religious policy, a strictly neutral position' was to be adopted. This was because, as the Inspector of *Napolas*, August Heissmeyer, put it, 'it is not a question of personal salvation of the soul, but of what becomes of Germany'.

Hitler's boarding-schools became increasingly godless places. In 1942, out of 6,093 *Jungmannen*, no more than one in four were still 'believers in God'. The proportion in Adolf Hitler Schools was similar. One of their pupils wrote in his diary on 1 March 1944: 'Went to the registry office. I am leaving the Church. My parents are against this; but one cannot go on paying one's dues to the opposition.'

In place of religion the *Erzieher* at the Adolf Hitler Schools taught sagas from the ancient Germanic pantheon or knowledge of the Party. Yet it was precisely in the latter subject that, in the first graduation examinations of an Adolf Hitler School in 1942, disaster struck. This was all the more embarrassing because it happened in front of the founders, patrons and financiers of the schools, organisation chief Robert Ley, and *Jugendführer* Baldur von Schirach. Both insisted on putting questions to the examinees themselves. Ley seemed to keep harping on the Party programme. At first he refused to face the truth, but with every question his suspicion became more of a certainty: not one pupil of the Adolf Hitler Schools knew what the Party programme was. 'To us, National Socialism meant much more than just the 24 clauses of the Party programme', explains Joachim Baumann, one of those who was baffled by Ley's questions.

So what *did* it mean? 'To us, National Socialism was faith in the idea of the strength and magnificence of Germany and the German spirit; it was the certainty that a world languishing under the spirit of Judaism would be brought back to health by the German character. And it was our task in this not only to win over the remaining doubters in our own ranks, but also to convey to the other Europeans of our race the message of a Germanic springtime until, to the benefit of all, a great Germanic empire would blossom from Greater Germany.' Thus blinded and seduced, after five years Baumann left Sonthofen as a qualified Adolf Hitler School alumnus. He had to prove himself as a 'bearer of ideas', and wanted to become a 'political manager'. Today he shakes his head over it all.

And not just over that. In his school magazine Joachim Baumann read again the topics on which he and his platoon had to write essays. And by the way, copying from others was unheard of, he says. That would have been 'dishonourable'. In classroom work the *Erzieher* wrote the topic or assignment on the blackboard and left the room. Anyone who 'cribbed' was reported by his classmates. This did not entail a punishment, just a firm admonition in the next lesson about the sense of honour. 'Boys, why do we practise this form of teaching in our classes? – It's because you're a select group, aren't you? – Well, then. Now we'll do something quite different. Write an essay on the topic: "Uprightness and Character." See you later.'

A harmless enough subject. Baumann also recalls other politically unambiguous essay topics. Simply posing the question suggested what the right answer should be. It had long been understood that 'Germany intends to replace Britain as a world power, and will do so'. There was no doubt that jazz had to be rejected as 'nigger music', that 'elements' of one's own blood, 'which threaten racial purity, have to be removed by sterilisation', that the 'political institution of the Christian teachings', had to be replaced by National Socialism and the people had to be freed from the 'clutches of the Catholic Church', that the Slavs had to be 'cleansed' from the annexed eastern territories. . . . When Joachim Baumann reads the essays today he is not especially surprised by the 'line-toeing and today rather ridiculous-sounding formulations and ideas' of that time. What depresses him more is 'the unbelievably casual matter-of-factness with which they were put forward', and the naturalness with which these arguments were soaked up by him as well. 'We were just gullible', says Baumann with a shrug. 'We just believed it all.' The school wanted to raise them as 'idealists', he says again and again. Today he is aware how criminal these ideals were, how much their thinking was clouded by images of hate which they did not only encounter in books alone.

One day Joachim Baumann's platoon was taken on an outing to the Munich suburb of Haar – 'to the loony-bin, as it was known in those days'. 'A professor showed us Adolf Hitler boys his patients', says Baumann, and guesses: 'This was probably meant to convince us that euthanasia would be an act of mercy for these poor creatures. They tried to sell us the idea that murder was a humane method of dealing with the mentally ill.' The *Erzieher* did not have to work very hard at convincing them. The merciless theory of the right of the strongest and of 'weakness unworthy of life' had long ago burnt itself into the brains of the schoolboy elite. 'We never learned that, among other things, we are on earth to help the weaker', says Ernst-Christian Gädke, then at the Spandau *Napola*, 'because their lives were considered unworthy of living.'

But what was the attitude of Hitler's schoolboys to what was presented to them as 'the Jewish Question'? Most of the alumni say that Jews were seldom discussed. Uwe Lamprecht, Plön

*Napola*: 'We never heard the words: the Jew must be killed. Only that we would and should have nothing to do with Jews.' That they were to be seen as enemies seemed as obvious as the expectation that before long there would be no more Jews in Germany. So why go on talking about it? Baumann describes the mood in the Sonthofen *Ordensburg* in this way: 'By the time it's our turn to take over the leadership, the Jewish problem will have been solved. There won't be any more Jews. Germany will be a Jew-free zone. Though of course we never thought about Auschwitz or about the gassing. To us, with our ideals, that was completely unimaginable.' Certainly he had known about marginalisation and emigration, Baumann admits, but nothing about the killings. All we heard about were 'Concert camps', says Uwe Lamprecht. This cynical euphemism he took to mean a type of penal camp, 'to which people were sent, who – as we saw it at the time – were totally pig-headed, who opposed Hitler, even though in our opinion he was doing good things for the nation.'

'The instilling of anti-Semitism was part of the programme', says Gerd-Ekkehard Lorenz, who then attended the Potsdam *Napola*, 'but not a word was mentioned about the "Final Solution of the Jewish question".' In history lessons, he recalls, Jews cropped up as 'well-poisoners', and there was discussion about Britain being ruled by Jews and the world by 'Jewish plutocrats'. They saw propaganda films which talked about 'Jewish nigger-jazz', where Benny Goodman 'maltreated his clarinet with criminal Jewish hands'. It was even drummed into the *Jungmannen* that the word '*Lametta*', meaning 'tinsel', was a Jewish word and that the correct German term for this Christmas decoration was 'Mother Holle's Hair'. They visited the propaganda exhibition 'The Soviet Paradise' in Berlin's amusement park, where they saw and believed how 'bestial' the 'Jewish commissars' were and what dangers 'Jewish Bolshevism' brought with it.

'Anti-Semitism was explained and justified as a historical phenomenon. We were told about the pogroms of Worms and Speyer. It was obvious that the Jews were evil. We didn't know *why* they were evil, just that they always had been. They once lived in ghettoes.' The fact that when the war broke out Jews in the east were forced to live in ghettoes once again, therefore seemed 'normal' to the elite schoolboys. From there hundreds of thousands were transported to death-camps such as Auschwitz and Treblinka. In August 1941 *Jungmannen* on agricultural service in the Wartheland, a region of occupied Poland, were taken on an excursion to Lodz, then known as Litzmannstadt. The platoon leader noted in his report: 'The *Jungmannen* were fascinated by the Ghetto.'

At the scene of the crime the leaders of tomorrow were to see and learn what happened to 'enemies of the Reich'. Thus pupils of the Adolf Hitler School in Thuringia went on an outing to the Buchenwald concentration camp. One of them was Harald Grundmann. His account lets us see deep into the psyche of the Adolf Hitler School boys. 'We went there by bus and saw the gateway with the inscription "To each his own". Then we went in. We couldn't move around freely but were escorted by an SS man.'

The camp had been well prepared for the visit. The Adolf Hitler boys had to be shown 'exemplary conditions': clean barracks, an absence of violence, in fact an innocuous labour camp. There was nothing to suggest that Buchenwald was the murderous billet for 56,000 people who were forced to work themselves to death or had to endure the torture of terminal medical experiments. Hitler's schoolboys remained oblivious to all this. Instead, they were introduced to Dutch scientists who were experimenting with shrunken heads. 'We were told', Grundmann recalls, 'that in the Dutch colonies, now Indonesia, the head-hunters carried out similar experiments on the heads which they cut off their foes, and that the Dutch scientists were continuing these experiments. For what purpose – I have no idea.' They were the heads of Polish prisoners. But none of the boys enquired about the victims.

'We saw people with different coloured badges on their chests. We saw how people were only allowed to go down the so-called Karacho Avenue at the double, and whenever they saw someone in uniform they had to remove their headgear. We took all this on board under the general principle that they were enemies of our nation, who during our time of struggle – war, to you and me – had to be "taken out of circulation".'

On their tour of the concentration camp the elite schoolboys also came upon a group of buildings with a tall, black chimney.

'We were told it was a crematorium and when we enquired further they said: the number of staff and inmates here is as large as the population of Weimar, that's to say about 50,000. Weimar has its crematorium and we have one, because of course there are mortalities here too. We were happy to accept that.'

Today Harald Grundmann realises that he had been taken through 'Potemkin villages'. In other words, he and his schoolmates had been presented with an artificial stage-set, which they took for reality. Today he can see what this 'education' was intended to make them into: 'We were to accept the thinking; as far as possible we were not to feel any sympathy or pity for the victims. The *Erzieher* wanted to make us insensitive to pain, both our own pain and that felt by our fellow-men. And I would say that they succeeded. It was not until the end of the war that we understood what had been taken away from us.'

The crimes, the terror, the day-to-day existence under the dictatorship scarcely penetrated the *Ordensburgen* and other educational establishments. The 'elect' lived in complete isolation. 'We in our *Ordensburgen* are very cut off from real life and all that goes with it', wrote the Adolf Hitler pupil Reinhard Wild in his school magazine in 1941. 'We only experience the events of the war at second hand. What do we know of food-rationing, of clothing coupons, of all the hardships of war and the privations they bring to the individual? Only in the brief holiday periods do we gaining a fleeting impression of them. Here we have our own "state", which is subject to very different conditions.'

Expeditions into the real world were a rarity. For twelve weeks every *Jungmann* had to work in a coal-mine, in order to acquire leadership skills and to learn something about the 'national community'. If, therefore, the *Jungmann* 'is later placed in authority over these German working men', explained *Napola* Inspector August Heissmeyer, 'he will not regard himself as their superior, but will stand at the head of his men as their leader. He can do that more easily if he himself was once one of their workmates.' When engaged in this underground drudgery, each elite pupil was meant to ask himself: 'How should I treat these men, so that in spite of their arduous work and cheerless existence they will hold dear their German homeland with the last fibre of their being?'

On agricultural service quite different questions came to the minds of numerous *Jungmannen*. For many, the weeks spent on farms were the first time they were put to the test as bearers of the Nazi ideology. But theory came up against hard reality. 'So how's it been since the Jews have gone?' a *Jungmann* from the Oranienstein *Napola* enquired of a Sauerland farmer. The answer he got certainly did not fit his image of the doughty German yeoman. Things were pretty bad, came the reply, seeing as the livestock trade was no longer functioning. Taken aback, the *Jungmann* attempted to argue his case. One shouldn't take too narrow a view, but should look at the fundamentals behind it all. The farmer was not convinced. Practicalities prevailed, and of those Hitler's pupils knew but little.

Again and again such contradictions arose. Why was war being waged against our Germanic brothers, the British? Why against the Soviet Union, when surely it said in *Mein Kampf* that there should never again be a war on two fronts? Why were the Jews considered 'inferior' when they had survived 2,000 years of persecution? Were not *they* really the 'superior race'? In the Adolf Hitler Schools such questions were indeed asked. Even some of the great figures of the Old Guard could scarcely be said to fit the ideal image. Was the bloated and drug-riddled Hermann Göring really one of the Germanic master-race? Likewise, Robert Ley, the Reich organisation chief and founder of the Adolf Hitler Schools, was hardly an example to the pupils. True, he liked to put on a jovial front, and promised many of his charges a career as the captain of one of his 'Strength-through-Joy' vacation-ships ('I'm building a hundred of 'em, and you'll be one of the skippers, m'boy!'). Yet his weaknesses were an open secret. Everyone knew when one of Ley's drinking binges was taking place in his apartment in the Sonthofen *Ordensburg*. 'He was often under the influence of alcohol', are the carefully chosen words of Heinz Giebeler, a former Adolf Hitler pupil. It was no accident that Ley's nickname was 'Reich-Dipsomaniac'. Hardly anyone dared challenge him about this. But one person who had the courage to do so was, all of things, an Adolf Hitler School boy.

'*Reichsleiter*, did you know that the general public consider you a heavy drinker?' It was the tensest moment in all his schooldays, says Joachim Baumann. Apparently Ley winced visibly and said rather hoarsely: 'My lads, you can be whatever you like except one thing: drinkers.' So low did Robert Ley sink in the estimation of his pupils that they were not afraid to indulge in little attacks on him. It must have been in late January or early February 1945, Theo Sommer recalls: 'Suddenly a car appeared at the main entrance to the Ordensburg; it was a VW Beetle.' Behind the wheel sat Robert Ley and beside him was an actress. 'She was one of Ley's mistresses, and apparently he wanted to spend the night with her in one of the three ski-huts belonging to the Ordensburg. We were absolutely furious about it and vented our anger by opening up the engine and kicking it with our heavy ski-boots. To us he was the personification of a fat cat.'

Contradiction was built into the elite schools themselves. Only one man escaped any breath of criticism: Adolf Hitler. To find fault with him was tantamount to sin. 'There was no God, but the Führer was a gift to us from Providence', says Hans Müncheberg, of the Potsdam *Napola*. 'To us he was a higher kind of being', recalls Hans-Günther Zemplein, *Napola*, Oranienstein. Simply to be a bearer of Hitler's name was both an incentive and an obligation for them. 'He has placed great trust in us', wrote an Adolf Hitler pupil in his diary for 1940. 'To us it means acting in such a way that we can stand before the Führer at any time. He is our example in all things. We are proud to bear his name. To step up before him, to experience his immediate presence, is something which nearly everyone dreams of.' Yet Adolf Hitler never once showed his face in any of the elite schools.

The disappointment which this occasioned was great. To some it caused considerable hurt. 'Unfortunately the Führer did not visit us at the castle', an Adolf Hitler School pupil wrote in his 1940 diary. 'However, we hope that in the coming years this wish will be fulfilled.' But Hitler was not particularly interested in 'his' schools. The fate of his 'heirs' did not begin to interest him until the final months of the war, when he was given a demonstration of the way many elite school alumni 'acquitted themselves in the face of the enemy'. Thus the only opportunity left to the schoolboys of catching a glimpse of the Führer was at official occasions – speeches, parades, ceremonies. Joachim Baumann can remember the exact day on which his dearest wish was granted: it was on 9 November 1937.

Baumann and 300 school friends travelled by special train from Sonthofen to Munich, where Hitler paraded, as he did every year, with a row of 'old campaigners' to commemorate the 'the Movement's Dead' in a chilling cult ceremony. Baumann, the Adolf Hitler pupil, knew about the failed putsch of 1923 from the readings of *Mein Kampf,* which were given at breakfast-time every day. Now he was standing expectantly on the kerbstones edging the circle of lawn around the obelisk on the Karolinenplatz. Along with tens of thousands of Müncheners he waited for the ceremony to begin, for the procession of the 'bearers of the medal of blood' with Hitler at its head. Flames leapt from the bowls of fire mounted on pillars, which lined the route to the Feldherrnhalle. Muffled drumbeats heralded the climax of the ceremony. Everything that Joachim Baumann had learned at the *Ordensburg* was here a tangible cult. The glorification of death, the morbid emotion of joyful self-sacrifice – Baumann knew all this from his classes. To this day he can still recite, word for word, a verse from the 'Edda' epic: 'Possessions die. Clans die. Thou thyself shall die as they do. I know but one thing that lives for ever: the famous deeds of the dead.'

Duly impressed, Baumann stood on the Munich kerbside. 'Everyone was as quiet as a mouse', he recalls. 'Then came the man who, on 9 November 1923, had carried the banner, now called the Banner of Blood. About twenty yards behind him came Hitler in a plain brown shirt, his left hand on his belt-buckle, staring straight ahead of him.' Hitler's gaze remained fixed, even at the moment when he passed Joachim Baumann. So that was it, then? Glumly, Baumann wrote to his parents that same day: 'Just imagine, I've seen the Führer. He went past really close. Next to him were Hess, Göring, Goebbels and Julius Streicher. But I only got a glimpse of them, because I wanted to look straight at the Führer, in the hope that our eyes would meet. But he just stared rigidly ahead. I was so very disappointed.'

> I order that in future the active-service officers and junior leaders of the army and the *Waffen-SS* must, before joining the Wehrmacht, be educated . . . at a National Political Education Institution, an Adolf Hitler School or at the Reich School, Feldafing.
>
> *Adolf Hitler, 1944*

Not only pupils but even officials like the Inspector of *Napolas*, *SS-Gruppenführer* August Heissmeyer, saw themselves being contemptuously bypassed. When Heissmeyer was visiting the Oranienstein *Napola*, Hans-Günther Zempelin overheard him 'complaining bitterly that he had only been received by Hitler on one occasion, when the latter, as commander-in-chief of the army, had received reports that *Napola* pupils were distinguishing themselves as young officers and ensigns. Then he had spoken with Hitler for just one hour.' From that time on Heissmeyer had never again been ushered into the Führer's presence. However, he never gave up hoping that Hitler would enhance the status of the *Napolas* by paying them a visit. In preparation for this, Oranienstein Castle was renovated. But Hitler never did appear.

To compensate for this, Hitler's henchmen concerned themselves all the more intently with the school, none more than the *Reischsführer-SS*, Heinrich Himmler. His efforts to achieve complete control over the *Napolas* culminated in the Führer Order dated 7 December 1944, quoted above. Hitler made his chief executioner, Himmler, principally responsible for educating young officers. Since the outbreak of war Himmler had been increasingly active in setting up new *Napolas* – as preparatory schools for young cadres for the regular SS and *Waffen-SS*. He wanted to extend the network of *Napolas* not only across the Reich, but also into conquered territories, in order to recruit 'a selected few among the youth' and inject young Dutchmen, Danes, Norwegians and Flemish Belgians with 'Reich thinking'. In 'trawls for good blood' Himmler wanted to sift out 'children of good stock' from the subject peoples and send them to boarding-schools such as the *Napolas*, thus gaining potential leaders – for wars of the future. Himmler's objective, to multiply the number of *Napolas* to a hundred within five to seven years, had already been approved by Hitler as early as 1940.

Hitler's order, that only pupils of the elite schools should be made officers, was exactly what most of those pupils wanted. Admittedly, they had the freedom in principle to choose their own career, but the majority knew what was expected of them and aspired to 'armed professions', as is clear from a secret memorandum of the SS central office dated 26 May 1942. This trend became even more pronounced. With every day of war the wish grew among the schoolboys to become officers, finally to be able to prove their worth. Only greater was the fear of missing out on the war altogether. 'After the French campaign', Hans-Günther Zempelin recalls, 'our *Erzieher* came to us and said: "Right chaps, down to work; prepare yourselves for the peacetime graduation." We found the very idea horrendous.' According to the Inspector of *Napolas*, August Heissmeyer, speaking after the war, 75 per cent of the graduates chose the career of officer.

Everyone who was drafted was envied by his comrades. 'Boy, we thought to ourselves', says Gerd-Ekkehard Lorenz of the Postdam *Napola*, 'they've got all the luck, they're in there already.' Regular reports from former *Jungmannen* about supposedly heroic battles fanned the flames of their zeal still further. One *Jungmann* sent a letter to his mother for her birthday, from the field post office: 'Dearest Mother, I cannot thank you enough for making me what I am: a staunch soldier, loyal to you and to the Führer – though it may be to my death. Around us echoes the call of our fallen comrades: fight for victory and die, if need be, for the great cause of the Führer! We belong to him. Heil Hitler, your loving son.'

Battle-cries romanticised with a diabolical appeal the supposed 'sweet death for Führer and Fatherland'. Paradise lay in 'in the shadow of the swords'. Hitler's schoolboys greeted news of their comrades' deaths with the hymn of the poet Hölderlin: 'Harbingers of victory descend: the battle is ours! Live on supreme, O Fatherland, and count not the dead! For thee, dearest country, not one too many has fallen!' But the real meaning of war was something of which the 'elect of German youth' knew virtually nothing. 'No-one mentioned the fact', says Harald Grundmann, 'that people actually got shot in the stomach and died a horrible death.' Even those awarded the *Ritterkreuz*, the Knight's Cross, and other war heroes, who were sent to the schools to further fan the patriotic flame, left the young hopefuls with the naïve belief that war was a harmless game. 'We admired those men', says Hans Müncheberg. 'We envied them, and they tried to comfort us by saying: cheer up, young comrades, we won't drag the war out much longer and after the final victory there will still be plenty to do.'

The fear of missing the war gave them scarcely any rest. Anyone who was finally allowed to enlist felt that, as one of the chosen, he had to stand out from the all the others. In March 1944 August Heissmeyer reported to Himmler: 'The young intake of leaders have in recent weeks proved themselves fully in the face of the enemy: four have been awarded Oak Leaves, 33 the Knight's Cross, 96 the German Gold Cross, and 1,226 are dead or missing . . .' In the *Napolas* there were more and more parades at which the names of fallen *Jungmannen* were read out. 'To start with we were proud', says Uwe Lamprecht, 'proud that one of us had been allowed to give his life for Germany. Or so we thought at the time. Later it began to disturb us that so many younger chaps, whom we knew, were dying. And it was not just our friends who were being killed, it was our fathers as well.'

'By the time the war ended', says Hans Buchholz, then at the Naumburg *Napola*, 'I had learned how to die for my Fatherland, but not how to live for it. Our ideas were so shaped in one direction: "You are nothing. Your Volk is everything. Germany must live, even if we have to die. Germany, thou shalt stand and shine, though we may be destroyed."' In his will, one former *Jungmann* from the Köslin *Napola*, wrote from the Front: 'If I should die [he did die], then I wish that this event be seen as nothing other than what in reality it is: a necessary sacrifice, and one I make gladly, for the victory of Germany is the fulfilment of my life as a soldier.'

As early as the autumn of 1944, *Napola*-Inspector Heissmeyer wanted to turn all the institutions into 'solid fighting bases', the last bulwarks in a war that was long since lost. By January 1945 even he could see that defeat was inevitable. He withdrew to the

*Napola* in Berlin's Spandau district. Other *Jungamnnen*, who were threatened by the advancing Red Army, had by now been evacuated. Only in the Adolf Hitler Schools did things continue according to schedule. A new school year was being prepared and the *Reichsjugendführung* expressed confidence that in two to three years every *Gau* would possess its own 'elite school'. The next Adolf Hitler School was to be opened in February 1945 in the Wartheland district of Poland.

For *Jungmann* Gerd-Ekkehard Lorenz, in the Potsdam *Napola*, the beginning of the end started on 19 April 1945. His platoon was transferred to Spandau, with Heissmeyer. On bicycles, with grenade-launchers on the handlebars, with steel helmets on their heads and carbines or machine-pistols slung over their shoulders, the *Jungmannen* headed out on 'class deployment'. Heissmeyer greeted them at 'Radeland Base', as the Spandau *Napola* was now called. Five days later the game became deadly serious for Lorenz and his friends.

It was not their first experience of 'war deployment'. Once already they had driven some Red Army soldiers out of a stretch of woodland, and they felt like victors. But on 24 April 1945 something happened which no-one had reckoned on. The schoolboy elite had taken a position which, a short time beforehand, German troops had lost to the Red Army. In the dug-outs lay young Luftwaffe men and anti-aircraft gunners, their bodies run through by four-edged Russian bayonets. The sight of the mutilated corpses was a violent shock to the *Jungmannen*. They had never seen dead bodies before. 'None of us dared speak out loud', Lorenz recalls. 'Would we soon be lying like that as well? We were also disturbed to see photos lying on the ground beside the dead men. Mother, girl-friend, sister?' The *Jungmannen* still believed that the 12th Army under General Wenck would break through the 'cauldron' around Berlin and turn the tables. Hadn't Heissmeyer promised that? 'We just have to hold out for 24 hours', were his words, as Hans Müncheberg recalls. 'The Führer is in Berlin, and you chaps must stay loyal to the Führer. The Wenck Army is on its way. Another 24 hours, 48 hours at the most, and fate will be reversed.'

The next morning began with heavy artillery fire. Then the howl of Russian rockets started. Batteries of rocket-launchers, known as 'Stalin's Organs', brought the 5th Platoon of the Potsdam *Napola* under fire. The *Jungmannen* were trapped, defenceless. Towards evening screams and groans could be heard above the din of machine-gun bursts and exploding grenades. Otto Möller, an *Erzieher* at Potsdam, screamed for morphine in a voice racked with pain. A grenade had shattered both his legs. 'For God's sake, give me some morphine!'

Rumours abounded. The Wenck Army was getting nearer by the hour. On the other side, it was said, there were 'Stalin Schoolboys', one elite fighting another. Someone said that Heissmeyer and his wife, the Reich Women's Leader, Gertrud Scholtz-Klink, had set off for the west, leaving them in the lurch – 'the bastards'.

On the night of 25–6 April the *Jungmannen* of the 'Heissmeyer combat group' took their chances in a breakout. Lorenz and his comrades made their way through to the airfield at Gatow. It was encircled and being bombarded by the Russians. Some of the boys tried to break out again. That was the last anyone saw of the children from Potsdam. In 'class deployment' in the defence of Berlin, one *Jungmann* in three from the 5th Potsdam *Napola* platoon was killed. Seduced, bemused, and expendable: 'We would never have surrendered. We would rather have got ourselves shot', says Harald Scholtz, who at the time was an Adolf Hitler School boy, just fifteen years old.

It was especially the products of the *Ordensburgen*, those who bore Hitler's name, who felt duty bound to sacrifice their lives in the 'final conflict', like 'knights facing death and the Devil'. On 11 February one Adolf Hitler pupil wrote: 'Ten days ago I joined voluntarily in an assault mounted from my home town. We dislodged "Ivan" from a nearby village. Between 40 and 60 *Hitlerjungen* attacked with us. They volunteered. Most of them were Adolf Hitler pupils from Wartha, the others were from the teacher-training college. It was a pleasure for me to watch these guys, the heroic way they fired their weapons, leapt around and went right out in front. The regular infantry stayed 200 yards in the rear. Our boys were singing as they attacked, they shouted and cheered, and they had the most casualties. The youngest were fourteen-and-a-half years old. This is the way we turn our ideals into reality.'

On a picture of Hitler found in the pocket of a dead Adolf Hitler pupil were written the words: 'When others begin to waver, I believe all the more firmly in you.' Fanaticism was taken to the point of death: in February 1945, two other Adolf Hitler School boys were dropped as 'Werewolf' partisans behind enemy lines in the Eifel mountains. SS men had given the boys a radio-set to take with them. Their task was to find out which British and American units were deployed in the battle-zone, in what strength and with what weaponry.

They were to pass the information back to the Wehrmacht by radio. But the *Waffen-SS* had deposited the schoolboys a long way behind the lines. Near the Vogelsang *Ordensburg* and around the dam on the River Urft, intense battles were raging. On the second day of their mission the two 'Werewolves' were picked up by a US patrol. They were first sent to a prisoner-of-war camp near Aachen, then taken before a military tribunal of the 9th Army. After a one-day hearing the officers reached a clear verdict and passed sentence: death by shooting, on the grounds of espionage. It was the exaggerated Allied fear of 'Werewolves' operating underground that had been the deciding factor.

The boys were returned to gaol in Aachen. The US officer defending them submitted a plea for clemency. It took weeks for a decision to be reached. On 30 May 1945 they were taken to Braunschweig. On 31 May a spokesman for the US military administration announced that the appeal had been refused and the execution was scheduled for the following day at 10 a.m.

The Americans allowed the boys to write a last letter to their parents. One of them, whose name was Franz, searched for words to explain to his father and mother why he had been in action in the northern Eifel: 'I did not do it for the government, who have lied to us and betrayed us, but in the hope and belief that I was serving my beloved German Fatherland and my people.' He was proud, he said, to die for his country. When he lay in his grave, everyone should know that he died 'not for Himmler and

Goebbels but for Germany'. He ended the letter with these words: 'A priest came to see me and so now I am prepared for it all. In fact, in my two months in prison, I have realised what it means to believe in God, to be able to say, there is someone there who helps you over all your troubles, who stands by you in your hour of greatest need, when no human being can comfort you.'

On the morning of 1 June 1945, a Sunday, American soldiers tied the two boys to posts in a gravel-pit near Braunschweig. Wooden coffins lay ready beside them. At 10 o'clock the shots of the firing-squad rang out. Franz was sixteen years and five months old, his friend Herbert was seventeen.

With the collapse of Hitler's Reich all the hopes and dreams of the 'leaders of the future' fell apart. 'That is something I haven't got over even today. A world had collapsed all around me and inside me', is how Hans Buchholz, of the Naumburg *Napola*, describes the shock of capitulation. 'Everything that had worth and value for me was suddenly no longer worth anything. The men I had looked up to were branded as criminals. The ideas by which I had lived, and for which I had been prepared to die, had become the products of criminal minds.' The news of Hitler's suicide came to many like a bolt from the blue and shook them out of their hypnotised state. Hans Müncheberg admits: 'I cried my eyes out.'

A world lay shattered. Leopold Chalupa, then at the Naumburg *Napola* and later NATO Commander-in-Chief Central Europe, puts it this way: 'A world in which I believed to the very end that the Greater German Reich could be victorious and could survive, thanks to the "miracle-weapons" which we had by then.' This fatal belief in miracles remained with many, even in the PoW camps. Ernst Lorenz, of the Potsdam *Napola*, was already a prisoner when he felt a breath of wind on a sunny day in May: 'And what did I think? Well, I thought, it's the last ripple of the pressure-wave from a miracle-weapon. The draught had to come from somewhere, didn't it?'

The years of brainwashing, the ideological polish and the drill had left their mark. For years afterwards many found it difficult to shake off the illusions and legends on which their education was based. Ernst-Christian Gädke, *Napola* Spandau, became more aware year by year that 'all those things they did to us, and which we were sometimes happy to go along with, had a definite objective – the hero's death'.

Half of all the schoolboy elite died that death – seduced and blinded by an inhuman educational system. Nevertheless, many of that former 'elect' still stress the advantages of their education. For example, Hans-Günther Zempelin believes: 'We were well educated for a wretched cause.' And Uwe Lamprecht of the Plön *Napola* is of the opinion: 'In that criminal age of blood, death and havoc, it was as if I were living on an island. I was protected. I had plenty to eat. I didn't have to hang around on the streets.' Certainly, much about the *Napola* life was uncomfortable. But was he harmed by it? Lamprecht later became a successful doctor. His education, he says, has helped him 'get through life pretty well'. An amazing number of the elite pupils have gone remarkably far in life. They have made their mark – as they were taught to do – through discipline, toughness and stamina. Lamprecht says he was quickly able to rid himself of the ideological baggage. As a young film star, Hardy Kruger was able to bring Jews to safety in Switzerland. Martin Bormann Jr became a priest and worked in the Congo. The great majority of the schoolboy elite shook off the stench of Nazism.

What remains? 'Scars on the soul', says Hardy Krüger about his time in an Adolf Hitler School. 'What has grown within me since those days is an incredible, almost exaggerated urge for justice, a tolerance towards unorthodox thinking, towards every religion, which is often hard to explain to many people. What has happened is the opposite of what they tried to teach me.'

Hans-Günther Zempelin, whose professional career took him to the top of a mammoth corporation, is left with 'the memory of many fine and likeable young people, whose lives ended at the age of eighteen or nineteen. They were the sacrificial victims of a criminal regime.'

# CHAPTER 4

# WAR

## KNOPP/SCHLOSSHAN

We *Hitlerjungen* were trained to march, to sing and to kill.
*Volker Fischer, born 1928*

They surgically removed not only God but also virtues like loving one's neighbour or love of truth, and placed loyalty to the Fatherland – equated with the Führer – at the centre of their ethic. Of course it was a false ethic.
*Manfred Rommel, born 1928, son of Field-Marshal Erwin Rommel*

It would have been the most emotional moment ever for me if Hitler had come into our air-raid shelter, placed a heavy, godlike hand on my shoulder and said: You are a young German soldier.
*Klas Ewert Everwyn, born 1930*

In those days it was dangerous to be eighteen years old. One of us had an eye shot out, and another lost an arm – altogether we had a casualty rate approaching 50 per cent.
*Franz J.Müller, born 1925, member of the 'White Rose' resistance group*

At that age you cannot really envisage death, because you don't relate to fear. But we would have accepted death – for Germany and for Hitler.
*Günter Adrian, born 1925*

I kept thinking: Jesus, I'm only just eighteen. I don't want to die.
    *Kurt Palm, born 1925, soldier in the Battle of Stalingrad*

To be human means to be a fighter. To be German means to
be a hundred times a fighter. To be a National Socialist means
to be a thousand times a fighter.
    *Hans Schemm, President of the NS Teachers' Federation*

When the Teuton sees no way out, all that is left is to go
down in a blaze of glory, the Twilight of the Gods. Heroism
to the last man was touted as courage and not as the height of
self-annihilating stupidity.
    *Franz J. Müller, born 1925, member of the 'White Rose'*
    *resistance group*

We were raised in the belief that a real man only proves
himself in war.
    *Klaus Bölling, born 1928, 'flak' auxiliary*

Anyone fighting for Germany was also fighting for Adolf
Hitler, of course. It was almost the same thing. Only towards
the end of the war did these attitudes begin to change and
lose their hold, but Hitler retained his extraordinary authority
right to the end.
    *Paul Kehlenbeck, born 1926*

The Front expects the Hitlerjugend, in the severest and most
fateful of battles, to continue to see it as their supreme task to
provide the fighting forces with the best of the young
generation of soldiers.
    *Adolf Hitler, 1943*

Führer, place your trust in your youth, and you, the young,
have every reason to pray for your Führer: God preserve him
for us, for we need an eternal Germany.
    *Josef Bürckel, Gauleiter*

It is up to you, whether you want to bring things to an end, and be the last of a worthless race, despised by posterity, or whether you want to be the beginning of a new age, one more glorious than you could ever imagine.

*Artur Axmann, Reichsjugendführer, 1944*

We always thought our Wehrmacht, our soldiers, were certain of victory. Then all at once we realised that they weren't. They said to us: 'Keep your heads down, kids. We'll need you to rebuild this country. Living for Germany is a lot nicer than dying.'

*Karl-Heinz Böckle, born 1929*

I never again want to see those children's faces – with steel helmets on their heads. Child labour is bad enough, but making children into heroes is even worse. I never want that to happen again.

*Dieter Hildebrandt, born 1927*

❖ ❖ ❖

On the eve of the Second World War the gateway to a deceptive kind of happiness opened for the Danzig *Hitlerjunge*, Werner Gottschau. Shortly before 11 p.m. the sixteen-year-old was ordered to report, in uniform, at the headquarters of the local HJ troop. There two men were awaiting him: an officer of the German Wehrmacht, wearing grey leather gloves, and a leader of the SS-*Heimwehr* (Home Defence Force) in a black steel helmet. Werner had to stand to attention and repeat a number of swearing-in formulas. Then he was told to remove his HJ armband and put on a yellow one with the words *Deutsche Wehrmacht* on it. 'There's going to be a war and you're being drafted as a messenger. There's a bicycle for you outside. Now, off you go.'

The enthusiastic *Hitlerjunge* took a leather bag full of letters, swung himself on to the bike and darted tirelessly around to various German positions in the Danzig area, delivering his messages. In the early hours of the morning he suddenly heard a deafening explosion. 'It was fantastic. I saw the *Schleswig-Holstein* firing its big guns. The shells exploded and the walls went sky-high, trees as well. The smoke and the din – it was really something.' It was 4.45 a.m. on 1 September 1939, and the German armoured cruiser *Schleswig-Holstein* had just opened fire on the Polish Westerplatte fortress. At the same moment German soldiers were crossing the frontier on to Polish soil. The Second World War had begun. From the first moment Hitler's youth were a part of it.

For *Hitlerjunge* Werner the war was a cause for rejoicing. Danzig and the German minorities in Poland would be 'brought home' to the German Reich, as Hitler had loudly demanded time and again. Hitler's 'final settling of accounts' with Poland was merely the overture to a programme of conquest which would soon spread terror and suffering right across Europe. But Werner had no inkling of that. 'Danzig isn't what this is all about', the dictator had secretly revealed to his generals. 'This is about expanding our living-space in the east and guaranteeing our food supplies, as well as resolving the Baltic problem.' While the warlord was beginning his all-or-nothing gamble for world domination, Werner believed in a just war. Even when he heard that one of his classmates, also serving as a messenger, had been shot, his enthusiasm did not wane: 'We're fighting now so that we can return to Germany, and sacrifices have to be made. That was clear to us right from the start.' Werner was filled with pride, that as a sixteen-year-old soldier he was allowed to do his bit for Germany. 'I rode around our town all day long with my left arm held well to the fore, so that everyone could see the armband and would think: "My word, Werner Gottschau's in the Wehrmacht." But no-one took any notice. I was really disappointed.'

Not until some German dive-bombers mistakenly bombed his home town of Neufahrwasser did a crack appear in the hard carapace of this ardent *Hitlerjunge*. He was seized by naked fear. 'I cried so much, and I screamed and trembled so much that I had to push my bike; I couldn't ride it because I was so terrified by this frightful roaring and the dust and the stones raining down . . . the houses had disappeared, roofs were lying on the street, it was terrible.' A doctor administered some tranquillisers to the boy and said: 'You're a German lad. Not going to cry now, are you?'

Werner thought about it, 'then of course I realised he was right, and I was a young German again'. He flung himself with ardour into the next assignment – and once again the harsh reality of war dragged him out of his reverie.

Poland was virtually defeated: by 19 September Hitler was making a speech in Danzig and on 27 September Warsaw surrendered. Werner was given the job of walking around the whole of the Westerplatte recording the dead and wounded. 'I have never got that tragic picture out of my mind: the brave, exhausted Polish soldiers, with shoulders drooping as they came out from their bunkers and gave themselves up. They carried their dead past us in overcoats. It was then that I saw for the first time that they had been fighting too, for Poland. They were soldiers like ours, but in different uniforms. You see, I'd never seen people dead before. But here they were, lying on the ground, dirty and covered in blood. Those were things which at the time I just couldn't handle.'

Yet Werner remained on duty. For seven days and seven nights he never took off his fatigues. The years of indoctrination were having their effect. Werner, too, wanted to be 'as fleet as a greyhound, as tough as leather and as hard as Krupp steel'. 'We are the future', he believed, as the propaganda had taught him, 'we're marching on, and whatever stands in our way will fall. We're marching on and when we come to a wall, we'll break it down. We want to set an example.' There were many *Hitlerjungen* who thought as Werner did. Now they were to prove themselves in the war for which over the years, in the *Jungvolk* and the *Hitlerjugend*, physically and mentally, they had been prepared. The seeds of indoctrination were now to bear fruit.

'The youth were not caught up in a passing brush-fire of enthusiasm. Their steadfast willingness to serve was to be tested in a war lasting six years.' Those words were spoken decades later by Artur Axmann, who from August 1940 onwards was *Reichsjugend-führer* of the Nazi Party and *Jugendführer* of the German Reich. 'So when I took up the post, it was my prime duty to help win the war with all the forces I could muster.' Victory at any price – with the aid of a nine-million-strong army of cheap labour and willing cannon-fodder.

Artur Axmann succeeded the aesthete and confidant of Hitler, Baldur von Schirach, as Youth Leader. Throughout his life this son of a Berlin manual worker, whom the Party liked to parade as their 'token proletarian', was tormented by complexes. Easy access to the Führer, such as Schirach enjoyed, was denied him for a long time. Like Schirach, he devoted his energy to turning the youth into a tool of the regime, and used it as a weapon to gain the favour of his lord and master. 'To Axmann Hitler was an idol, the great hero of the German people, a superman', believes Armin Lehmann, who at the end of the war served as the *Jugendführer*'s messenger. 'Axmann was obsessed with showing the Führer how loyal the youth was.'

The top Nazis never tired of stressing that war service should be performed completely voluntarily, as a 'service of honour to the German people'. The fact that only a few months before the outbreak of war, Hitler declared that service in the HJ was a legal obligation made no dent in their hypocrisy. In any case, from the voluntary origins of the service had grown an inner sense of obligation which had become a matter of course for most young people. Otto Bartel, a section head under Axmann, wrote: 'Since the youth of Germany considers the performance of their service neither as compulsory nor as a duty, but as an honorary national right, of which it must continually show itself worthy', the HJ was not, he wrote, an organisation imposed by the state, but remained *the* German youth movement.

Now people could read in black and white what was already the accepted practice anyway: the entire youth of Germany was encompassed by the HJ, and any breaking away from Hitler's strict youth organisation brought sanctions with it. Volker Fischer, then a committed *Hitlerjunge*, recalls: 'They would go to your parents' house and threaten them by saying: right, if your son doesn't turn up for duty this coming week, you can expect unpleasant penalties.'

'Youth must be led by youth', was the high-sounding creed of the poetically minded pioneer of the Hitler Youth, Baldur von Schirach. Among themselves the youth could be pretty savage if need be, when individuals resisted group pressure: 'Boys who didn't feel at ease in this community, who didn't fit in, were shunned, tormented, slapped about or beaten up', Fischer recalls. Like a giant octopus, the regime had stretched its tentacles out to the youth and held it in a suffocating embrace. For years the Reich youth leadership had been working towards a monopoly of the young; for years the HJ had already been trying to control every spare minute of its members' time. For most of them, escape from HJ service was unthinkable: 'But in those days it was not considered demeaning to do what everyone else was doing. It was rather the reverse. If you stayed away and did something different from all the others, *that* was demeaning', as the former *Hitlerjunge* Paul Kehlenbeck recalls.

This attitude was to continue into the war. The young were ready for active service and for sacrifice – not simply out of conviction, but because of the lack of any alternative. 'We are convinced that our youth will not deteriorate in the war', boasted Axmann in a speech to the Wehrmacht High Command. 'It is growing more and more to meet the demands of the war. The young will no longer be able to make the comparison with peacetime. They will regard the state of war as normal. They will see this war as their mission.'

That was what Hitler liked to hear, for he needed the youth: 'November 1918 will never again be repeated in German history', he had prophesied in his speech to the Reichstag on 1 September 1939. The traumatic experience of the German collapse was still in his bones. Never again would there be a surrender, nor a revolution like that after the First World War. Then an uprising had led to the republic being set up. The monarchy was swept away – though the population, weakened by hunger and disease, scarcely shed a tear at its passing. Together with the rebels, the government had stabbed the supposedly victorious army in the back, as others besides Hitler wrongly believed. He ignored the fact that the generals themselves had asked for an armistice and made the democratic government bear the consequences of the military defeat. This kind of 'treachery' was something the dictator would not tolerate. The youth were to see to it that, in spite of the war, the population suffered no privations and would stick up for him during his campaigns of conquest. In order to keep up the morale of the Germans the illusion of life continuing 'normally' at home – while bloody battles raged at the Front – was to be conjured up for them.

Despite the protests of many parents, the HJ succeeded in laying claim to even more young people than it had in the pre-war years and, outside school or working hours, in pulling them in for duties lasting several hours, days or even weeks. While their fathers and HJ leaders went off to the Front, the boys were to supplement the depleted workforce and plug the gaps at home. They were put to work in government, Party and Wehrmacht offices and in air-raid patrols and health services; they dashed around the cities as messengers, distributed propaganda material, issued food-ration cards, and helped in the Red Cross or public authorities such as the Post Office. In the 'Business and Industrial Service' they unloaded trainloads of food or coal and delivered goods to shops. In winter young people were put on to clearing snow and gritting the roads. HJ orchestras played in military hospitals, in order to motivate the wounded to return and fight new battles for the Fatherland.

The girls cooked food for air-raid victims and refugees, darned and patched in the sewing rooms, and knitted socks and gloves for soldiers. In 1940 some 319,000 girls were engaged in domestic work, 64,000 worked in the Red Cross, 60,000 cared for the wounded in military hospitals, 100,000 worked in railway stations and 3,500 as flight control assistants.

> Later I worked out that I was twelve years old when I last had free time to play. After that I probably forgot completely how to play and just to laze around.
>
> *Telse Zimmermann, born 1929*

Most of all, collecting was the order of the day in the war economy. Like an army of ants the children tripped off and lugged back anything that could be of use in the war. *Pimpfe* and *Jungmädel* collected medicinal plants and herbs for infusion by the ton, and thus supplied almost the entire needs of the pharmaceutical industry during the war. They gathered fallen fruit, mushrooms, berries and beech-nuts to help the food supply, and hunted down Colorado beetles. Sometimes this passion for collecting reached grotesque proportions. The children went from door to door demanding not only waste material like paper, metal, leather and bones, but even persuading women to pick the hair from their brushes and combs. This 'high-grade' raw material was used in the manufacture of thermal clothing for submariners.

---

As previously announced, this year the Hitler Youth is solely responsible for the collecting of: lime-flowers, birch-leaves, hazelnut-leaves, camomile and foxgloves. Other herbs for drinking and medicinal use will not be collected by the Hitler Youth.

*From circular 51/44 of Branch 737 Zabern of the HJ, 1944*

Now we were collecting scrap instead of singing, and medicinal herbs instead of hiking.

*Telse Zimmermann, born 1929*

---

The Nazi 'Winter Aid Programme', instituted in 1933, had long been a cornerstone of NS social policy. The collecting of money and clothing, door-to-door and in the street, the monthly 'Stew-pot Sunday', deductions from wages and salaries, and collection boxes for the 'Winter Pfennig' – all served to support those needy who were considered politically, racially and genetically 'worthy'. But they had another purpose: these appeals to the 'ethnic community', to 'national solidarity' and 'the spirit of self-sacrifice' killed two birds with one stone. The aim was both to trigger a national mood of 'going for it' and also to involve everyone, even in their family and private lives.

The plan worked: in the winter of 1942 the total sum collected was 1.6 billion Reichsmarks. Compared to the 680 million Reichsmarks in 1939 this was a rise of 135 per cent – thanks not least to the collecting zeal of the Hitler Youth. 'We were called on to collect for Winter Aid, and had to promote the idea that people should donate generously', a former *Hitlerjunge* remembers. 'Then we were spread around in the Market Square and in the lobbies of various apartment blocks. When a whistle blew we dashed up, shouting horribly loudly, to attract people's attention. Then we would go up to them and recite: *Leute, zückt das Portmonnaie, spendet für das Ve-Ha-Ve!* (Everyone, pull out your purses, give to the WHW!). Or the macabre variant: *Leute spendet unverdrossen, wer nicht spendet, wird erschossen*! (Roughly: Be sure to open up your wallet, otherwise you'll stop a bullet).'

The faster the warlord drove his war of aggression onward and the more of those eligible for military service who went off to the Front, the greater was the shortage of working people at home – especially on the farms. With the invasion of the Soviet Union in 1941 the Front suddenly lengthened by thousands of miles. In order to guarantee food supplies, in April 1942 basic regulations were issued for the 'war service of the youth to ensure the feeding of the German people'. From then on, between April and November each year, entire classes of boys and girls could be obliged to work on the land for several weeks at a time. In 1942 alone about 580,000 boys and 1.3 million girls were drafted for farm work. And to ensure that Bavarian beer continued to flow down thirsty throats a good 90 per cent of the hop harvest was, according to Axmann, brought in by the Hitler Youth.

Particularly bizarre was 'Operation Barefoot' introduced by Axmann in the summer of 1942. Since the 'war forced upon the German Reich places great demands on war production', and leather and textiles were of critical importance for equipping the fighting soldiers, the HJ was to 'play its part in conserving these important raw materials for our soldiers', and to take care of their clothes and shoes, as Axmann wrote. The HJ was required to go around barefoot in the summer. The 'tattered look' was *de rigueur*: from now on it was to be chic to 'wear things that are faded, worn out or patched'. The Second World War was to be fought out on the soles of children's shoes.

After years of preparatory indoctrination, after being drilled, put into uniform and taught to obey, the youth had become Hitler's willing tool, which only had to be put to use. 'It was the strength of the Third Reich that we were led to such an extent that we never got to think for ourselves. We were simply told: "You must all do your bit to help win the war, and you must be better than anyone"', recalls a former *Hitlerjunge*. With pride the Reich youth leadership reported in 1940 that 'over five million German boys and girls are working in the service of Führer and *Volk*'. It is certainly the case that without the tireless and versatile deployment of the Hitler Youth Germany's economy and social structure would have collapsed sooner. The young contributed significantly to the prolonging of the war.

> A young generation who had been brought up to be activists could not but enter the war with the unquenchable desire to take over as many tasks as possible.
>
> *Herbert Reinecker, from* Young Germany, *August 1943*

In the early years of the war the active service of the Hitler Youth was still a long way from the murderous Front. All that changed dramatically when the war came to Germany. On 10 May 1940 the hawkish Winston Churchill, the energetic proponent of a policy of strength in the face of Nazi Germany, replaced the 'appeaser' Neville Chamberlain as British prime minister and gave notice of inflexible resistance. On 11 May Churchill gave the go-ahead to the Royal Air Force to attack the German heartlands. The first bombs fell on the Ruhr, Berlin, Hanover, Hamburg, Bremen and other German cities. On 20 February 1942, with the appointment of Arthur Harris as chief of Bomber Command, Britain committed itself fully to a terror strategy. In Germany the name of 'Bomber' Harris soon became synonymous with fear: his stated objective was to 'wear down the morale of the German people' with the carpet-bombing of German cities.

This began with a raid on Lübeck in March 1942, in which for the first time incendiary bombs were used on a large scale, in addition to the more usual high-explosive bombs. In May 1942 the devastating '1,000 bomber raid' on Cologne showed what the British were capable of. When the RAF began to receive support from the Americans in 1943, a ceaseless bombing terror began at the same time: the Americans flew precision bombing raids by day, and the British laid down their carpets of bombs by night. Incendiary and high-explosive bombs, sometimes dropped in conjunction with phosphor canisters, set off those infernal fire-storms which reduced cities like Hamburg and Dresden to ashes and rubble.

Wherever things got really hot, the *Hitlerjugend* were now to be seen in action. Day and night they stood by, ready to rescue the wounded and those buried under rubble – and risked their own lives without a second thought. The HJ Fire Brigade would often go out while the bombs were still falling. 'As soon as the air-raid warning sounded, we went to our positions. In those saturation raids, a fire-storm was very dangerous. In the middle of the street you couldn't move around more than a metre above ground, because above that level all the oxygen had been burnt up. When big apartment blocks collapsed there were a lot of dead. But we had to help. We were working under the toughest conditions', remembers Werner Steinberg, then a member of an HJ fire service unit.

Training in air-raid precautions, which in peacetime had been a tiresome obligation, now became deadly serious. After the raids *Pimpfe* and *Hitlerjungen* were drafted in for clearing up and rescue work, and were themselves in constant danger of being killed by unexploded bombs or falling debris. For many boys the shocking experiences were engraved in their memory: 'The first time I saw a dead person in the war was in Bremerhaven – a young woman whose whole body had been ripped open from the abdomen up to her arms, presumably by a bomb-fragment', Lothar Gulich recounts. 'We were told to carry her away, but I was a bit squeamish; it wasn't very nice seeing a dead woman, all ripped open like that, and I didn't want to touch her. An NCO nearby shouted at me: "Hey, Lothar, if she was alive, you'd like to touch her, I bet!" Then I lost my inhibitions and helped pick her up and carry her away.'

A total of four million homes were destroyed. Some 500,000 people in Germany died in air raids, and an even greater number were wounded. The omnipresence of death insidiously invaded the daily life of the young. 'I lost my childhood sweetheart in a bombing raid and the same night I pulled a lot of other people out of a cellar, people I had been at school with', an air-raid auxiliary recalls. 'One day you were playing with someone or talking to him, and the next day he was lying like a heap of nothing, burnt up, carbonised. He had to be carted off in a bathtub. It's then that you begin to think about the meaning of life and about dying.'

> If fathers and brothers are making sacrifices in the field, it is the honourable duty of each individual boy and girl to conduct themselves in such a way that every age-group, which may yet be called to the defence of the Reich, is standing ready, strong and healthy.
>
> *Baldur von Schirach, 1936*

The Nazi leadership now tried, from autumn 1940 onward, to take as many children and young people as possible from the areas threatened by bombing, to places of safety. According to the official jargon of the HJ press, the purpose of this measure was 'to protect young people from risks to their health that might arise from frequent air-raid warnings and spending time in inadequate air-raid shelters, and also to ensure uninterrupted schooling and communal education'. Lofty, humanitarians aims – or so they might seem at first glance. Yet in truth this *Kinderlandverschickung* (KLV, Despatch of Children to the Countryside) finally provided the regime with the chance to get their hands on young people 'totally, in a broad context and for a considerable period of time'.

> By order of the Führer, however, there is to be no use of the word 'evacuation', but rather of a 'despatch to the countryside' of children from the big cities.
>
> *From a circular issued by Martin Bormann, 27 September 1940*

Children aged from ten to sixteen arrived as complete schools or classes in KLV camps, of which there were some 5,500 by the end of 1943. They were housed in youth hostels, rural education hostels, hotels and guest houses. There were reception areas in villages and small towns throughout Germany, and there were also camps in the Reich Protectorate of Bohemia and Moravia, in the *Generalgouvernement* of Poland, in Slovakia and in ethnic German enclaves in Hungary, Romania and Yugoslavia. Theoretically, parents had a free choice about sending their children away. But many only did so under pressure, unhappy about being parted from their offspring. Panicky rumours were going around that the armed forces might no longer protect German cities once the children had been compulsorily evacuated. Placatory words from Hitler's propaganda chief, Goebbels, and propaganda films such as *Hands Up*, which showed camp life in a romanticised light, were intended to calm the wave of anxiety. But in any event, the terror of the air raids, the shortage of food in the cities and ultimately the closure of many schools from 1943 onward often left parents with no choice.

The man Hitler placed in charge of the evacuation of children was the former *Reichsjugendführer* and now *Gauleiter* of Vienna, Baldur von Schirach. He in turn handed the organisation of it over to the HJ, in collaboration with the NS Teachers' Federation and the NS National Welfare Service. In practice this often meant that, depending on the Party orthodoxy of the teachers and heads of the HJ camp staff, the 850,000 boys and girls were exposed more heavily than ever to Nazi indoctrination in camps far from their parental homes. As a document from the teachers' federation put it: 'The educator can return home full of inner satisfaction, if he can say of himself: I shaped a youth at risk into a faithful National Socialist community.' When parents got wind of these aims and began to complain, Martin Bormann, head of the Party office and Hitler's shadowy right-hand man, felt obliged to 'counteract the rumours that the evacuation of children from the cities is to further the aim of taking the children's upbringing out of the hands of their parents'.

To be on the safe side, however, it was better that the parents never found out how their evacuated children were really faring. In the deceptive idyll of the KLV, the strictest censorship prevailed. An eye-witness, Frieder Schott, remembers: 'Once, I had written a wrong address on a letter and it was returned to me.

Then I saw that parts of my letter had been blacked out. That meant that they were checking on whether I was writing nice things, or things that others were not supposed to know about.'

Many who were children in those days have happy recollections of their peaceful, carefree times in KLV camps in Bavaria and Austria, for example. In the country, the children were indeed protected from the bombing. And yet these experiences only reveal a part of the truth. The real objective of their 'country holiday' remained hidden from the children, caught up as they were in the net of a treacherous system. They had no idea that this was the fulfilment of the dream of every totalitarian regime: unhindered access to its youngest citizens in camps specially set up for the purpose.

> We were certainly protected from a lot of things . . . But in my personal experience, it was a bad time, really dreadful, and I wouldn't wish it on any future generation.
> *Mildred Scheel, 1932–85, wife of leading postwar politician Walter Scheel*

The very selection of the HJ camp team-leaders, who were often recruited from the *Napolas*, and who had distinguished themselves by 'conduct or deeds especially steeped in Nazism', betrayed the actual aim: 'physical, mental and moral' education as a suitable member of the Nazi 'national community'. The strictly regulated daily routine and a specially designed KLV uniform were more indicative of a barrack square than relaxation in the country. 'The drill we had in the KLV camp was something few soldiers would have known. We were sent camp-leaders who had been stood down for recuperation. They came from the SS, from the Reich Labour Service and from teacher training, where they had just learned some stuff by heart, and now they wanted to try it out on us. I can tell you, the first ones to arrive made us work our balls off', in the colourful words of Wigand Kusitzky.

Flag parades, marching, ideological schooling, as well as farm work, harvesting and preparation for the army, were all part of a day's work. All too often the young HJ leaders took control of the camps and shamelessly exploited their position of power. Usually, schoolwork played only a minor role. From time to time teachers had to teach subjects they knew nothing about. There was a lack of classroom materials, and cancelled classes were a regular occurrence. The children's educational standards sank rapidly. 'We were brought up as barbarians', remembers Jost Hernand, who became, in a very obvious way, the victim of overstretched and miscast camp staff. 'We weren't just trained in all kinds of war-games and toughness exercises, we were even trained to kill animals, to chop the heads off chickens, to butcher hares and wring the necks of pigeons. Those were the really quite barbaric tactics used to toughen us up.' Jost Hernand tells of unpleasant harassment of boys by other boys, of beatings and even rapes – which the camp staff did nothing to prevent.

The smallest misdemeanour brought the risk of draconian punishment: 'If you dared to swipe a little spoonful of pudding before it was served, you were immediately punished. The head of the camp staff had a truncheon and he used it. There was also a smoke-house for curing ham and things. You were locked in it until you couldn't breathe. Or you had to stand for hours in the stench of the lavatory. It was out in the yard, very hot in summer, and had nails all over the walls, so that you could neither sit, nor lean against them.'

Thus in the KLV camps the rule which Hitler had always commended, the law of the strongest, held sway. As the battle-front moved ever closer even the youngest in the camps were affected by mobilisation. From March 1944 on, they were transferred to pre-military training-camps run by the HJ, the Wehrmacht or the SS, where they would be prepared for a future as cannon-fodder.

> Courage and how to be heroes, those were the things that were drummed into us. Not quiet heroes, but only those who had done something military. There was no other kind of hero.
>
> *Joachim Ellert, born 1928*

The organising of the *Kinderlandverschickung* seemed to make the leaders of the HJ ideal candidates for other assignments: led by a blindly fanatical *Reichsjugendführer* some members of the HJ took an active part in the crimes driven by Nazi racial policy. HJ leaders played a part in almost all the cruel measures introduced by *Gauleiter* and the SS in the occupied regions of the east. They even made decisions about resettlement or expulsion, life or death. This shocking discovery is something new: it has been documented in a recently published study of the Hitler Youth by the historian Michael Buddrus.

> We want no shrinking violets, no toadies or creeping hypocrites; we want our youth, our German youth, to become an open and straightforward generation.
>
> *Adolf Hitler, 1937*

Acting as supreme executive of the deportations, resettlement and Germanisation operations in Poland was the *Reichsführer SS*, Himmler. As early as October 1939 this ardent proponent of a Nazi utopia of noble Teutonic warriors was appointed 'Reich Commissioner for the Consolidation of German National Culture'. A secret decree by the Führer entrusted him with the task of 'removing the harmful influence of alien sections of the population'. His job in the east consisted of Germanising all 'suitable social strata', to push out all 'non-Germanisable groups of alien race' and attract new German settlers.

At last Himmler had an opportunity to turn into reality his crazed obsessions about a 'paradise of the German race' in which men of 'Nordic blood', wedded to the soil, would indulge in a peasant idyll. With a brutal zeal he did everything he could to force a mass migration. In order to 'Germanise' western Poland, not only were new settlers lured in from the 'Old Reich', but ethnic Germans from the Baltic states, and the old Habsburg border regions of Volhynia, North Bukovina, Bessarabia and North Dobrudja were also brusquely ordered to abandon their adopted homes and were transplanted to the 'Wartheland'. At the same time, by the summer of 1941, a million Poles had been driven from their farms and 'resettled' further east in the *Generalgouvernement*. There they were to be 'at Germany's disposal as a leaderless population of labourers and to provide seasonal migrant labour and a workforce for special requirements' – in short they were to be enslaved.

Sensing new assignments, Axmann had issued the slogan 'Eastern deployment and land service' for his Hitler Youth. In the occupied regions of Poland the 'eastern volunteers of Germanic youth' were to win over for National Socialism the Germans already settled there as well as the ethnic Germans who had immigrated there from Russia and the Baltic states, and to confirm them in their 'Germanity'. The aim was to overcome the 'cultural and social disadvantage of the east vis-à-vis the west' and to contribute to the 're-creation of eastern German peasant life'. What was commonly known as 'eastern service' was generally targeted at looking after the resettled Germans and seeing that they made themselves at home in the new eastern regions of the Reich. This task fell to the BDM in particular. In 1942 some 16,000 girls were working with families, in domestic and agricultural work, in kindergartens and schools. They organised coffee mornings, singsongs and children's parties, founded local groups of the HJ and BDM and made every effort to become 'the strongest possible propagandists for the East'.

Although many of these girls saw themselves as caring, hard-working angels of charity, they were nevertheless also part of a ruthless Germanisation of the east. In the newly established *Reichsgau* of Wartheland especially, the girls took part in the expulsion of the Polish population, in order to open the way for the settlement of ethnic German *Volksdeutsche*. The camp-leader of the BDM's eastern service, Melitta Maschmann, wrote about their deployment in Poland:

An SS leader explained to us what we were needed for: we were to clean out the empty houses and get them ready for the arrival of the German farmers who were usually expected the same day. Early one morning we were once again roused from our sleep and taken to a village earmarked for clearance. The SS officer who was in charge of the operation explained that he didn't have enough men at his disposal and he hoped we would leap into the breach. The Poles were still there, packing their things. They had to assemble with their wagons at the edge of the village by 6 a.m. Each family could only take with them what they could load on to one wagon, and a specified minimum had to be left in the houses for the next occupants. I was immediately to distribute the girls around the farms and they had to make sure that the Poles abided by the rules. The Poles were our enemies. We had to exploit the fact that we were more powerful than them, in order to weaken their 'national fabric'. We described arguments of that kind as *Realpolitik*. I think we all felt that we were 'doing our duty for Germany' and that this fact granted us security of action and secretly protected us.

In contrast to the incoming settlers the Poles were known in Nazi jargon as people of 'grovelling mentality' with a 'low level of indigenous culture' and were classified as not 're-naturalisable'. In plain language: 'Their penetration of Germany's bloodstream' would result in 'a destabilising of the German people'. The target was their 'complete removal'. However, when the deportation of 'racially undesirable' people to the new regions ground to a halt and even 'Germanic' settlers could only be drummed up in limited numbers, the Nazi race-politicians were forced to lower their sights: the trend was now towards Germanisation, which meant compulsory adaptation by the population, particularly the young. The idea was to rescue German blood, wherever it flowed. 'The parents of children of good blood will be offered the choice, either to hand over their children or else to go to Germany and there become loyal citizens', Himmler wrote in a 1940 memorandum. 'Each year all children in the *Generalgouvernement*, aged six to ten years, will be sorted into those with blood-value and those with no blood value.' A 'German national list' was set up, in which all persons of German origin were classified as to their suitability for 'Germanisation'.

For a long time there had been close links between the Hitler Youth and the *Schutzstaffel* (SS). As early as December 1938

Himmler had reached an agreement with the Reich youth leadership that volunteers in the so-called Land Service – which in any case was directed, just as Himmler wanted, towards agricultural and settlement work in the east – would be given preference in recruitment for the general SS and the *Waffen-SS*. In return for this, after their military service, they would be entitled to a piece of land of their own: they were to settle the conquered regions in the east and defend them as militarised farmers with weapon and plough. Furthermore, Artur Axmann was a fervent champion of the 'blood and soil' theories of the Nazi racialists and saw the Hitler Youth as 'carrying the banner of the German imperial idea'. 'On our eastern frontier we must erect a rampart of flesh and blood, which is even stronger than iron and concrete', he demanded in his New Year address for 1942. 'For deployment in the east, only the best are good enough. So let's have volunteers!' The setting up of a central department for the 'Consolidation of German National Culture' in the headquarters of the Hitler Youth put the seal on its complicity in the goals of the SS.

The task of the HJ on assignment in the east was soon extended to looking after and settling young people classified as 'worthy of Germanisation' in the annexed eastern regions – i.e. East Prussia, Danzig-West Prussia, the Wartheland, Upper Silesia, and in the *Generalgouvernement*. They were to be schooled in 'National Socialist thinking' in special camps, and prepared for their work on the land. These young people comprised, on the one hand, about 64,000 ethnic German immigrants who had arrived in Poland and, on the other, half a million young indigenous Poles who woke up one day to find themselves classed as 'worthy of Germanisation' in the 'German national list' and were now to be educated as 'good Germans'. However, since it was the declared aim of the Reich youth leadership to guard against 'any penetration by foreign blood' and also to 'recover German blood and prevent its further loss', HJ leaders took part, from December 1942 onwards, in the registration and classification of the new settlers according to racial criteria. They were thus in a position to determine who was *volksdeutsch* and therefore acknowledged as worthy of settlement – and who was not.

Since the spring of 1940 Litzmannstadt (Lodz) had been the location of Himmler's Central Office for Resettlement, which coordinated the evacuation, deportation and murder of the Polish and Jewish populations from the former eastern territories of Germany, and the Central Office for Immigration, which dealt with the settlement and naturalisation of ethnic German returnees. As part of these SS authorities an 'Action Commando' of the Hitler Youth carried out its 'selection process'. Between November 1942 and April 1944 some 30,000 young people were registered, examined for health, ethnic origin and political attitude, and in particular investigated for 'racial characteristics'. Of critical importance were 'height and body-shape, stance, length of leg, shape of head and back of head, shape of face, ridge, length and width of nose, position of eyes, eyelid aperture, flesh-folds around the eye, lips, chin, type of hair, amount of body hair, hair-colour, eye-colour, skin-colour'. Those who made the leap into 'Germanity' were as far as possible distributed to youth camps set up in remote areas where, under HJ leadership, they were given drill and Ideological schooling, and prepared for their settlement. For those who failed the test the future held expulsion from homes and farms, the ghetto, forced labour, deportation and at worst the gas-chamber.

In one resettlement operation, where people were moved from the Black Sea region to the Wartheland, the HJ leaders made their selection. Young people from 'mixed marriages' were judged 'not settlement-worthy' and – under HJ supervision – were sent to work in arms factories in the 'old Reich'. Even for young people of German extraction from places like Alsace or Yugoslavia, whom the HJ considered worthy candidates for German citizenship, this decision often led to privation and isolation. In many instances those affected were torn away from their surroundings, parted from their parents and put into HJ-run camps for further 'treatment'. In HJ jargon this would 'facilitate their adaptation into the German national community'.

When the desired volume of new settlers from Bessarabia, Volhynia, Galicia or the Baltic states was not forthcoming, the criteria for being 'German' were lowered. A frantic search began for 'naturalised Poles of German descent', who could be 're-

Germanised'. The HJ now set about tracking down 'submerged' German qualities among the Polish youth in order to preserve every drop of German blood for the Führer. They chiefly homed in on blond, blue-eyed children, since only those who fulfilled certain racial criteria were deemed 're-Germanisable'. Determining this qualification was also the job of the HJ. Youngsters who passed the test were unceremoniously separated from their parents and taken to 're-Germanisation' camps. Hitler's youth lined itself up in the ranks of his other diabolical disciples led by their insane belief in the superiority of the German race, to set themselves up as judges of 'valuable' and 'valueless' lives.

Thus there grew up, out of the spirit of the old National Socialist virtues and on the foundations of solidly constructed organisation, this young generation which soon knew nothing but the single watchword: 'Into action for victory.'
*From* Das Junge Deutschland *(Young Germany)*
*magazine, 1943*

'It's your job, Axmann, to guarantee a flow of young, combat-ready new troops and their officers and to train up a select body of youth. They will the elite of tomorrow. Do anything that will serve the Front and will be a help to those at home!' It was with these words that Axmann remembered being received by Hitler at his 'Wolf's Lair' in East Prussia, in March 1942.

Hitler's zealous disciple did not need to be told. He had already been planning for this for a long time. From the spring of 1942 the pre-military training of boys was sharpened up: in military preparation camps they were to undergo 3-week courses giving them 'further orientation for their political and military duties'. From as early as 1935 members of special HJ formations were intended as new manpower for the corresponding branches of the armed services. Boys who were keen on motorbikes and joined the Motor-HJ found themselves being trained for armed motorcycle units. The Air-HJ not only received basic glider training but also learned how to maintain powered aircraft.

The Naval-HJ anticipated the basic training for the navy. The Communications-HJ learned in the field, under operational conditions, how to lay land-lines and to pass on messages by field telephone or in Morse code by radio.

Now every boy aged sixteen or over had to expect his call-up to a military preparation camp. Command of the camps was given to former HJ leaders who had been wounded as officers or enlisted men and were no longer considered fit for front-line action. The trainers were from the Wehrmacht or the *Waffen-SS*, and the object was to gain the 'War-training Certificate of the Hitler Youth' and the silver HJ performance award. This covered fieldcraft and map-reading, camouflage and deception, communications, sentry and reconnaissance activities, small-bore rifle-shooting and ideological schooling. The last of these was thoroughly hammered into the boys. On the timetable were unambiguous subjects such as 'Compulsory school topic: "We are fighting"'; 'Morning ceremony: "Where the German stands, there stands loyalty"'; 'evening parade: "Let them all take me on! I will prevail, because I know how to believe and how to fight."'

In these camps the boys became familiar with a hard military grind, compared to which their service in the Hitler Youth seemed like a stroll. 'It started with them making a quick check of the bunk-rooms in the evening. They ran their fingers along the top of lockers and things, found some dust and threw the whole lot of us out. Then there was what they called "fancy dress", which means, in five minutes we had to be in our tracksuits, five minutes later in our best uniforms, five minutes after that in fatigues. Well, you can imagine – in a bunk-room . . . they were barracks, former Reich Labour Service barracks, with maybe 30 men in them – you can imagine what the place looked like. Then it was: bunk-room inspection in five minutes. Another much-loved trick was a cross-country march in the rain . . . big puddles everywhere. Suddenly they'd shout: "Dive-bomber alert, everyone take cover!" So we were all down in the mud. Then someone says: "What *do* you buggers look like?" We had to have our kit all clean in a couple of hours', remembers one of our interviewees, Peter Wacker. 'It was really hard graft. They were very tough and uncouth, the way they treated us. Well, you have to remember – that was in 1942, and we were sixteen years old.'

It sounded like a grotesque mockery when Schirach insisted at Nuremberg after the war: 'Nowhere in the Hitler Youth were the young prepared for war, because they did not go directly from the HJ into the army. Any kind of playing at soldiers in a youth organisation had always been anathema to me.' In those camps it was no longer a question of educating the youth. It was here that Hitler's future warriors were prepared for the real thing. 'Once we were taken into an area where they were shooting with live ammunition, and of course were instructed on how we should behave. So we had to go through our crawling exercises in the grip of fear. The live bullets were whizzing over us, which certainly made us maintain a very appropriate and precise attitude on the ground', Volker Fischer tells us.

What was most important to the Wehrmacht was 'that the spirit of the camp is soldierly and that the boys' exercises result in a strengthening of the armed forces'. In order to breed a thoroughly soldierly 'type', marching songs were bellowed out in 'ideological instruction', 'militaristic' topics and the progress of the war were discussed. The success proved the *Erzieher* right: 'The number of pupils who volunteer for the forces proves that the militant spirit is very much alive', wrote a liaison teacher.

The military preparation camps were nothing but a first stage in the training of recruits. Hitler saw them in exactly those terms. In September 1943, when the HJ's Military Preparation Day took place throughout the country for the first time, the Führer turned in person to Axmann: 'The Front expects the *Hitlerjugend*, in the severest and most fateful of battles, to continue to see it as their supreme task to provide the fighting forces with the best of the young generation of soldiers. National Socialist determination and action must find ever stronger expression in the attitude and demeanour of the young. Then there will grow up that hardened generation which will, in the end, successfully carry out all the tasks preordained by destiny for our nation.'

> The military life was glorified even before the war. To be in the armed forces was an honour, especially if you were an officer.
> *Paul Kehlenbeck, born 1926*

Hitler had been speaking with utter conviction when, at the outbreak of war, he declared: 'The young will in any event fulfil with a cheerful heart that which the nation, the National Socialist state, expects and demands of them.' But at the time the tyrant's courtiers were not quite so sure about that. In order to build up an enthusiasm for war in children, they were totally immersed in propaganda and patriotic appeals. As early as 10 September 1939 Hermann Göring made this appeal to the German people: 'There is no longer a mobilisation order for soldiers between such and such ages, today there is one mobilisation order for all Germans, as soon as they reach the age of sixteen, girls as well as boys.'

In the spring of 1940, the Party's chief ideologue, Alfred Rosenberg, was appointed to take over the 'supervision of the intellectual requirements of youth in wartime'. In a radio broadcast he called for 'courage in the sometimes difficult circumstances of daily life' and a readiness for action in the 'awareness that, in the midst of a corrupt world run by a capitalist Jewish mafia, you are carrying the banner of a great new European order of national culture'. A large scale operation of 'ideological support for young people at school and in the workplace' was aimed at 'maintaining and strengthening in the young an awareness of the greatness and harshness of our nation's struggle for survival, and at the same time calling for their commitment to this struggle'.

Subtle pressure was exerted by the threat that, in the event of defeat, young people would become 'labour-slaves of international financial powers and other deadly enemies of German liberty'. From the outset the boys were to keep in view a future as heroes in the field. Highly decorated men on leave from the Front were regularly invited to schools and HJ camps to give an account of their glorious deeds. 'Once a captain came down who had the German Cross in Gold, and the Iron Cross First Class. We were very impressed', Willy Rabe remembers, 'The German troops are fighting heroically, he told us; there's no better army in the world and we will win. We have superiority in weaponry.'

'Of course, we all wanted to be in the forces, and our idols were mainly pilots like Adolf Galland, who were all highly decorated and whose pictures could be seen all over the place in every magazine and every newspaper', Karl-Heinz Böckle adds.

However, the greatest exemplar was and remained Adolf Hitler. At HJ hostel evenings newsreels were used to ram home the message to the youngsters: 'Führer, we belong to you!' 'Führer, command, we will follow you.' That was the central imperative of the Hitler Youth. 'It is your duty to be healthy; your body belongs to the Führer.' Even Sal Perel, who became famous as '*Hitlerjunge* Salomon' was aware of the seductiveness of power. Perel, who was Jewish, escaped the Holocaust by entering the lions' den in the guise of a *Hitlerjunge* named Jupp Perjell. In this period he was constantly torn between his keenness to serve in the Hitler Youth and the fear of being exposed as an 'enemy of the people' and murdered.

> Primarily I wanted to be a young man in whom the state could place its trust, and after that I wanted to be a courageous airman who later would see service as a pilot in the German Luftwaffe.
>
> *Volker Fischer, born 1928*

War service was, according to Nazi ideology, to be the ultimate fulfilment of youthful plans for life, nothing less than a coming-of-age ritual. Goebbels, a film buff himself, also discovered the captivating power of the moving image as an instrument of propaganda aimed at the young. In Sunday film sessions the boys were shown documentaries with titles like *Victory in Poland*, the *The Luftwaffe's Baptism of Fire*, *The HJ at War*, or *The Lads Want to Go to Sea*. Feature-films such as *The Daredevils*, *The Young Eagle*, *Jakko* or *The Lads* were intended to arouse enthusiasm for special units of the naval or air branches of the HJ, and at the same time bring the boys into line ideologically. In one scene from *The Daredevils* an instructor bends the ear of a wayward *Hitlerjunge* with the words: 'I know it's never been easy for you to obey orders . . . We pilots are risking our necks all the time. *Schweinehunde* who question the reason for an order are no use to us.' Discipline and obedience were presented as values without which true comradeship was simply not possible.

In the film *Cadets*, which was premiered in December 1941, the Nazi propagandists appealed to the boys' keenness to fight. It told the story of a company of nine- to twelve-year-old Prussian cadets who were taken prisoner by the Russians in the Seven Years' War (1756–63). Of course the cadets manage to escape, do heroic battle with the Russians – presented as shabby and coarse – and succeed in breaking through to their own lines again. This epic did not fail to have its effect: 'It was a film which, if you like, was concerned with my generation', remembers Bernhard Heisig, who volunteered for the army. 'The song they sang: "I fancy a fight with the foe in the open field" was one we sang as well. This attitude of defiance at their age, seeing it through like that, certainly impressed us.'

The film *The Great King*, about Frederick the Great, appealed on the other hand to the spirit of sacrifice among the population as a whole, to see the war through either to victory or doom. As Karl-Heinz Böckle saw it: 'The whole film was telling us what fine chaps those Prussians were and how we ought to be like them. Frederick the Great, for example – he was practically surrounded by enemies and yet he still won in the end – and they were deliberately saying that's how we had to be. We are also surrounded by enemies on all sides, but in the end we will be the last battalions. What they didn't show us, naturally, was the great suffering, the bodies torn to pieces and the bloodshed. All we saw the whole time were radiant heroes.'

Inwardly the boys had long been prepared for war. 'When the war broke out, our teachers at school told us: "It'll be your turn soon." We hoped that would happen. We actually wanted it. I had a friend who said to me in all seriousness: "You know, I'd like to be killed"', remembers Bernhard Heisig.

War, combat spirit and endurance were to take the boys over, body and soul, and become part of them. Herbert Reinecker, editor-in-chief of HJ magazines and later script-writer of TV crime series such as *The Commissioner* and *Derrick*, wrote in *Junges Deutschland* in 1943: 'Brought up in absolute confidence of victory, determined to take every expression of doubt as an insult, every trial and vicissitude simply strengthens the defiant impulse in the heart of youth: "So what, we'll go for it all the harder." The

zealous soul of many a boy has matured beyond his years. The fact
that youthful souls have been shaped by the burdens suddenly
thrust upon them was the gift of activist courage, courage to take
the war on the chest and not to stand aside. Anything that brings
maturity is good.' And he continues: 'The service of arms seems to
youth to be the only goal worth striving for.'

Before long it was inconceivable for a 'good' German to be
anything else but a soldier. The fact that girls soon considered only
men in uniform worthy of a second glance was actually a more
decisive factor: 'The young ladies of our dreams would not even
speak to us if we didn't wear a uniform', reports Bernhard Heisig,
who was just sixteen when he joined the Panzer corps. 'No girl
would go out with anyone who wasn't a soldier. Better still if he
had a handsome uniform, like my Panzer uniform for instance,
and ideally a few medals as well.'

In order to create role-models the *Reichsjugendführung* never
tired of stressing that by 1940 no less than '95 per cent of HJ
leaders' were wearing the 'honourable dress of the soldier'. But as
the newspapers became increasingly filled with death notices, it
was impossible to prevent it dawning on some of the young
disciples that heroes ended up as a three-line entry in the daily
press. 'I can still see the board with the roll of war dead at my high
school', recalls Karl Kunze. 'The art teacher wrote six names on an
old drawing-board – that was after the Polish campaign. Then
about six more names after the French campaign, and quite soon
the board was full. So a second board was hung below it, then the
next one to the left, and another board on the right – it got faster
and faster.'

The fortunes of war had turned against Germany. Hitler's
*Blitzkrieg* strategy had come up against its limits: 'Operation
Barbarossa', the invasion of the Soviet Union, which was intended
to bring with it the 'smashing' of the deadly enemy, had failed.
Every day an entire regiment bled to death on the Eastern Front.
By the end of 1942 the army of the east had suffered casualties of
800,000 dead, missing or wounded. To make matters a great deal
worse, Hitler had declared war on the USA on 11 December 1941,
thus creating a new and powerful enemy. The long slow death of
Germany was about to begin.

> We were told by our superiors that we simply had to focus on one thing: that was the victory of the Third Reich, and for that we had to give everything.
>
> *Volker Fischer, born 1928*

It is certainly true that not all young Germans saw it as a blessing to be allowed to serve the Führer with loyalty and glad self-sacrifice. Not everyone considered marching in step to be the only acceptable means of locomotion. Despite compulsory service in the HJ, propaganda and pressure from official quarters, a few 'incorrigibles' dropped out of the ranks. In Hamburg and soon in other major cities young jazz enthusiasts got together in groups to put on swing records and have a ball. During the war dancing of any kind was pretty much forbidden. But dancing to 'decadent' American music was regarded as treason: not only did it originate in the USA and was mainly played by blacks – some of it had even been composed by Jews. As early as 1935 the Nazi newspaper, the *Völkischer Beobachter*, announced: 'As from today nigger jazz is banned from German radio.' The rhythmic sounds, to which a wild kind of jive, a forerunner of rock'n'roll, was danced, certainly did not fit in with the brassy marching tunes of Nazism.

The drab taste of that time, which regarded the waltz as the most ecstatic form of motion, is clearly revealed in a memorandum from the *Reichsjugendführung*: 'The sight of the dancers was appalling. Sometimes two youths danced with one girl, sometimes several couples formed a circle, where they linked arms and hopped around, clapped their hands, even rocked with the backs of their heads touching and then leaned forward with their torsos hanging down slackly, their long hair flapping wildly in their faces, and their legs flopping around. When the band played a rumba, the dancers went into a wild ecstasy, they all jumped around and gabbled the words of the song in English. None of the band players remained sitting down, they were all madly "jiving" around on the stage . . . They call each other "swing-boy", "swing-girl" or "old hit-boy". They end their letters with "swing Heil". Their favourite word is *lottern*.' [Roughly: 'hang loose' Tr.].

> At those swing parties a lot of smooching went on of course;
> there was even some heavy petting, so we were all 'sexually
> degenerate'. The Nazis found it completely unspeakable . . .
>
> *Uwe Storjohann, born 1925, member of the young*
> *Hamburg 'swingers'*

What sounds today like the description of a good party was, to
the dictatorship, proof of an 'illegal association of young people
hostile to the state and the Party'. From 1940 dances in
Hamburg's Alster Pavilion or in the Hotel Kaiserhof were broken
up by the Gestapo and the swing kids arrested. On one evening
the police counted over 400 partygoers, of whom just two were
over twenty-one years old. Since it was no longer possible to dance
in big venues, the swing kids grabbed their portable gramophones
and moved the parties into private flats or danced by the shores of
the Alster. The fact that at these parties there was actual erotic
contact between the swing boys and swing girls was clear proof to
the Gestapo that they were dealing here with depraved 'sex
monsters'. To make matters worse, with their casual appearance
the swing kids tried to differentiate themselves from the
standardised mass of the Hitler Youth. Their trademarks were
tartan jackets with long vents, shoes with thick crepe soles and
loud scarves. They smoked pipes and used long cigarette-holders,
and wore what in England would be called 'Anthony Eden' hats.
Whatever the weather, they carried umbrellas on their arms. Even
the girls wore their hair loose, in contrast to the well-behaved
BDM girls, and put on trendy gear and make-up.

> I was then asked why I wasn't in the Hitler Youth, and so
> I said: I'm not in the Hitler Youth because I want to be a free
> human being. And that phrase got me sent to a concentration
> camp.
>
> *Günther Discher, born 1925, member of the young*
> *Hamburg 'swingers'*

The swing kids were certainly not interested in political resistance. While the bombs were thudding all around and it was only a question of time before they were called up into the Wehrmacht, they simply tried to enjoy a few hours of freedom listening to the music of Artie Shaw, Louis Armstrong or Benny Goodman. They weren't political, just rebellious. There was only one organisation which they vehemently rejected: the Hitler Youth. Military-style drill, marching and any kind of compulsion were anathema to them. Many of them managed to trick and lie their way out of joining the HJ. And that of course led to repeated clashes with the feared HJ patrols.

In order to keep recalcitrant youngsters in check, Heinrich Himmler had issued, on 9 March 1940, the 'Police Regulations for the Protection of Youth'. These prohibited young people under eighteen from drinking alcohol or even hanging around in public places, such as cafés, cinemas, music-halls or nightclubs. Boys aged only seventeen could die a hero's death, but not go out for the evening. In order to be able to clamp down on infringements, the 'Youth Service Arrest' was introduced on 17 September 1940, whereby young people under fourteen were literally locked up on a diet of bread and water for up to one month. These 'Youth Protection Laws' were supervised by the police and the HJ patrol service.

As the result of an agreement in 1938 between Schirach and the *Reichsführer-SS*, Heinrich Himmler, this special HJ formation was closely tied in with the *Schutzstaffel*. It provided new recruits for the police and for Himmler's 'Black Order'. Selected on racial criteria, some of these boys later found themselves in SS 'Death's Head' units as guards in concentration camps.

During the war the HJ patrol service took on additional assignments in air-raid protection and in the fire brigade. This 'HJ police' worked closely with the regular police, the Gestapo and the security service (SD) and increasingly developed into a network of informers within the HJ. In the final years of the war, it had the job of taking action against cliques of young people which had formed outside the Hitler Youth.

'It was very dangerous to fall into their hands', remembers former swing kid Uwe Storjohann. 'They marched you along to the Gestapo, and the Gestapo did the rest.' Yet even the swing kids knew how to defend themselves. Admittedly, many of them were the sons of Hamburg's commercial 'upper crust'. But among them were also working-class kids who had won their spurs in street fights. So, if swing kids ended up in the Gestapo's interrogation cellars, quite a few members of HJ patrols disappeared in the murky waters of Hamburg's Alster Lake.

However, when these youngsters were caught, their smiles quickly faded. The Gestapo prison at Fuhlsbüttel (now Hamburg's international airport), soon became notorious among the rebels. 'They were tortured in the usual Gestapo manner: teeth knocked out, thumbscrew applied, and cigarettes stubbed out on their skin. When they came back, they looked terrible', Storjohann tells us. 'If a dictatorship needs the youth for its wars of aggression, it can't get anywhere with swingers like that', ex-swing boy Günther Discher believes. 'Quite apart from that, they were afraid that *Hitlerjungen* would leave and join the swing cliques who lived a different kind of life and wanted to free themselves from uniformity. The Nazi regime smelt resistance in the wind and wanted to prevent this creeping poison from spreading any further.'

The kids often listened to the 'enemy broadcasts' of the BBC, which made them 'radio criminals' and provided the authorities with a pretext for taking them out of circulation. Criminal regulations about intent to commit high treason, the 1934 'law against treacherous attacks on state and Party' and the imposition of 'custody orders', put young people into prisons and concentration camps. During the war, the law on juvenile crime was increasingly widened, making it easier to condemn young people to imprisonment or death, as 'pests upon the people'.

Even the harmless swing youth now had to be 'eradicated'. On the recommendation of Artur Axmann, Himmler in turn instructed the head of the SD, Reinhard Heydrich, on 26 January 1942, to despatch the young swingers to a concentration camp. 'Only by brutal intervention will we be able to prevent a dangerous spread of this Anglophile trend, at a time when Germany is fighting for its survival.' Swing kids were arrested by the Gestapo and were either put into punishment battalions for a probationary period at the Front or else, without any conviction in the courts, sent by the police, Gestapo or HJ to the 'youth protection camp' set up at Moringen in 1940. Günther Discher was one of those arrested and interrogated by the Gestapo. When he told them with naïve brashness: 'I am not in the Hitler Youth because I want to be a free human being', he was sent under a protection order to the concentration camp. The dance on the edge of the volcano had come to an abrupt end: 'We knew there were camps like that. But in 1939 we didn't yet know that people were forced to starve and die there.'

Beatings, starvation, forced labour in arms factories, sickness and humiliation were awaiting Günther Discher in Moringen. 'If you go to the Moringen cemetery today, you will find that 150 young men were buried in shallow graves by the SS. They died from exhaustion. By July 1944 a total of 1,386 boys were suffering the maltreatment of Moringen, some for alleged criminal activities, others on political grounds.'

In other major German cities, too, cliques and gangs of 'wild' youths were formed. In Leipzig they were the 'Mob', in Vienna the 'Shufflers' and in Munich the 'Blisters'. What they had in common was the desire to escape from HJ drill and to live a life of freedom. Other groups gave themselves outlandish names like 'Red X', 'the Navajos' and frequently the 'Edelweiss Pirates'. The last of these names soon became an umbrella term for all anti-HJ gangs. The tender alpine flower concealed behind their jacket lapel was their recognition sign. Their activities ranged widely from harmless afternoon dances to gangs of hoodlums roaming the streets during the blackout. These youngsters were pursued relentlessly and branded as political enemies, a fact which only served to raise their profile.

The reign of terror soon produced the result that common criminals became politicised and political activists were criminalised. Any kind of opting out from the tyranny was elevated to the status of a political act and characterised as 'disruptive', 'culturally Bolshevist' or 'anti-national'. Anyone who eluded the constraints of the HJ was considered nothing short of 'depraved'.

Even the Youth Alliance, banned by Schirach and absorbed into the HJ, continued its independent existence and was ruthlessly persecuted. Acting on information from the HJ the police arrested Robert Oelbermann, a co-founder of the 'Neroth *Wandervögel*'. He died after five years' imprisonment in Dachau concentration camp. Helmut Hirsch, a member of the 'dj11' movement was executed; the movement's leader Eberhard Köbel, alias 'Tusk', was arrested by the Gestapo but escaped abroad.

There was a clear political agenda behind the underground activities of the Socialist Workers' Youth – the banned youth organisation of the German Social Democratic Party – and the communist youth leagues. They distributed leaflets, painted anti-nationalist slogans on walls and supported the impoverished families of political exiles. True, they could not organise themselves on a large scale, since most of the associations had been broken up in the first months following the Nazi seizure of power. Thousands of young communists and socialists were already in prisons and concentration camps.

Members of Christian youth organisations also lined up against the regime. In 1942 a group of Catholic apprentices from Munich were charged with high treason before a People's Court. The leader of the group, seventeen-year-old Walter Klingenbeck, was executed in Munich's Stadelheim gaol in 1943. Helmut Hübener was also just seventeen when he was beheaded on 27 October 1942. He was a member of the Church of Jesus Christ of the Latter-Day Saints, better known as the Mormons, and had been protesting against the Nazis and the war in leaflets he drafted himself. He was condemned to death by a People's Court.

It was from the Catholic Youth and the Youth Alliance that the student resistance group, 'White Rose', grew up around Hans and Sophie Scholl. With leaflets and wall slogans they attempted to mobilise academic youth against the dictatorship. As Goebbels was addressing a hand-picked audience in Berlin's Sportpalast on the need for 'total war', the members of the White Rose were arrested in Munich. Hitler's hanging judge, Roland Freisler, condemned them to death.

On 10 November 1944, in the Cologne suburb of Ehrenfeld, six boys aged sixteen to eighteen were publicly hanged by the

Gestapo without trial. This was intended as a 'warning' and a 'deterrent'. They were left dangling from their nooses for almost the entire day. One of the six was a sixteen-year-old apprentice roofer named Bartholomäus Schink. The boys belonged to Cologne's 'Edelweiss Pirates' and had started to carry out active resistance. They hid escaped forced labourers and deserters, and mounted attacks on Gestapo and Party functionaries. During the war as a whole, at least 162 youths aged between sixteen and twenty-five were executed for opposing the Hitler regime and its criminal war policy. However, it was that regime which, without any help from its opponents, drove the 'Thousand Year Reich' to its destruction.

> An admirer at my dancing-class told me that there were young people who were just as idealistic as I was, but who put all their idealism into working against Hitler. I was utterly shocked.
>
> *Renate Finckh, born 1926*

The glorious victories of the 'greatest military commander of all time' were like the snows of yesteryear. Since the end of 1942 Hitler's 6th Army had been slowly and agonisingly bleeding to death at Stalingrad in the depths of Russia. The capture of this city on the Volga had become a paranoid obsession for Hitler. Yet it was less its strategic significance than its very name which represented a challenge to him. By taking Stalingrad he wanted to deliver a symbolic death-blow to the hated Soviet enemy: 'Communism must be robbed of its shrine.'

However, instead of being a defeat for Stalin, the battle became the writing on the wall foreshadowing Germany's catastrophe in the east. The desperate struggle lasted 75 days. The pleas of the generals, to be allowed to risk a breakout from the 'cauldron', were rejected by Hitler: 'Fight to your last cartridge!' was his fanatical order. The Red Army tightened its pincer-grip and closed off all lines of retreat for the German troops. They were caught in a trap and met a wretched end, from their wounds, from hunger and from the icy cold. In January 1943 over 180,000 German servicemen died on the Eastern Front. Of the 300,000 who had been encircled at Stalingrad, 90,000 became prisoners of war. Only 6,000 would ever see their homes again.

For former supporters of Hitler, who had gone off to war full of the spirit of heroism and sacrifice, the approach of death had a sobering effect. An embittered young officer wrote from Stalingrad: 'My battery has just 26 shells left. That is all, and there is no more to come. We crouch in a cellar and make a fire from furniture. I was pretty bright, was thrilled to get my officer's epaulettes and roared "Heil Hitler" along with you. Now we have to die miserably or be sent to Siberia. That would be bad enough, but the worst is that one knows it's all happening for a completely senseless cause. It makes one's blood boil.'

> Stalingrad was, of course, the first real defeat and we were very aware that the outcome of the war was all-important, and that it was now a matter of avoiding further defeats, and helping however we could.
>
> *Paul Kehlenbeck, born 1926*

Others attempted to maintain their illusions to the end: 'Becoming a nation, drawing a line under all history down to the present, these for me are the aims of the war. Only on those conditions can any sacrifice be demanded. For me, my people is my law on earth, for which I must take a stand under the direction of the Almighty.' These young men died because Hitler wanted it so. To the lord of the Hitler Youth even his own youngsters were mere tools with which to fulfil his insane obsession. If he could not drive them into war in the hope of victory, he would do so under the threat of destruction.

In January 1943 the US president, Franklin D. Roosevelt, and Britain's prime minister, Winston Churchill, met in Casablanca and demanded Germany's unconditional surrender. Rumours now circulated in the Third Reich, fanned by propaganda, that the Allies wanted not only to defeat Germany, but also to destroy it and annihilate its population. 'Our walls may break, but not our hearts!' was the slogan; fight to the bitter end, the motto. 'The young know today that all bridges have been burnt behind us', announced Axmann, 'and that for the people and for the youth, in faith and trust in our Führer, there is only one way to go: forward!'

Since early 1942 *Reichsjugendführer* Axmann had been working on a 'Führer decree' about the formation of war-service units of German youth, 'in order to provide unified control of the tasks which are to be carried out to an ever greater extent by the entire youth of Germany within the framework of war service'. Following in Schirach's footsteps, Axmann now wanted to anchor the totalitarian demands of the HJ in the education of youth, to organise war deployment centrally through the HJ and to exclude all competitors.

> War is best fought with young men, because they have no imagination. They hope to distinguish themselves and have a fear of failure.
>
> *Manfred Rommel, born 1928*

There followed two years of wrangling with the education minister, the Reich labour minister, the minister of the interior, the air ministry, the navy, the Reich labour service and the ministry of armaments and war production, all of whom laid claims to the young generation. None of these gentlemen wanted to give up their access to the available pool of young people in wartime. The 'regulation on the calling-up of German youth for the fulfilment of war tasks', which was finally issued on 2 December 1943 over the signatures of Göring, Lammers, Keitel and Bormann, was a compromise, and a defeat for Axmann. The Reich youth leadership had to accept countless restrictions on their influence and in the end had fewer powers than before the issue of the decree. Future war service as air or naval auxiliaries, early entry into the Reich Labour Service, the Wehrmacht and the *Waffen-SS*, or obligations in the context of the defence of the Reich, were increasingly taken out of the HJ's sphere of responsibility. Its influence was further diluted by the mass call-up of youth on the basis of emergency ordinances. Basically the job of the *Reichsjugendführer* was limited to recruiting, at great expense, young people for war assignments over which he had long since lost all control.

Schirach's plan to build up the HJ into a state within the state, had failed miserably. In the war everyone wanted to get their hands on this 'magnificent youth' which the *Reichsjugendführer* had already shaped for this purpose. In the fourth year of the war *Junges Deutschland*, a once respected nationalist journal taken over by the Nazis, summed things up in this way: in the face of an enemy which has 'sworn the destruction and annihilation of this youth, these boys and girls will thank the Führer that, under the inevitable restrictions of the war, they have not become feeble and inactive, but from an early age are allowed to toughen and condition themselves, and train themselves in body, spirit and mind'. Now this 'steel-hardened' youth would soon be permitted to prove their endurance in battle as well.

> We sat there and fired our weapons and saw nothing of our own youth. But in the midst of it all there were a lot of things like comradeship, for which we perhaps developed more of a feeling, and we saw what was going on under the surface. So I can't really pass judgement on that period; it was simply part of my life.
>
> *Joachim Redlin, born 1928*

With the disaster of Stalingrad in February 1943 there also came a turning-point in the war service of the young. Hitler called for the mobilisation of the last reserves – from ten-year-old *Pimpf* to grey-haired pensioner. With his rallying-speech in the Berlin Sportpalast, full of fanaticism and a diabolical eloquence, Goebbels the firebrand succeeded in mobilising his audience for the final struggle: 'Do you believe, along with us and the Führer, in the final, complete victory of the German people?' he cried in a voice cracking with emotion. 'Are you determined to follow the Führer through thick and thin in his fight to achieve this victory, accepting even the severest personal hardships? Do you want total war? Is your confidence in the Führer today greater, more trusting and more unshakeable than ever?' A wave of enthusiasm swept through the Sportpalast, in which every last seat was filled. The crowd went wild. As if in ecstasy the people jumped from their seats and replied to every fiendish question with a frantic yell of '*Ja!*'

Looking back, the former *Hitlerjunge* Reinhard Appel, who subsequently became chief editor of ZDF, Germany's second national TV network, has this to say: 'They all leapt enthusiastically to their feet, these grown men, and said, yes, we want total war. It is incredible how people can be seduced, and most of all the young, of course.'

The next morning Goebbels wrote happily in his diary: 'The mood is like that of a wild popular frenzy. I bring the meeting up to a state resembling a total intellectual mobilisation. At the end the meeting breaks up in a complete shambles of wild excitement. The people are ready to give everything for war and for victory. I hope that the words I spoke at the end of my speech come true: "Now let the people arise, let the storm break!"'

> After fourteen months on the flak batteries we already thought of ourselves as veterans. We had lost all enthusiasm and were just waiting for the war to end.
>
> *Manfred Rommel, born 1928*

By 1943 Hitler's dream of extending Germany's 'living space' had – at least for the ordinary infantryman – became a reality. German soldiers were deployed from Norway's North Cape to North Africa, from the Atlantic coast of France to the snow-covered Russian steppes. Yet for a long time now the effects of war were being felt at home. Here, around German cities, airports, industrial plants and arms factories, soldiers were manning anti-aircraft guns to ward off Allied bombers. The reservoir of 'human material' was almost drained when the Luftwaffe chief, Hermann Göring, had an idea for a new source of 'fresh meat supply': would it not be possible to draft complete classes of schoolboys born in 1926 and 1927 (who would now be as young as fifteen), from the upper and middle schools, to man the flak batteries? Each 100 boys could replace 70 regular servicemen without difficulty. The navy was immediately in favour of sending children to the guns and urgently requested that their own flak batteries should not be forgotten. Bormann, Hitler's *éminence grise*, protested. Enemy propaganda could claim that Germany was at the end of its strength, he argued, and was obliged 'to recruit children as a last resort'. However, Göring succeeded in persuading Hitler. The 'decree concerning auxiliary war service of German youth in the Luftwaffe' dated 22 January 1943 made deeper inroads than ever before into the ranks of the HJ. The calling-up of air and naval auxiliaries was the prelude to increasingly direct involvement of minors in military assignments in the Wehrmacht and *Waffen-SS*. By the end of the war nearly 200,000 boys were serving as flak auxiliaries.

A legal loophole was provided by the Emergency Service Ordinance, which had been gathering dust in a drawer since 1938 and was now applied with a liberal wartime interpretation. Admittedly Göring stressed that 'air force auxiliaries were not to be regarded as soldiers in a legal sense. Even during auxiliary war duties they were still considered to be schoolboys.' The Reich youth leadership also insisted that the flak auxiliaries should be given the additional initials 'HJ', should wear the uniform of the Air-HJ and when off duty should put on their HJ armbands. At a swearing-in ceremony they had to promise at all times to do their duty 'with loyalty, obedience, courage and readiness for action, as befits a *Hitlerjunge*'.

Reams of documents were printed with regulations about 'Ideological Schooling', 'Physical Exercise' and 'Preparation for Military Service', which the flak auxiliaries had to go through in addition to their battery duties. In fact, the HJ hardly retained any influence in the flak batteries. Even the school lessons, which the education minister had insisted on for the flak auxiliaries, usually fell by the wayside. Fundamentally, Hitler's henchmen knew that the flak auxiliaries were nothing but the dictator's youngest servicemen. According to Schirach, they formed 'the bridge between probation on the home front and active war service'. Göring stressed that 'these young people are proud that even though below military age, they are being actively deployed for Germany's victory, within the framework of the Wehrmacht'. It was the task of their superior officers 'to intensify this pride, keep alive the enthusiasm for the military life and raise it to a zeal for active service'.

Certainly, many of the boys needed no further encouragement. Their Nazi education was bearing fruit: 'We broke into cheering when we got our call-up. We were very happy about it', remembers Lothar Gulich. 'Our German teacher, who had just been giving us a class, stood there tapping his forehead with his index-finger. "You idiots!" he shouted.'

> During the war we regarded ourselves as the so-called Home Front. We thought about the great job our troops were doing at the battle-front, and we wanted to live up to them.
>
> *Friedhelm Busse, born 1929*

The service began with four weeks of basic training. The instructors were usually NCOs from the units in question. In addition to the usual field exercises and drill the schoolboys were given a crash course in handling searchlights and anti-aircraft guns. They were posted on range-finding and fire-control equipment, as gun-loaders and gun-aimers, they operated the machines for setting the detonators or dragged shells weighing up to 90lb over to the guns. They manned the heavy 88mm and 128mm guns as well as light 20mm cannons. 'I won't forget the specifications of the guns as long as I live', says Lothar Gulich. 'We really had to bone up on them. Sometimes an NCO would even come round on an inspection at night. He would tear your blanket off and shout: "What type of gun are you being trained on?" Then I would growl back at him: "The gun I am being trained on is a 105mm SKC32NL in 88mm MPLC30D."'

After training they went to action stations. 'There were 24 lads in a hut with two-tier bunks, and we wore the same clothes as newly recruited soldiers wore', recalls Joachim Ellert, who was sixteen at the time. 'But they were too big for us – especially me. The long-johns came up to our armpits; the shirts hung below our knees.'

For many of the boys this was the realisation of all they had dreamed of ever since Nazi propaganda had tried to deprive them of independent thought: they were to be allowed to be soldiers. The fact that they still had to wear HJ armbands was felt by most to be a humiliation. They no longer wanted to be *Hitlerjungen* but rather, since they were daily risking their lives on the gun-batteries, to be recognised as fully fledged soldiers. Whenever they went off duty they removed their HJ armbands – the last fraudulent indication that, as far as the state was concerned, they were still regarded as children.

Now, in the heat of battle, Hitler's child-soldiers were experiencing the brutal reality of war. Particularly in major cities like Berlin, where they were assigned to protect industrial plants and airports, they lived in constant danger of being targets for enemy bombers. 'When I was sixteen I was first put on the roof of the Siemens-Schuckert factory with a 4-barrelled 20mm flak cannon. That was uncomfortable. That's when I got the first inkling that war was not just a kind of tempering process in which the German male had to be hardened. Then, as a kid, I felt the fear of death for the first time.' Such were the feelings of Klaus Bölling, a flak auxiliary in Berlin.

The ordeal by fire in Berlin was also a shock for Peter Boenisch. 'I was in a searchlight battery and what we did was amusingly called "Operation Shroud". The trick was to turn the searchlight over and remove the reflector. The light was not then focused in a narrow beam but shone in a broad inverted cone up to the cloud-base. With a low cloud-base this was good for the German fighter-pilots because then it was easier for them to pick out the approaching enemy bomber formations. The trouble was, for those down below it was very unpleasant. When you shine your light like that you present a perfect target. Then of course all hell broke out around us. Many of those kids – we were only fifteen years old, remember – had genuine nervous breakdowns and blubbed their eyes out. Needless to say, in these air raids a lot of auxiliaries copped it.'

Hitler's schoolboy soldiers were children who had been promoted to men from one day to the next. Like children they played tricks on their teachers in the intervals between firing, enjoyed card-games until the alarm sirens wailed, were given special rations of sweets instead of cigarettes, cried in bed at night and asked for their mothers. And if, from time to time, they felt proud to be regarded as soldiers, then they also had to die like soldiers. Axmann's summing-up bears witness to a contempt for humanity, whether he intended it or not: 'Many a flak battery manned by Luftwaffe auxiliaries was wiped out by a direct hit. All one could do was award the dead posthumous medals for bravery. In the Reich capital we experienced the appalling sight of Iron Crosses being fixed to the coffins of Luftwaffe auxiliaries.' Medals for dead children who – thanks to Axmann – would never know what it was like to live in a time of peace.

Young men are thoroughly suited to being given orders, if at the same time their status is enhanced and they are complimented.

*Manfred Rommel, born 1928*

A storm-girt island in the German Bight became a hell for 150 schoolboys from Schleswig-Holstein, East Prussia, Silesia and Pomerania: it was called Heligoland. On this isolated platform of rock the German navy had built a massive fortress with U-boat pens and a modern radar range- and direction-finder with a range of 600 kilometres. Fatally for the garrison, Heligoland also lay in the corridor for Allied bombers flying to and from Germany. Night after night the sirens wailed. But it was not until three weeks before the end of the war that the inferno broke over their heads. On 18 April 1945 the British launched a massive air attack on the island, one of the highest concentrations of bombers in the Second World War. For two long hours the deadly cargo of some 1,000 bombs was unloaded on to Heligoland.

Lothar Gulich, flak auxiliary on the 'West Cliff' battery, remembers: 'I was sitting at this powerful telescope and could see the approaching aircraft opening their bomb-doors and the bombs flying out – right at us. Within a few minutes all the guns were destroyed. One of them was blown right over the cliff with its whole crew – all killed, of course. And then the CO shouted: "Every man for himself." So I ran like hell across a field of craters, towards the flak command-post – as best I could between exploding bombs – and then I flung myself into a bomb-crater. At the bottom lay an older man, a sergeant, bleeding to death. I guess he had internal injuries, a lung or something. I wanted out, but the bombs kept on dropping. I wanted to try and get to the command-post because I knew that in the bunker there I would be completely protected. But he kept saying – and I'll never forget this – "Stay with me, kid." Then he died. Until the end of the attack, which lasted about two hours, I lay with him in the crater. When I came out in the open again I saw all the dead bodies. The ones in my battery who were still where they'd been when the raid started – they were all dead. The majority of my class- mates lost their lives there.'

We were loaded on to goods-wagons and sent off into the Eifel mountains. There we could already hear the rumbling from the front line. It was spooky, at night, with the mountains brightly lit up by artillery fire. You got the feeling of war. Now we're really there, we thought, it sort of gave us the shits.

*Klas Ewert Everwyn, born 1930*

Despite the losses, most boys were fighting in the firm belief that they had to defend their Fatherland and their families against the 'enemy'. At the same time they forgot that it was only Hitler's war of aggression that had turned these countries against Germany. The boys' actions were driven as much by a sense of duty, discipline and obedience, as by pride in being able to report an aircraft shot down. True, the enemy was not destroyed by their fire but was certainly made to feel it. Concentrated anti-aircraft fire made as great a contribution to defence against Allied bombing raids as did the fighter sorties. In one night attack on Essen in March 1943, only 153 out 422 RAF bombers reached the target zone. In the Battle of the Ruhr between March and June 1943, out of 18,506 RAF bombers 872 were shot down and 2,126 damaged. Even in the massive raids on Berlin in August 1943, the RAF suffered 176 aircraft shot down and 114 damaged, a casualty rate of 14 per cent. Boys who could prove they had shot down an aircraft received a medal.

As we know, Hitler wanted his boys to be 'as tough as leather and as hard as Krupp steel'. Daily exposure to the horror of war had its way of making some of the boys display a hardness and insensitivity towards death which appals them today. One witness recalls with a shudder an event in his flak days: 'My unit had shot down a British Mosquito fighter-bomber and we immediately ran over to the aircraft. We could see how both the pilots had died. They had been strangled by their control cables. In those days we were familiar with death, had known horrible situations and had seen people die. And, well, I suppose we just sort of accepted it. It was pure curiosity that made us run over to the plane. In addition to which we were interested in the armaments and the ammunition of those aircraft and even the pilots' clothing. We were even nasty enough to pull items of clothing off the dead bodies: boots, overalls and things, which we then made use of ourselves. In wartime we weren't the least bit concerned or put off by that. I certainly didn't lie awake in bed thinking about it. I didn't say to myself: "Man, that was a terrible thing to do." I'm sure it was because we had been trained over and over and brought up like that.'

> War is horrible, but having to experience it at such a young age is even more horrible.
>
> *Peter Boenisch, born 1927*

In a state in which *Gleichschaltung*, or Nazi standardisation, reduced daily life to the lowest common denominator, in which marching in step was the normal means of locomotion and individuality dissolved in mass uniformity, the cry 'To be part of it is everything!' applied to the young more than in any other system. Even worse than being put through harsh assignments, along with others, was not to be part of them at all. Klaus Bölling had first-hand experience of that. At first he was a *Hitlerjunge* like all the others. Like his school friends he joined the *Jungvolk* and was even promoted to *Jungendschaftsführer*. He looked on officers as his role-models, lined the route on Hitler's birthday and served bravely as a flak auxiliary in Berlin.

Then suddenly his world collapsed around him: 'My father came to me and said, your mother has been arrested and taken to a transit camp, and you have to take off your uniform. Any day you'll get your discharge notice because now, on account of your mother being Jewish, you are considered unworthy of military service.' This was the first the boy had known of his mother's Jewish descent. He had to learn that, for this reason alone, he was no longer held to be worthy to fight for the Führer. It was this ostracism that first revealed to him the true face of the perfidious system. 'Two weeks later I did indeed receive my discharge papers. Earlier I had a chance to visit my mother in the transit camp before she was taken off to Auschwitz. So I went there wearing my flak-auxiliary uniform. She held my arm tightly. She looked worn out, absolutely wretched, almost transparent and she immediately began to cry. She did try to suppress her tears but she just couldn't. And I, who had only an inkling that from that moment on something dreadful was going to happen in my mother's life and in mine – I began to cry too. I was not crying for myself now, or because my swastika armbands had been torn off; I was crying for my mother. That was the moment when, even with my minimal knowledge of the nature of the regime, I just had this instinct: you have been excluded, you don't belong any more.' Klaus Bölling had to remove his uniform. Instead, he was now classed as a 'half-caste of the first degree' and drafted into the *Organisation Todt* labour force, to work on building the Westwall defences.

> Lads! Our homeland is under threat! A barbaric enemy stands at the Westwall and is bound to try and storm it. This means that for us the order of the day is: get those trenches dug! Dig, dig and dig again!
>
> *Daily orders of the HJ regional leader to the male youth of the Cologne-Aachen region, September 1944*

The deployment of the flak auxiliaries for Hitler's devastating war made heavy inroads into the youngest age-groups. But that was just the beginning. By the end of 1943 the Wehrmacht's casualties had reached the figure of 4.2 million. Over 1.8 million had been killed and countless more maimed. Hundreds of thousands were missing or prisoners of war. For the young, volunteering became a form of conscription. Officially, according to military law, liability for military service began at the age of nineteen. But now call-up was starting at an ever earlier age. In 1941–2, eighteen-year olds had to join up, and in 1943–4 the seventeen-year-olds were drafted. And in 1945, in some cases even sixteen-year-olds. Youngsters could volunteer for military service in their seventeenth year. In 1944 the youngest volunteers, born in 1928, were just sixteen.

Increased pressure was placed on sixteen-year-olds to join the Wehrmacht or the *Waffen-SS*. If Axmann had named the year 1943 as the year of general conscription, then by 1944 at the latest the Hitler Youth was to become a movement of war volunteers. In some 120 military preparation camps batch after batch of young soldiers was turned out, conveyor-belt style, for the Wehrmacht. This was admittedly observed with some misgiving by the SS, who for their part were interested in a new young intake for the *Waffen-SS*. After reaching agreement with the *Reichsjugendführung*, the SS equipped 40 preparation camps of its own, for 'its' *Hitlerjungen*. However, the head of the SS Central Office, Gottlob Berger, complained to Himmler that 'we cannot get the *Reichsjugendführung* to ensure that we only receive boys who are racially suitable'.

> We had to parade in the yard and an SS officer came along and said: 'Right, now I expect you're all going to volunteer for the *Waffen-SS*. Or is there anyone here who *doesn't* want to volunteer?'
>
> *Burkhard Köttlitz, born 1929*

The SS organised elaborate advertising campaigns to attract boys into the *Waffen-SS*. These 'volunteers' did not always land up in Himmler's 'Black Order' of their own free will. The SS resorted to all kinds of subterfuge in order to lure the boys into their clutches. Ulrich Krüger, a medical orderly in the HJ, tells us about a health examination in which the boys were tested for TB. 'After they'd been through the X-ray, they went up to a desk and were given a form to fill in: "I hereby confirm that I have taken part in a screening examination, etc." Date, location, signature. But below the line was written in very small print: "I hereby state that I wish to volunteer for the *Waffen-SS*." So I thought to myself: It can't be true, you know, that these boys are being made to do something, willy-nilly, without being informed about it.' Lothar Schmitz is another who describes a recruitment event put on by the SS in the Reich Labour Service, where all was not as it seemed: 'They were handing out beer and sausages. Everything we wanted was there. Including application forms for the *Waffen-SS*. But that was all right, because they promised faithfully to anyone who didn't want to join: OK, you can join the navy or the cavalry or have an office job. Then they crossed out "Waffen-SS" with a pencil and wrote underneath the name of the chosen service. But I'm certain that it wasn't there ten minutes before they rubbed it out again.'

> One had an inner resistance to the *Waffen-SS*; somehow you knew that they were up to things which you wanted nothing to do with. Not that we had any precise knowledge of the facts which became known later – it was just an unconscious feeling of unease that we had.
>
> *Günther Adrian, born 1925*

The *Waffen-SS* was considered an elite unit. At the same time, because its numbers had been inflated to a full-sized army towards the end of the war, it had long since lost the character of an exclusive order. What is more, it was preceded by a reputation for the fanatical, even ruthless, way it fought the enemy. For this reason, in the rush to the flag, many boys preferred to volunteer for the Wehrmacht. That way they could choose the arm of the services they preferred, and would initially be taken in for training – and so escape the pursuit of the SS. Nevertheless, it would be wrong to say that all boys who joined the ranks of the SS were forced to do so. The promise of being allowed to be part of an elite made many a young heart beat faster. Albert Bastian received an invitation from the HJ to be examined as to his suitability for the HJ Patrol. But it was doctors from the *Waffen-SS* who examined him. 'When I went in, three or four men were sitting at a table, and one said to me: "A chap like you, tall, well-built, healthy – you'd be just right for the *Waffen-SS*. Wouldn't you like that?"

I swelled with pride. "Yes, of course I want to join the elite force", I said and clicked my heels.'

But when Bastian, beaming with pleasure, told his mother about his enrolment, her reaction was one of horror: 'My mother stared right through me; then tears rolled down her cheeks, and finally she burst into a rage: "But they're all criminals", she said. Then she went out, slamming the door behind her, and I heard her shouting in the courtyard: "They're only children. Have those men no respect left for anything?"' Albert Bastian's mother saw to it that her boy did not go into the SS. Others were not so fortunate.

> If you joined up as a volunteer, you didn't have to do labour service, and I certainly hadn't the slightest desire to do that. So I volunteered for the tank corps.
>
> *Bernhard Heisig, born 1925*

The only thing Artur Axmann had any respect for was the wishes of his Führer. The young were the 'miracle weapon' with which he wanted to impress Hitler. After the defeat of Stalingrad he saw his chance. 'For the first time in many years of war we asked ourselves if the war could still be won. We did not want to lose it. We could not remain in a state of inaction and lethargy. We had to act. The young generation in particular, who saw their future threatened, had to set a positive and encouraging example.' Axmann developed the hair-raising idea of forming an elite unit from Hitler Youth volunteers – as a birthday present for Hitler. A perverse gift indeed. 'It was to be a symbol of the spirit of sacrifice of German youth and an expression of their will to see things through', was how Kurt Meyer, known as 'Panzer-Meyer', justified the proposal. The SS *Brigadeführer* had become, on the death of his predecessor Fritz Witt, the youngest commander of the HJ Division at the age of thirty-three, and thus the youngest divisional commander in the Wehrmacht. After the war he was obliged to account to a war-crimes tribunal for the cold-blooded murder of dozens of Canadian prisoners by the division under his command.

Hitler was delighted to welcome the new division as a reinforcement of his fighting forces. On the other hand, Goebbels noted sceptically: 'It will surely be concluded from this that we are now drawing on our youth in order to find the manpower to wage our war.' In 1943 the 12th SS Panzer Division 'Hitlerjugend' was formed from sixteen- to eighteen-year-old *Hitlerjungen*. Their cadre was made up of officers and NCOs of the SS-*Leibstandarte* 'Adolf Hitler', the Führer's dashing elite troops. However, since there was a shortage of officers many platoon commanders were rapidly promoted to lead companies. *Hitlerjungen* who made their mark in the military preparation camps were briskly despatched on 3-month courses in the *Waffen-SS* school at Lauenburg and subsequently posted as NCOs in the Hitler Youth Division. Thus they had no more combat experience than those they were supposed to command. In addition, Wehrmacht officers who had served as HJ leaders were seconded to the division.

In the end a total of 20,000 'volunteers' was recruited directly from the military preparation camps. Although not all of them had joined the division of their own accord, but had in some cases been 'persuaded' to do so, as 'Panzer Meyer' cautiously put it, most of the boys were indeed fired with enthusiasm for the fray. Bernhard Heisig had actually applied for the Panzers. But when it came to the medical he found himself facing an SS officer: 'He only had one arm – obviously something which made a big impression on me – and he asked me: "Wouldn't you rather join *us*?" So I say: "I've already applied for the Panzers!" "Oh", he says, "we've got lots of tanks too – or have you got something against us?" That was the catch question. Of course I didn't have anything against them. So I said: "OK, why not?" We knew that those SS divisions were better equipped and better supplied.'

In fact the boys received a training – that under the circumstances of the time was pretty comprehensive – for up to one year at Beverloo in Belgium. Admittedly there was still a shortage of equipment. The *Hitlerjugend* Division initially had only four Panzer IV and four 'Panther' tanks at its disposal. To begin with the artillery regiment had to make do with light field howitzers, and they had almost no motor vehicles. Only towards the end of the war did the supply of matériel improve and the boys could carry out field manoeuvres as a division.

With time they were imbued with the feeling of belonging to an elite force. Whereas Bernhard Heisig felt insulted at first by the name 'Hitler Youth Division' because it reminded him of his days as a *Pimpf*, he later wore the armband with pride. 'We thought we were something special: we're special heroes, we're the best division in the Wehrmacht.' The first commanding officer of the unit known by the opposition as the 'Baby Division', was the 34-year-old SS *Brigadeführer* Fritz Witt. In June 1944 the unit was thrown in to the defence of the Normandy beaches. D-Day, standing for Decision-Day, or perhaps Dooms-day, was to prove to be a death-knell for the Hitler Youth Division as well.

When, in the early hours of 6 June 1944, the sun shed its pale light on the waves of the English Channel, the outline of a gigantic war fleet took threatening shape on the horizon. For those in the German observation-posts there could no longer be any doubt: the Allied landings had begun. As early as 3 a.m. the earth of Normandy had begun to quake. Thousands of Allied bombers and fighter-bombers released their deadly load. Acres of land were churned up. The coast was transformed into an inferno of explosion and fire. As dawn broke, from seawards heavy naval guns opened fire on the German positions. At 6.30 a.m. the first of over 4,000 landing craft hit the beach.

The surprise was complete. To the last Hitler had expected the assault to be mounted across the narrowest stretch of the Channel, between Dover and Calais. Even before he could be informed of the Allies' masterly move, the critical battle was already raging in Normandy. It became a slaughter for both sides; the coast was laced with massive emplacements of concrete and steel – a system of hundreds of bunkers, dug-outs and coastal batteries with heavy guns, barbed-wire entanglements, underwater obstacles and mine-fields. The Germans put up a bitter resistance against the crushingly superior forces of the attackers.

On that day the Hitler Youth Division was ordered into action. The Americans, British and Canadians on the beaches had to be 'thrown back into the sea'. All along the 75-mile route from the assembly area north-west of Paris to the battle-zone around Caen, Allied fighter-bombers were swooping down on the troops like hornets. Then heavy shells fired by warships offshore came whistling over the boys' heads. They suffered their first casualties.

In the next few days they had their baptism of fire: thick smoke, explosions, hungry tongues of flame, devastating artillery fire, tanks being blasted to smithereens. In their first action against the Canadians, troops of the 'Baby Division' knocked out twenty-eight tanks and only lost six of their own. In the days that followed every yard of ground around Caen, every village, was bitterly fought over by both sides. In an action involving tanks, artillery, shrieking multi-barrelled rocket launchers, grenade launchers, anti-tank mines, machine-guns and often hand-to-hand fighting, the boys of the Hitler Youth Division crept through the thick undergrowth or dug themselves into foxholes. The green and pleasant landscape of Normandy was transformed into a mass grave.

The war has not even spared our youth. They are in the very first line. They are performing with confidence at home, they are fighting on the Fronts. In inspired hearts lives and glows their faith in Germany.
*From an article, 'Faith of Youth – Guarantee of Victory', July 1944*

Yet the commitment of the *Hitlerjungen* was in vain. Against the overwhelming superiority of the Allies on land, at sea and in the air, they were powerless. In their heart of hearts the commanding officers knew: 'The war can now only be won by political means.' As early as 16 June 'Panzer Meyer' summed up the position thus: 'The division's casualties are considerable. In this situation one can already calculate on the division being completely wiped out.' Reinforcements had not yet arrived. The Division had to manage on its own. Yet the order came from Hitler: 'Caen is to be defended to the last shot.' The 12th SS Panzer Division 'Hitlerjugend' stayed in position – and on 30 June even managed to recapture from the British the strategically important Hill 112 outside Caen. At the beginning of July, after hard fighting and heavy losses, Kurt Meyer defied Hitler's orders and pulled his troops back to the south bank of the River Orne. The Allies took the town.

The fact that to Hitler the children were no more than human war material is made clear in a letter dated 21 July 1944 from Himmler to the Reich Labour Leader, Konstantin Hierl: 'Having learnt that the SS Panzer Division 'Hitlerjugend' had already lost 3,000 men, the Führer asked me what replacements I had . . . I informed the Führer that I would get in contact with the *Reichsjugendführer* with the object of getting him to provide, once again, a fairly large number of volunteers for the SS Panzer Division 'Hitlerjugend'. The *Reichsjugendführer* promised me 6,000 volunteers . . . The 'Hitlerjugend' Division now has casualties of 6,000, including 2,000 dead. The painful truth is that, at the lowest estimate, one third of the wounded are amputees, since most of the injuries have been caused by artillery and dive bombing. We must see to it that these divisions do not bleed to death totally, since they are – and this is a phrase I seldom use – in the truest sense decisive for the war.'

> The young were exploited; they were cannon-fodder driven into a war that was criminal in the first place, and then, in a way that made a mockery of all military principles, their lives were squandered.
>
> *Karl Kunze, born 1926*

The boys' pugnacity and willingness to die soon gave rise to myths surrounding the 'Children's Division', which built them up as Hitler's most fanatical fighters. How much is legend, how much true? Wolfgang Filor, a soldier in the *Waffen-SS* Panzer Division 'Das Reich', was then fighting alongside the *Hitlerjungen*: 'When we saw them fighting, first of all we thought: my God, now they're starting on the children. I myself, as it happened, was in the Saint-Lô sector; I had an American tank in my sights and was about to knock it out. To my horror a German soldier suddenly raised his *Panzerfaust* (grenade launcher) as a signal to hold our fire. Then the tank blew up and him with it. He had sacrificed his life. He had made a hole in the tank from underneath with his *Panzerfaust*. The kids were like that.'

Bernhard Heisig, who can only look back on his time in the HJ Division with anger and grief, tells us: 'Sometimes we saw the casualties as proof of how tough we were, how hard we could be pushed. That was a crazy ideology.' Yet he does not see himself and his comrades at the time as fanatical fighters: 'With people who are still half children, that's exactly what you can do. They run straight towards disaster, because the others are running. It's that lemming-like behaviour, where thinking is not required. At least not at that age.'

Nor does Wolfgang Filor see the boys as the glorious heroes that are still revered and celebrated today by SS veterans' organisations: 'All right, they were bigger heroes than us – through their stupidity and utter inexperience. If they'd spent any time at the Front, been wounded, seen the corpses, then they'd know what it's all about. I was shot up five times, the fifth time I wanted out of the Panzers. I sometimes wet my pants. It was that fear that made me recognise the dangers; most of the HJ Division didn't. They went bravely to their deaths because they hadn't thought about what could happen to them.'

> I just read the name 'Tiger Panzer' and wanted to join. I wanted to win a big medal as soon as possible with the Tiger Panzers. I dreamed about it all the time. So I went to my parents one evening and said: I'm volunteering for the HJ Division.
>
> *Günther Adrian, born 1925*

They were children who had been licked into shape for war and brought up to be heroes. The Battle of Normandy was a quasi-religious sacrifice. Within a month the Hitler Youth Division had forfeited a quarter of its strength. Half its tanks and armoured cars were gone. In July the division was granted a brief breathing-space. But six days later it was thrown back into the firing line, when the German positions between Maltot and Vendes threatened to collapse. In the Falaise Pocket the 12th SS Panzer Division 'Hitlerjugend' ended in a sea of blood and tears, after it had fought to keep open an escape corridor for thousands of German troops. In seven days the division lost about 1,000 men. Having been created after the Stalingrad debâcle, the 'Hitlerjugend' now had to live through a Stalingrad of its own. In autumn 1944, when the HJ Division got back to German territory once more, its numbers were reduced by half. Yet these child soldiers were by no means the youngest to be expended in this war.

The more clearly the end came in view, the more desperately the regime resorted to its youngest citizens. After the opening of the second front in the west, the armaments industry could not keep up with demand, and from the autumn of 1944, girls especially were obliged to leave whatever they were doing and go to help out. A 60-hour week was fixed by law for sixteen-year-olds. All the propaganda stops were pulled out in order to round up children for arms work. The film *Young Eagles*, which was shown to school classes and HJ units in 1944, depicted a group of apprentices doing additional night work of their own accord in order to reach production targets.

In the final phase of the Third Reich some six million young people were working in industry and agriculture, the majority in arms and munitions factories. For the functioning of Germany's war economy and for the continuation of the war, employment of the young was as important as that of the 7.5 million foreign workers and prisoners of war.

The Front moved ever nearer with menacing speed. In autumn 1944 the Americans were on the German border near Aachen and the Soviet troops were in the Baltic region. With a last desperate effort the regime tried to protect its borders from the onslaught of the enemy. Once again young children had to jump into the breach. In an emergency decree issued by the *Reichsjugendführung*, all available boys aged fifteen or over and girls aged sixteen or over were drafted from the arms industry and put on to trench-digging duties. Almost half a million youngsters, including 125,000 girls, had to work on dug-outs and gun emplacements and dig tank-traps.

Being so close to the Front, death showed its true face even to the youngest, since the trench-diggers were being attacked by Allied dive-bombers: 'The first dead German soldier I saw was lying on a dung-heap, with his chest bare and with his identity-disc. I thought to myself, now his company commander will write a letter to his mother saying: Your son died a hero's death for *Führer, Volk und Vaterland*. No-one will know that he was lying here on a dung-heap – those were the first sort of doubts that came into my mind.'

Trench-digging was gruelling work for the youngsters. In all kinds of weather the boys and girls stood in the mud and dug until their hands blistered. 'Digging foxholes was just about OK', recalls Theo Nicolai of his trench duties near Königsberg on the Baltic, 'but when it came to digging tank-traps, that was really hard graft. It was really tough, and there was no getting out of it.' Boys who ran away in desperation were pursued mercilessly and had to submit to brutal reprisals: 'They were beaten and sent straight back to the section where they had been digging before. Then they had their heads shaved. That was a great dishonour. In our eyes they were ostracised because we really believed we were fighting for Germany.'

In the construction of tank-traps, field emplacements and bunkers, on the '*Ostwall*' alone, in regions like East Prussia, Pomerania and Silesia, Hitler's young people shifted millions of cubic metres of earth. For this they received just one Reichsmark per day. Mothers at home were anything but thrilled about what their boys were having to do. Apart from anxiety about their children's safety, the Security Service (SD) also reported doubts as to the military usefulness of the trench work. The word on the street was: 'If not even the Atlantic Wall could hold, how ever can these earth ramparts and ditches?'

The Allies had reached the same conclusion. Even back in 1939 British soldiers had jokingly sung: 'We're going to hang out our washing on the Siegfried Line.' It would not be long before Anglo-Saxon laundry would be fluttering in the wind from Kleve on the Lower Rhine, to the Swiss frontier.

Even as the Third Reich lay in its death agony, Hitler's henchmen showed no mercy towards the young. 'Germany has secret weapons at its disposal. One of the greatest of these weapons is a youth educated in National Socialism by the Führer', Axmann had once said. Brought up by an inhuman regime to be cogs in a machine, the youth were now expected to function smoothly, no matter what the assignment. One event in Soltau brings these circumstances vividly and tragically to life.

The small town on the Lüneberg Heath was notable for two reasons. Firstly it was a rail junction: one of three main routes from Hamburg southward intersected here with the important east–west line from Bremen to Berlin. Secondly, Soltau was only a few miles from two concentration camps, Bergen-Belsen and Westerbork. For years the people of Soltau had watched goods trains passing through, laden with people, either bound for the east or for Bergen-Belsen. As one witness tells us: 'All kinds of rumours were flying around. Goods trains run through Soltau at night, you know, and you see people looking through the gaps at the top, you see faces.'

In the final days before the end of the war the shipments of human cargo became more frequent. But now they were arriving from the east. These were the inmates of concentration camps abandoned as the battle-front approached, and who were being transferred to the west. When attacked by bombers the trains stopped. So it was that at noon on 11 April 1945 British pilots dropped about 200 bombs on Soltau. A train carrying concentration camp victims came to a halt and, as the guards took cover, the prisoners were able to escape. Where the train had come from and where it was heading, no-one knew. The inhabitants of Soltau were afraid of the prisoners, afraid of looting and the spread of disease. The good citizens had been told again and again that concentration camp inmates were criminals. On that day a group of Soltau's *Hitlerjungen* were given the order to recapture the now completely exhausted prisoners. It is no longer possible to establish who gave the order – it may have been the local army commander.

'So at least 40 or 50 *Hitlerjungen* were detailed off for this unpleasant task', one of them tells us. 'Towards evening we had rounded up about seventy prisoners. They were taken to the edge of town and kept under guard by us *Hitlerjungen*, who were armed. The shootings began as it got dark. The prisoners were made to stand in rows and then we were given the order to shoot those poor, wretched people. Obviously, at the age of seventeen, we felt that something dreadful and wrong was happening.' Overcome by emotion, our interviewee broke down in tears at the memory of this ghastly occurrence.

This *Hitlerjunge*, in great distress, went the same night with his father to the local Party headquarters. 'There we spoke to two top officials, and my father asked them: "Why was this asked of the children? Why them, of all people?" The laconic reply was: "We want to educate the young to be tougher and not to shy away from any horror." The next morning the executions were resumed.'

The dishonest education system had the effect that even in such extreme situations the boys never questioned their leaders. After years of brainwashing they were expected simply to function without thinking. 'The order was all that mattered', admits the former *Hitlerjunge* from Soltau. 'In those days I would have got myself shot for *Führer, Volk und Vaterland*. Even in small matters orders were all-important in the Hitler Youth. If orders were given, they had to be carried out.'

Only a few days later the British marched into Soltau and discovered the prisoners in their mass grave. In front of newsreel cameras they forced the people of Soltau to disinter the corpses. About 90 dead bodies were found in and around Soltau. Today a simple memorial recalls their suffering.

Only one of the shootings led to a conviction before a war-crimes tribunal. The defendant was sentenced to five years imprisonment. The chief culprits could not be identified. The *Hitlerjungen* who were actively involved in the shootings are left with the memory of the horror which for nearly all of them is rooted in recurring nightmares. Their exceptionally terrible story showed once again what became of Hitler's children during Hitler's war: they were victims and perpetrators at the same time.

# CHAPTER 5

# SACRIFICE

## KNOPP/BRAUBURGER

Through their deeds, the young want to show themselves
worthy of the Führer's trust. The great majority of those
born in 1928 have volunteered to serve the flag and, in the
sixth year of the war, have reached the highest level of
volunteering so far. They have thus shown evidence of their
willingness to fight and thereby given great pleasure to the
Führer.

*Artur Axmann, Reichsjugendführer, 1945*

We tied the Panzerfaust grenade launchers to our bikes,
as though we were strapping on our rucksacks for an
outing. We jumped on to our bikes and headed off to the
battle-zone, always trying to get into action as quickly as
possible.

*Werner Hanitzsch, born 1929*

It is my wish that the young recruits born in 1928, the
youngest and most valuable of our youth which the nation
has under arms, be treated with every consideration . . .
I urge that intelligent supervision be applied in order to
ensure that recruits who are non-smokers are not taught to
smoke through the issuing of cigarettes.

*Heinrich Himmler, 1945*

My longing for action was extraordinarily great, and I was glad that I was finally being used to drive out the evil enemy. My blinkering and indoctrination by the state had achieved their purpose. I wasn't in a position to make a realistic evaluation of the facts. Our chests swelling with pride and armed to the teeth, we set off.

*Werner Hanitzsch, born 1929*

The SS Panzer Division 'Hitlerjugend' which has been sent into action in the west has proved itself heroically and after a brief spell of fighting has already earned the recognition of the Führer. Contrary to the concerns of many, that a division comprised only of young soldiers with no experience of the front line would not be up to the demands placed upon it, the HJ Division has proved that it knows how to fight with heroism.

*Recruitment advertising for the SS Panzer Division 'Hitlerjugend', 1944*

The Hitler Youth has a fine spirit. Within six weeks the *Gau* of Franconia has established a regiment of anti-tank troops of the HJ. So far they have fought superbly on various fronts. However, it is a great pity to see this young and precious blood being shed in such battles. One battalion has already been nearly wiped out.

*Situation report from the Gau of Franconia, 1945*

The bulk of the boys will still be physically unable to withstand the principal strains of war – hunger, lack of sleep and abnormal physical exertion. On military duty serious damage to their health is bound to occur, which throws doubt on any fully active deployment later on.

*General Siegfried Westphal, Chief of Staff to the Commander-in-Chief West, 1944*

The position had been abandoned. The soldiers and boy-soldiers, demoralised by the earlier rocket-attacks and the tanks, must have fled in sheer panic. Apparently this often happened with poorly trained beginners. I would have run as well, of course, but had missed my chance and now knew that to be too far forward or to one side was not to be recommended either.

*Wolfgang von Buch, born 1928*

The enemy stands in our homeland and is directly threatening our lives. Rather than let ourselves be annihilated or enslaved, we will fight hard and doggedly until the final victory. Those born in 1929 will receive a long-term, varied and conscientious training. This training will later combine with their courageous conduct to give them superiority over the enemy.

*Artur Axmann, Reichsjugendführer, 1945*

I was sixteen. I had no insight whatever, no overview of events, no understanding and no experience. I was a frightened child when all that was going on. And in that situation you feel most comfortable in the herd, in your own group. Everyone's doing the same thing. You get told what to do – of all the possibilities open to us, this was the best, or so it seemed at the time.

*Hans-Rudolf Vitter, born 1929*

I die with a joyful heart in the knowledge of the inestimable deeds and achievements of our soldiers at the Front, of our women at home and of the historically unique contribution of our youth, who bear my name.

*Adolf Hitler, 29 April 1945*

We were sitting in the bunker and heard about Hitler's end; it's something I'll never forget. A world collapsed then. The news was that Hitler had died outside the bunker of the Reich Chancellery, apparently at the head of his troops in a heroic battle for Berlin. Well, that left us with a feeling of emptiness – the Führer had fallen.

*Lothar Loewe, born 1928*

❖ ❖ ❖

The war was entering its sixth year. For a long time the German Reich had lain in its death agony. Yet the warlords could only conceive of total victory or total defeat. From the autumn of 1944 onwards the death-rate in the Wehrmacht rose to 5,000 men per day. With the child-soldiers of the Hitler Youth the dictator was mobilising his very last reserves. In 1944–5 over two million young men aged from seventeen to twenty-five were enlisted with the Wehrmacht or the *Waffen-SS*. In the months before capitulation hundreds of thousands more fifteen- and sixteen-year-olds were drafted in to fill the depleted ranks. Sometimes boys who were not yet fourteen were involved in the fighting, and to begin with actually enjoyed the deadly 'field-games' of the war.

The regime's 'man-catchers', whether it was Goebbels the propaganda minister, Himmler the SS boss, or the *Reichsjugendführer* Artur Axmann, all extolled the dreadful bloodshed as an epic of martial heroism. Axmann did more than evoke the mystic celebrations of the solstice, which had long been an article of Nazi faith: 'We intend to obey the law of battle. In the world of plants and creatures there is no life without struggle. That which is weak falls, that which is strong survives. Vital energy is the morality of nature.' In the crazed world of the Hitler regime there was only victory or defeat. And if at the end the Führer himself should pass away, then the German people, seeming to be unworthy of him, would immediately have to follow him – the morbid cynicism of the senior warlords no longer knew any bounds.

The sacrifice of children is one of the last criminal chapters in the war that Hitler unleashed. As the former flak auxiliary, Gerhard

Häfner, sums it up: 'The youth were sacrificed or, in their blindness, let themselves be sacrificed, at a time when the war had long been lost, simply to allow their Führer to live a few days longer.'

The clarion-call to the last contingent was given in October 1944 as under cover of darkness posters were nailed on trees, ruined houses and wooden fences throughout the Reich. On the morning of 19 October Germans read the latest decree from their Führer: 'In the *Gaue* of the Greater German Reich the German *Volkssturm* is to be formed from all men aged from sixteen to sixty years, who are capable of bearing arms. It will defend our home soil with all weapons and means.' It was a final stand, making use of the last available reserves and a time-honoured image of the enemy. 'The known intention of our Jewish-international enemies to destroy us totally, must be opposed by the total engagement of all German people.'

It was the 131st anniversary of the Battle of the Nations at Leipzig, against Napoleon. 'Just as in those days of the War of Liberation', declared Heinrich Himmler, who held military responsibility for the civilian reserves, 'the *Volkssturm* today has the task of engaging the enemy with fanaticism and if possible wiping him out, wherever he steps on to the soil of our homeland.' Since those in charge of the 'total war' effort had already combed the population several times in search of final reserves, and since all those men fit for combat and who could be spared from other duties in the Reich had been fighting for some time at the Front, this call could only be meant for those who for good reason had been spared from active service, namely the old, the injured, women and especially boys.

In fact this summons amounted to a confession of military impotence. Was this to be the 'vengeance' which had been portentously proclaimed in Nazi propaganda – a last 'contingent of the halt and the lame, children and old men'? as Hitler's opponents mocked. However, the Nazi newspaper, the *Völkischer Beobachter*, praised the decision as the 'greatest, proudest and most uplifting act of valour that Germany has ever been capable of'.

The regime could rely on the young, or more precisely on the willing self-sacrifice to which they had been educated. 'To die for *Führer, Volk und Vaterland* was after all an honour and a duty –

that's what we had been taught.' Hundreds of interviewees give this as the reason why they went uncomplainingly into that senseless battle. This was the fruit brought forth by the seeds of monopolisation and indoctrination from childhood onward.

The cult of sacrifice had in fact been a continuing ritual of the Hitler Youth ever since its foundation. How often had boys marched in silent groups past bowls of guttering flame, or paraded by torchlight in front of memorials; how often had they sung patriotic songs with feeling or watched free movies about German martyrdom, listened to heroic medieval sagas at historical gatherings or the hymn to the sacrifice of young warriors at Langemark in the autumn of 1914? How often had they rehearsed for war in the field and yet knew nothing of what it was to be in a real battle?

The *Volkssturm* was admittedly an auxiliary arm of the Wehrmacht, but because the Nazi leadership had mistrusted the General Staff since the attempt on Hitler's life by army officers on 20 July 1944, the Party was to exercise control over it. 'In each *Gau* the *Gauleiter* will take responsibility for the establishment and leadership of the *Volkssturm*', the order read. It was the *Gauleiter* who, as local 'Reich Defence Commissioners', had ever greater influence on the conduct of the war.

The man with political and organisational responsibility for the *Volkssturm* throughout the Reich was Hitler's *éminence grise*, Martin Bormann. But the 'People's Battalions' were under the military authority of the new commander of the reserve army, Himmler. This hybrid position – half Party, half military – led to power struggles at the expense of the young.

Anyone who did not join the *Volkssturm* could be recruited directly by the Wehrmacht or the *Waffen-SS*. Both were becoming dependent on an ever younger intake, as the strength of their armies bled away. When Hitler's Germany invaded Poland the youngest men enlisted were nineteen- and twenty-year-olds, born in 1918 or 1919; from 1943 onward seventeen-year-olds were called up for the Wehrmacht. In 1944, and even more so in 1945, those with birth-dates in 1928 and 1929, which meant some sixteen-year-olds, were liable for service. During the last turbulent weeks of the war, in many places *Hitlerjungen* aged only twelve were fighting, admittedly not under express military orders – in their blind loyalty most of them had gone into battle voluntarily.

What motivated us at the time? Perhaps a little bit of pride. But we didn't race into the army with banners flying, as our fathers had apparently done in 1914. In short, we weren't filled with enthusiasm or patriotism. Was it a feeling that the final victory could only be won through and with us? No. I think that what marked us out then was scepticism and fear.

*Hans-Rudolf Vilter, born 1929*

The year 1944 had been declared by Axmann to be the 'Year of the Volunteer'. He sent out his best public speakers to promote enlistment in the Wehrmacht at ceremonial rallies. To begin with the volunteers were accorded special honour: at their first inspection they were saluted respectfully, they received a special document and a lanyard on the shoulder-strap of their HJ uniform; on parade they stood in the front rank. Later, all that went. As soon as they were inside the barracks, the drill started. 'There was endless shouting. We were totally exhausted and were hassled and bullied until we didn't know whether we were coming or going', the comedian Dieter Hildebrandt remembers.

Often entire Hitler Youth groups enlisted together. Anyone who refused was immediately labelled a coward. 'In our lot, no-one would have thought of dropping out. That wouldn't even enter our heads.' Many of our witnesses gave similar evidence. The war-weary soldiery shook their heads sadly at the heroic hype surrounding this recruitment sweep, seeing their youthful reinforcements as no more than 'prolonging the war' and 'suicide candidates'. But in fact many of these adolescents went off to war with enthusiasm. Quite a few even feared that it would all be over before they could prove themselves as soldiers. 'We were just stuffed with propaganda, and we knew we had to win. "You lads have been specially chosen for this", they said.' Those are the words of Johannes Schröder, who was thrown into the Battle of the Bulge.

For many there was the lure of heroic self-sacrifice for the apparently good cause of 'the Fatherland'. But 'what kind of Fatherland was it?' asks Reinhard Appel, who was eighteen at the time. 'They only realised later that what they were sacrificing themselves for was a criminal regime.' But most people saw things differently: 'We did not doubt for one minute that the war was a just one. We were taught that life was a continual struggle, a nation must fight to survive, and we were under threat.' The national community meant 'everything', you yourself were 'nothing'. One of the typical slogans on the walls of Hitler Youth hostels read: 'We were born to die for Germany.'

> I was just a very ordinary kid, obedient, docile, compliant, someone who never kicked over the traces, wasn't ambitious or a rebel either, just a tiny dot in the mass of brown, ready for duty at all times, available and, ultimately, willing to die.
> *Dietrich Strothmann, born 1927*

Nevertheless, the attitude of youth to the war varied greatly, depending on when and where one saw service. Many young men in the east heard from refugees or saw on newsreels the cruel impact of the war on the people in whose name it had been unleashed. Meanwhile, the deliberately well-circulated reports of atrocities, murders and mass rapes by Soviet troops in places like Nemmersdorf in East Prussia or Lauban in Silesia spread like wildfire. Many youngsters now simply believed they had to act in self-defence: 'We had only one thing in our minds: to protect our mothers and sisters from the Russian soldiers.' Nazi propaganda was quick to exploit such motivation – it was necessary to mobilise fresh forces in order to delay a little longer the fall of the Nazi regime.

Those who had doubts about a successful military outcome were branded by the propaganda as traitors, 'creatures who undermine our struggle for life, deadly enemies of the people.' They 'deserve the bullet or the gallows. Anyone who believes he can resist the national imperative will fall.' In the end even children were sent into battle at gunpoint or under threat of the death penalty; the guardians of the 'sacred national war' knew no mercy.

Whether convinced of victory or soberly realistic – it was a strange procession which arrived at the recruitment office, in the barracks and finally on the battlefield: white-haired men and downy-faced youths – war-wounded, students and schoolboys.

As soon as the recruits were handed their yellow armbands with the words *Deutsche Volkssturm – Wehrmacht*, and a pay-book, they were 'soldiers within the meaning of military law'. This meant that they enjoyed the protection of the 1907 Hague Convention on war. As combatants they were formally protected, if taken prisoner, from being summarily shot – as distinct from partisans, who could be. The western Allies recognised the status of the *Volkssturm* as soldiers, in October 1944. However, it would be of little help to those taken prisoner in the east. Accounts of acts of extreme brutality or the summary execution of *Volkssturm* men by the Red Army spread like the wind. Thus many were driven by fear to choose enlistment with the regular army or the *Waffen-SS*.

But there were other reasons as well: there was no question of providing the *Volkssturm* with adequate weaponry. The Nazi leadership quickly realised they did not have the capacity to equip the new million-strong army effectively for battle. The large-scale purchase of black market arms and ammunition from Italy was considered, but until that happened the men of the *Volkssturm* would have to make do with captured weapons. These were jealously hoarded by the regular troops; the same was true of uniforms and other necessary equipment. As a result there was frequent reference to a government directive of October 1944, under which 'the establishment of the *Volkssturm* must not cause either weapons, articles of clothing or items of equipment to be withheld from the active Wehrmacht'. In all this the impression was bound to arise that the front line soldiers set no great store by their young auxiliary riflemen. After all, these poorly armed men of the *Volkssturm* in their disreputable civilian clothes were not fully fledged 'brothers in arms'. The 'last contingent' were presented with ridiculously outmoded equipment, some of which dated back to the nineteenth century. The boys took up their positions at the Front fitted out with carbines and a handful of cartridges. It is true that thanks to their 'military preparation' many knew how to handle a gun, but their experience of battle was non-existent.

> We scarcely had time to introduce them to the most basic essentials of the Front, and I hardly managed to memorise their names – because we could be pretty sure that by noon the next day most of them would no longer be alive.
>
> *Hans-Günther Stark, Wehrmacht officer, born 1929*

The grandiosely heralded 'fight to the last drop of blood' began for many with service in the supply or transport corps, went on to construction and trench-digging work and ended with the guarding of frontier and fortified emplacements as well as the defence of towns, villages and individual installations. The 'last reserve' was also deployed in mine-clearing units. However, in the middle of 1944 a massive slaughter began on the Fronts, thousands of adolescents went through their baptism of fire, and many did not survive their first action. 'The flag means more than death' – under this watchword the youth were sacrificed, whether in the Battle of Normandy, in Hitler's last offensive in the Ardennes, in the 'emergency battalions' which were supposed to defend the Oder breach against the Red Army, in the defence of the 'fortress cities' to the rear of the front line – such as Königsberg or Breslau – or finally in the battle for Hitler's centre of power, Berlin, where child-soldiers had to remain in their positions when Hitler's paladins were already making their getaway or else – like their Führer – taking steps to remove themselves through suicide from the responsibility for millions of deaths.

There are people who survived in all these theatres of war and who have told us of their experiences. They bear witness to the fate of a youth misused, of a senseless sacrifice in the dying days of a criminally inspired war. Their statements reflect the destiny of an entire generation. Their faces show what it meant for youngsters, either driven by fear or blinded by propaganda, to kill and die for *Führer, Volk und Vaterland*.

> Their mothers came up to me and said: please look after our kids! I retorted: What do you think this is? Take them back home with you! They replied in terror: No, we can't do that. We'd be shot.
>
> *Willi Rabe, Wehrmacht officer, born 1925*

The long farewell began with a battle which was actually intended to turn the war in Germany's favour: Hitler's last offensive in the Ardennes. It was to have turned the wheel of history back once more. 'Fortress Europe' had failed, in June 1944, to withstand the onslaught of the Allied invasion forces. The German Army Group West had been swept back from the Atlantic to the borders of the Reich. Hitler's orders had been to throw the enemy troops back into the sea. Now the 'fate of the German people' would be decided in the Ardennes. In early December, almost unnoticed, the German High Command brought up a powerful force of 250,000 soldiers, armed with tanks and artillery, to positions along the edge of the Eifel mountains. The last reserves of the Wehrmacht were mobilised for this battle, while to the rear the elderly men and boys of the *Volkssturm* plugged the gaps in the German army. The self-appointed 'supreme warlord' had decided to gamble everything on a single card.

Two seventeen-year-old *Hitlerjungen* who had joined the Wehrmacht as volunteers, Johannes Schröder and Günther Münz, barely escaped with their lives in this mid-winter battle. Like many boys of their age, they had first had to watch their comrades being killed in droves. Then they themselves were wounded. Johannes Schröder received a bullet in the head, and on Christmas Day Günther Münz lost a leg. Both were lucky; they survived – Schröder with the help of an American orderly. '*Hitlerjungen*, heroism, final victory? You must be joking. That's when I learned how to cry', says Günther Münz.

The Nazi newsreel for December 1944 spoke only of victory, and showed the beaming lads on their way to battle. 'The song died on my lips as we set off', says Münz. 'We were told: "It's your age-group that will turn things round, you've been called on to do it . . ." We *had* to win. Whether we wanted to or not – we couldn't pull out of it', recalls Johannes Schröder.

On the morning of 16 December the conditions were just what the German High Command had been hoping for to cloak their attack: 'Führer's weather' – a low cloud-base and fog made it impossible for the Allied air forces to get their fighters and bombers into the air. At 0630 no fewer than 3,400 guns opened a murderous, non-stop barrage along a 70-mile front. It took the Americans by surprise. In Germany the Reich radio gratefully seized on the news from the first day of battle and in its usual pompous way announced the 'rapid collapse of Allied resistance'. Yet the early successes were principally attributable to the fact that western air power could not be deployed due to the low cloud cover.

At Christmas all hell broke out. As Münz describes it: 'It was a still, clear night. We were starving and dead tired. I didn't even want to think about Christmas Eve, and fell asleep from exhaustion. Then the bombers came. There were explosions all around me. Bombs making craters everywhere. Then a terrible, penetrating pain, and the blood was kind of shooting out. One of my legs had been shattered, and I stopped the flow of blood by holding my trouser-leg tight at the bottom.'

> *Hitlerjungen*, just kids, were literally jumping at tanks with their grenade launchers. My God, how they were mown down . . . Beside a wrecked tank on the road lay a heap of dead or dying kids in their brown uniforms. One was crawling round in circles. His face was nothing but a mass of blood . . .
>
> *Gerd Häfner, born 1928*

Film taken by US army cameras shows the fear on the faces of the young German soldiers taken prisoner. They look like utterly confused and helpless children. Meanwhile, the Nazis' Christmas newsreel transformed the horror of the Front into an idyll with shots of soldiers handing out presents to children. The cynicism still disgusts those who survived. 'Forget Christmas; it was the worst day of my life!' says Münz. 'What were they doing to us?'

At one spot on the edge of the battle, peace made a brief appearance. On Christmas Eve two young American soldiers with a wounded comrade were wandering through the Hürtgen Forest, having lost contact with their unit. They knocked on the door of a farmhouse, and it was opened by the farmer's wife. She saw that one of the GIs was wounded and tended him. To celebrate the festival a Christmas dinner of goose was prepared. Suddenly, there was another knock at the door. This time four young German soldiers were standing in the snow. The woman said: 'You can come in but we have visitors who you may not look on as friends.' 'Why, who's in there?' snapped the NCO leading the group. 'Americans.' Grim looks all round. But before the young men could reach for their guns, the woman said with a disarming forthrightness: 'Listen to me. You are young enough to be my sons. So are the ones indoors. One of them is wounded and fighting for his life. And his comrades are just as tired and hungry as you are. Tonight of all nights, let's not think about killing.' For a few moments there was silence. In the end they all sat down peaceably around the table and sang Christmas carols. The following day the Germans showed the Americans the way back to their unit.

I found it extraordinarily depressing psychologically to see how these young people broke down emotionally, when the fighting virtually became hand to hand. Many of them were weeping, screaming, running away and – something which affected me deeply – crying for their mothers.

*Hans-Günther Stark, Wehrmacht officer, born 1921*

By now the German withdrawal had begun. The second retreat from the Ardennes within a few months revealed once again the absurdity of Hitler's conduct of the war. The German armies pulled back to their old positions. Johannes Schröder was lying in a dugout in the forest when he heard the deafening noise of engines. 'There were fourteen of us against 100 tanks. What hope did we have? Near me, one man dropped after another. The guy next to me in the trench got a bullet in the neck and I was shot in the head.' His comrades thought Schröder was dead and left him lying there. But American medical orderlies rescued the severely wounded boy. 'He's just a baby', said the nurses in the field hospital when Schröder 'came back to life' after an operation on his head.

More than 60,000 German and Allied soldiers lost their lives in the Ardennes. For many young Germans captured by the Americans, imprisonment in camps across the Atlantic was an eye-opener. 'Gradually we found out what had been done in all our names. There were many moments when I was ashamed to be German', Schröder says. At home in the Eifel, his relatives held a memorial service for him in March 1945. But as they were coming out of the church the postman beckoned to them; he had a letter from the United States. 'Our boy's alive!' The portrait of the deceased, which the family had had printed for the requiem, showed the child-soldier for whom a second life was now beginning. He had been lucky. But Schröder is still filled with anger. 'Throwing fourteen- and fifteen-year-olds into battle was criminal. They were walking over corpses.'

Even after the Ardennes offensive had failed the propaganda of the Nazi regime continued untiringly to conjure up a final victory with hollow phrases: 'We have put a year behind us that is unique in German history', declared Reich Minister Goebbels in his Christmas address. 'In this war the German people are showing a degree of moral stamina which can only earn admiration. It is the guarantee of the victory which will eventually come.'

And yet the propaganda seemed unwilling to trust its own slogans. The Red Army had long since crossed the frontiers of the Reich. With a commentary containing tirades of hate, Goebbels' newsreels repeatedly showed appalling images of Soviet brutality in some German villages that had been temporarily recaptured by the Wehrmacht. Mutilated corpses, women who had been raped, whole families slaughtered in the devastated rooms of their homes.

These pictures were certainly not faked. 'Revenge' was the battle-cry – for example, in the rousing poems of Ilya Ehrenburg. Many Soviet units made this their business, especially in the first weeks – revenge for the millions murdered in their homeland. However, it was these excesses by the Red Army which unwittingly helped to mobilise Germany's child-soldiers: 'I went into a school and behind the door I saw a woman lying smeared with blood, her legs splayed. She had literally been raped to death, and her husband was lying in the hall, shot through the neck', remembers Theo Nicolai, who was just sixteen at the time. 'When you saw that, the hate rose in you, and you could have massacred those responsible without hesitation.'

'Just let those Russians come; they'll learn a thing or two', *Hitlerjunge* Martin Bergau had overconfidently thought, when he heard the din of battle for the first time as the Front approached Königsberg. The Red Army was now on German territory and was spreading alarm and terror. The essential motive for those who volunteered to defend the Eastern Front was to protect their own families from the violence of the intruders. 'We really felt it was a matter of life and death.'

> I wanted to fling a grenade at the first Russians I saw. But then an experienced sergeant dragged me back and shouted: Are you crazy or what!?! You'll get us all killed! Then he hoisted a flag and we surrendered. If it hadn't been for him, I probably wouldn't be alive today.
>
> *Reinhard Appel, born 1927*

In the winter of 1944–5 it was the 'fortress cities' which were intended to act as bastions protecting the homeland. The knell was sounded with the battles for Königsberg and Breslau. Right on cue for the start of this struggle for survival, a spectacular colour film was completed, which was mainly aimed at impressing the young. Its title was *Kolberg* and it glorified the victorious stand of the citizens of this Pomeranian city, besieged by the French in the Napoleonic War. Just as they had then, the fortress cities now had to hold out against the Soviet troops. The film was full of resounding phrases like: 'You have a duty to defend and to die' or 'There is always pain in bringing forth greatness'.

Officially, the task was to secure lines of retreat for the hordes of refugees on the move as well as to hold off the onslaught of enemy forces on the Reich. But in the final weeks of 'total war' it was the army commanders, with their overestimation of their own abilities, their ideological obtuseness and their obedience no matter what the cost, who were to blame for the fact that so many more people were driven to their deaths.

A tragic example of this was Königsberg, the easternmost 'fortress' of Hitler's Reich (now Kaliningrad, the Russian enclave on the Baltic). It was the seat of the fanatical *Gauleiter* of East Prussia, Erich Koch. In the last days of January 1945 the besieging Russians completely encircled the old royal city. Fear spread among the population, from mouth to mouth went to the most incredible rumours about Soviet brutality. Königsberg tried to huddle down under the continuous Russian artillery barrage. More than 100,000 civilians as well as some 15,000 foreign forced labourers took cover behind makeshift tank-barriers, in hurriedly dug trenches and foxholes and at fortified street intersections.

Everything they needed to defend themselves was lacking: heavy weapons, light artillery, ammunition and trained personnel. Patrols in search of deserters combed through the burnt-out houses, the cellars half-filled with rubble and the overcrowded shelters. On the streets the lack of anti-aircraft defence meant that every step was taken at the risk of being killed by dive-bombers.

And yet a former *Hitlerjunge* remembers it in this way: 'It was obvious to us that we had to defend Königsberg. We weren't in the slightest doubt about that. It was our homeland', Erich Schwarz tells us. 'The film *Kolberg* raised our spirits. If you can hold out as they did then, the film told us, then victory is yours. And we believed it.'

Whenever a film was *not* a propaganda tool, then going to the cinema at all presented obstacles. 'One time a romantic film starring Heinz Rühmann was showing and we queued up with the other soldiers. Then our passes were checked and we were promptly shown the door. It was an "adults only" film and we weren't allowed in. But getting ourselves shot for the Fatherland, that was OK, of course.'

> It was a mad game of numbers. All these boys had been
> sent to war, simply so that Hitler could be told that we had
> x number of divisions and that these divisions each had
> such-and-such a number of fighting men.
> *Hans-Günther Stark, Wehrmacht officer, born 1921*

In Königsberg, as in many other parts of the Reich, the field gendarmerie searched houses again and again for potential soldiers to fill the thinned-out ranks at the Front. Sometimes the basic military training of the young recruits lasted only a few hours. Often it was not only the *Hitlerjungen* who stood helplessly in the advance positions, but also the soldiers they had been put alongside. 'The Russian barrage on Königsberg was incredible. Even the old stagers had never known anything like it. The youngest kids who were with us in the trenches – one was twelve and two were fourteen – screamed "help" and "Mum". Then the infantrymen were howling and bawling at us: "Chuck those kids out of the trenches!" It was a shambles', Theo Nicolai tells us.

Hans-Günther Stark was commanding a local group of *Hitlerjungen*. 'Whenever we recruited a few more of the lads, I said: "Write down all your personal details for me", because we had to assume that by the following noon most of them would be dead. It was completely insane to send young people like that into the front line. It was verging on the criminal. Basically, there was no way you could justify it.' In that case, why had he allowed them to go into battle? 'One way or another, we had to do something to maintain at least the hint of a defensive capability.' Many officers found themselves under similar compulsion, which is why thousands of boy-soldiers died right up to the final day of the war.

Erich Schwarz from Königsberg survived the murderous battle because he lost all illusions just in time: 'I had an important message to deliver: level four alert. I went down to see the acting battalion CO in his command-post. There I found him with a glass of wine in one hand and the other arm round a Russian girl. I thought: What's he up to? That's racial misbehaviour – or something like that. And then he bawled at me: "Whadda you want? Why aren't you up top with the others? I'll have you shot!" So I ran for it and said to myself: "Nope. That's it. I'm not doing this any more!" I went home and said to my mother: "I'm quitting the *Volkssturm*." She was very pleased. I changed out of my uniform and threw it in the bin, and I was a little boy again.'

Others who wanted to get away from the senseless dying, paid with their lives. While Erich Schwarz was going home to his mother, some young soldiers were hanged at Königsberg's North Station, as alleged deserters.

Siegfried Jankowsky, who was born in 1928, was the son of a local official of the Nazi Party in Königsberg. He had had a strict National Socialist upbringing and since the end of 1944 had been a member of the *Volkssturm*. Although older soldiers warned him that the war had been lost long ago, he and his comrades continued to believe in victory. 'We were the hundred-percenters', he admits. 'We were still singing "Victory will be ours".' But then one of his friends was so badly maimed by an artillery shell that Siegfried lost all desire for a final heroic struggle.

The propaganda machine rolled into action against any form of defeatism, and in the process all connection with reality was lost. 'It gives us pleasure and creates a mood of confidence to see how Königsberg is being defended. The composure and calmness of the people radiates security', wrote the *Völkischer Beobachter* as late as the beginning of April 1945.

On 6 April the destruction of the Baltic city reached a crescendo. The besieging Soviet army opened fire with every barrel on the beleaguered citizens. The *Gauleiter* Erich Koch had resigned a few days earlier. But in telegrams to Hitler he continued to make a pretence of holding out unflinchingly in the Königsberg pocket. Some of the trapped German troops managed to break out and reach the Baltic port of Pillau. Some *Hitlerjungen* were withdrawn by this route. They were intended to survive in order to be available for the final defence of Berlin.

Not far from Königsberg, in Palmnicken, the *Hitlerjungen* who were located there had to take part in a 'special' assignment. 'We went to the mayor's office', Martin Bergau tells us. 'There were three SS men there, disguised in other uniforms. They looked sinister and didn't say a word. Right from the start I didn't like them. Then it gradually dawned on me. These three men were going to take us somewhere. On a special assignment. We had been selected – at least that was the feeling I had – for something very special. Then everything began to happen very fast. Some Jewish women were made to line up in two ranks, and us *Hitlerjungen* in the *Volkssturm* had to escort them.'

The column was taken to a quarry near the sea. 'They had to kneel down beside a trench that was already full of bodies. Then they were killed with a bullet in the neck. Many of them gave a death-rattle, their last dying gasp. I saw it all happen. I even saw a boy putting some of them out of their agony with a carbine. Maybe then he could say one day: at least I didn't shoot *at* them, those Jews.

'Then I went home – feeling ashamed and wretched. I heard the rumbling from the front. What will become of us now? Obviously, when the Russians get here we will have to defend ourselves. To the bitter end. They'll kill us all; we're all guilty.'

That was how many *Hitlerjungen* became accessories and accomplices in the crimes of the regime – the greater their fear of revenge by their opponents, the more determined they were to go on fighting. Goebbels' minions in the east were able to make capital out of this. Breslau, the capital of Silesia, was vaunted by propaganda as a bulwark against the 'dehumanised Bolshevist hordes'. Until well into the last year of the war the city had not had to suffer a single air raid. Yet the Front was coming inexorably closer.

Anxious suspicions seized the townspeople when, on 21 January 1945, the *Gauleiter*, Karl Hanke, declared Breslau a 'fortress': in order to tie up enemy troops the city had to be held at all costs. This fateful decision was the first step on the way to large-scale destruction. In the three months that followed it was this fanatical obsession with defending it, rather than enemy fire, which turned the 'Pearl of Silesia' into a mass of rubble. Holidaymakers, business travellers, the sick and the wounded, were all recruited as soon as they set foot on the station platform. Everyone available ended up in the *Volkssturm*, including the Hitler Youth. Christian Lüdke has particular memories of the day he was drafted: 'I went to my mother and said: "I'm a soldier now." The first thing she said was: "My God, now they're even taking the children." I'd only been a soldier for a week when the order came – exactly on my birthday – for me and my mates to report to a particular sector of the Front. As it was my birthday, we decided not to go until the next day. And when we did go a guard was waiting for us at a bridge. "Lüdke", he said. "You're under arrest! You're not fit to wear the German uniform." And he tore my jacket off me.'

His case was then dealt with personally by the regional leader of the HJ, Herbert Hirsch, at his headquarters in Breslau. While the city was collapsing under a hail of shells, there was a debate as to whether, in the case of Lüdke and friends, mercy should prevail over justice. 'And then they came over to me and said: "Well now, we will regard your behaviour as ill-considered and foolish and will therefore refrain from taking the severest measure – there will be no summary execution. However, since you are the ringleader, we will not be satisfied with twenty strokes of the cane. You'll be given twenty-five. So grit your teeth." Then he beat me. After the tenth stroke I began to whimper and couldn't stand any more. Then he said: "Right lad, off to the Front now, and show what you're made of. I hope I'll soon be able to pin an Iron Cross on you."'

It was a grotesque scene, in view of the imminent destruction of the city. Lüdke was given the honour of again being allowed to sacrifice himself for the Fatherland. Other youngsters who absented themselves from the ranks without permission were given shorter shrift.

Breslau, too, had those who were notable for their particular fanaticism. The city was held until 2 May. Admittedly, the Front had long since moved westwards. But time and again new Soviet formations attempted to take the city. In the middle of February the encirclement of the remaining 200,000 defenders was complete. Advancing from the south, the Red Army fought bitterly for every street, every building and every storey. Huge fires painted blood-red reflections on the clouds. Gandau airfield, west of the city, was one of the main targets of the Soviet attacks. When it was captured, all contact with the outside world was cut off. Churches were converted into miniature strongholds, cemeteries flattened to create a 'better field of fire', and gravestones torn down for use in building barricades.

The battle became a bitter struggle for every inch of ground. In the city centre a second airstrip was improvised, since right to the end many believed that relief would come – and many of the young still believed in victory. They saw action in units of the Wehrmacht, in the *Volkssturm* and in the specially created 'Hitler Youth Regimental Group'. This had been established by Hirsch, the regional chief of the HJ. The unit comprised about 1,000 boys, organised into two battalions. They were relatively well-equipped and were commanded by experienced NCOs. They attacked and recaptured the Rüttgers plant and the Pöpelwitz Station. The corner of Kaiser-Wilhelm-Strasse and Augusta-Strasse was soon renamed 'Hitler Youth Corner' by the Breslauers, because the boys had built catapults there to fire hand-grenades.

However, the stubborn resistance took a high toll in blood. In the street-by-street fighting half the boy-soldiers were killed. Hundreds of *Hitlerjungen* were literally driven into battle along what was known as the main defensive line, the railway embankments in the south of the city.

Ten of us lads in the 'tank destruction force' dived into the trenches we had dug around our position, looked out over the parapet, whenever we dared, and saw with amazement, rather than horror, the flashes from the barrels of the tanks' cannons. We saw and heard and felt the shells being fired, which rapidly carpeted the entire farmstead, and soon we couldn't make out anything in the thundering din.

*Carl Damm, born 1927*

Manfred Preussner was wounded in an attack on Soviet machine-gun posts. He was lucky. 'A gigantic sergeant stood over me with his pistol levelled. "What's up with you?" So I say: "I caught a piece of shrapnel." He takes a look. And it was in fact bleeding a bit. Anyway, I was allowed to go down into the bunker, and some others wanted to retreat as well. But he just raised his pistol and chased them back – they weren't wounded. They had to go up that embankment again.'

What awaited them on the battle-line is described by Roman Schäfer: 'The Russians were lying on the top of the embankment and we were supposed to drive them back off it. You can imagine what it was like; them lying up there with their machine guns, mowing everyone down. People were just being sacrificed. I mean, it was sheer madness.' Christian Lüdke, the boy who had been flogged for being absent without leave, was also in that action. 'The operation we had to carry out there was hopeless. We could hardly keep count of our losses. There were quite a few who cried – not only because many of them were severely wounded, but also from fear of death.'

Official statements made it seem possible that this human tragedy might yield military advantage. The army command in the city issued the following message: 'Thanks to the stubborn defence and the proven battle-spirit of the fortress, with the powerful support of the Fatherland, and in the deep conviction that we will win in the end, we will hold the fortress until the war turns in our favour.' Yet despite the bombastic war propaganda the 'iron discipline' was visibly evaporating. Every day, soldiers would enter those churches that were still intact, to kneel in silent prayer. No longer did anyone try to prevent them.

Early in April the last act in the drama began. In the Easter holiday period Breslau experienced the full harshness of 'total war'. What was still left of the city was bombed flat by the Red Army. Breslau was transformed into a blazing inferno. Still the fortress commanders would not give up. They were hoping – in vain, of course – for help from outside. 'Our confidence, founded on Hitler, grows all the greater, the longer we hold out.' Such was the extravagant praise for the Führer, uttered by the fanatical army commanders on his birthday, 20 April.

With a ceasefire lasting several days, the Soviets gave the city a final chance to surrender voluntarily. But the German defenders stubbornly refused to budge and lost this opportunity of saving at least some human lives. Not until the beginning of May did German negotiators set out from the city, among them Arthur

Grossmann. And of all people it was the Hitler Youth who tried to prevent them from taking this one sensible step. Grossmann tells the story: 'With our white flag we were clearly recognisable as civilians and were intending to go over to the other side to negotiate a surrender. However, we had to pass several blocks where the Hitler Youth were in position. And they couldn't understand it. To them something was collapsing here. They didn't want to stop. They even shouted, we're fighting on, we'll never surrender. But we had to get past them. Of course, it felt strange, but it was no good trying to give them orders or to say "we've got to get through". They just stood there and refused to let us past. So then we notified the CO of the *Hitlerjugend* battalion, who was in the vicinity, and telephoned the fortress command, to say we were having problems getting across the line. Thereupon the general spoke to the battalion commander, and only then were we able to cross the battle-line amid the jeers of the *Hitlerjungen*. Even then there were still expressions of disapproval. They called us traitors and cowards and kept on shouting: "We're fighting on." That was the kind of mentality prevailing in that battalion.'

> The fighting spirit of the young is the guarantee of ultimate victory and of Germany's joyous future.
>
> *Nationwide order of the Reichsjugendführer,*
> *6 November 1944*

After months of fighting an eerie silence at last fell over the city. On 6 May 1945 the last shot was fired. 'Fortress Breslau' had fallen two days before the general German surrender. *Gauleiter* Hanke, who up to that point had presented himself as a particularly rabble-rousing 'defender', now revealed his own notion of 'utter fearlessness'. Several days before the fall of the Silesian 'fortress' he had sneaked away surreptitiously, leaving his 'comrades in arms' in the lurch.

During the spring of 1945 the Western Front also pushed closer and closer. A symbolic date was 7 March 1945. For the first time since the age of Napoleon enemy troops crossed the 'German stream'; the 9th US Armoured Division made a crossing of the Rhine at Remagen. Hitler flew into a rage on receiving the dire news. That did nothing to alter the military reality: the 'Greater German Reich' had dwindled to a single country between two rivers. The Soviets were on the Oder. After further Rhine crossings the western Allies advanced in six large wedges, thrusting deep into German territory.

In the west, many *Hitlerjungen* now saw that the hour had come for them to prove their worth. One of them was Rudolf Helmich, aged sixteen at the time, and a pupil at the Steinbart high school in Duisburg. Because of the air raids on the cities of the Ruhr he had been evacuated several times since 1940, under the *Kinderlandverschickung* scheme, nearly always with the same group of friends. Thus a tremendous comradeship had developed between the boys. They made all their decisions together. In January 1944 Helmich and his friends had been sent off to Bad Mergentheim; and early in 1945 the entire youth of the town were drafted into the *Volkssturm*. The *Bannführer* asked if anyone was 'not' volunteering for duty. As expected, no-one spoke up. Helmich could only smile at the barefaced deceit. That he and his friends wanted to contribute of their own free will to the defence of the Fatherland was, however, not in question.

On 31 March the Americans unexpectedly approached Bad Mergentheim. The growing alarm roused the curiosity of Helmich and some of his schoolfriends. They heard that the 'Dirnagel battle-group' had succeeded in driving back the leading American armour at Neunkirchen with heavy losses – the 88mm guns had knocked out six American tanks. The boys seized this opportunity; they showed young SS soldiers, unfamiliar with the area, how to get to Neunkirchen. The SS men impressed the high-school boys because they showed discipline and decisiveness, while other elements of the Wehrmacht were streaming back in unplanned retreat. 'Then the *Waffen-SS* men asked us: "What are *you* doing here then?" So we replied, as quick as a flash: "We want to make ourselves available for the defence. We want to join in the fighting." One of these soldiers said: "OK, if you want to volunteer for action, that's fine. We'll take volunteers, but your decision is final. Anyone who says yes, stays. There's no backing out." So, without having to think about it, we all said yes.'

In the days of waiting for a renewed attack by the Americans the group of volunteers were restless – now and again someone failed to return from the defensive line, and boys would be sent to take their place. One mother tried vainly to fetch her son home from the lines. One of the youngest boys, having tried to get away, was brought back again – straight from his bed. Both boys were later killed.

---

The older fighting men had more common sense than we did. They didn't want to get themselves shot. We boys simply didn't think about it. We only started worrying when the Americans arrived.

*Wilhelm Meissermann, born 1929*

---

On 5 April the Americans pushed forward again and captured the nearby village of Stuppach. The war-weary villagers welcomed the conquerors with relief. However, that night the Americans pulled out again and camped outside the village. The *Waffen-SS* soldiers exploited this chance to ensconce themselves in Stuppach. The next day the Americans returned. They were not expecting any resistance. The leading jeep carrying an officer was shot at and the occupants taken prisoner. The boys from Duisburg now moved in as reinforcements. They split into groups. Helmich's section, eleven schoolboys and a seasoned NCO, were to take up position on the road out of the village towards Lustbronn. There was little cover and they had no entrenching tools. The NCO sent Helmich back into the village to borrow some shovels. But the inhabitants refused to hand any over.

By now the tanks of the US 10th Armoured Division had surrounded Stuppach, some distance off. As Helmich tried to return to his section a barrage opened up. The boy took cover in a shed. From his hideout he could not see his comrades, yet he knew they were barely 100 yards from him, without cover and exposed to the American fire – it was a traumatic moment for him. 'I was aware that they were all completely unprotected and that I had in fact been sent to fetch help. And now I couldn't help them. I couldn't do a thing.'

The exchange of fire dragged on for hours. None of the *Waffen-SS* soldiers thought of surrendering. When the Americans finally moved into the village, Helmich had to conclude that none of his friends were left alive. In the centre of the village, where the prisoners had been assembled, he found only one schoolmate, Walter Kremer, and his NCO. Sixty-three German soldiers were dead, among them nine of the Duisburg schoolboys.

The bodies of the dead boys, like those of the adult soldiers, had to lie in the sun for ten days. The Americans wanted to make an example of them. 'When we were allowed to bury the dead, they were half decayed, their organs were bursting out of their bodies', a villager tells us. Rudolf Helmich brooded for a long time about the death of his comrades. 'We were friends. Everything that mattered we did together. It causes me infinite pain to think of what happened to us, but that was how we wanted it. We ourselves wanted it. Each one had to be responsible for himself.'

> We had some there who weren't yet fifteen. They'd received even less training than we had. And their casualties were correspondingly high.
>
> *Günter Prätorius, born 1928*

Yet the excessive zeal of the *Hitlerjungen* dragged others, as well, to their death. In Brettheim, near Rothenburg-ob-der-Tauber, it was on 7 April that the sound of American tanks could be heard. The population had hoped to survive the war unscathed. But then a tank destruction unit consisting of four *Hitlerjungen* appeared outside the village. As one of the inhabitants recalls: 'The boys said: "We're going to defend this place." The people of Brettheim were afraid their village might come under fire. At this point a farmer named Hanselmann and a helper took the grenade launchers and carbines from the boys, boxed their ears, chased them off and threw their weapons into a pond.' Their honour slighted, the *Hitlerjungen* marched straight off to the nearest SS command-post. The general in command of the XIII SS Army Corps, SS *Gruppenführer* Simon, and SS *Sturmbannführer* Gottschalk, set up a drumhead court martial to investigate the matter.'

The eye-witness continued: 'The court martial condemned the farmer to death for subversion of the armed forces. However, mayor Gackstetter, and the local head of the Nazi Party, Wolfmeyer, refused to sign the death-warrant.' A second court martial was summoned to try Gackstetter and Wolfmeyer, who were finally sentenced to death as well. The three condemned men were hanged from the lime trees outside the cemetery and their bodies were meant to hang there for three days – but within two days the Americans arrived. The *Hitlerjungen* had placed the nooses around the men's necks and kicked away the chairs they were standing on. Before and after the execution one of the boys played tunes on an accordion. They left the corpses swinging to and fro. To this day Brettheim suffers under this trauma; it has become a symbol of the blind fanaticism of youth, who even in the face of defeat were prepared to go on denouncing and humiliating their fellow Germans.

Yet in most cases their youthful impetuosity led to their own deaths. Franz J. Müller, a member of the 'White Rose' anti-Nazi resistance group, who was liberated from prison by the Americans, recalls a horrifying scene near Stuttgart: 'I was being driven in a jeep which was escorting a column of Sherman tanks. Suddenly we heard a huge explosion. We drove up and saw an American tank with its left-side track shot away, and the hatch at the top was open. In the road near the tank, lined up almost in a row, lay four HJ boys. They were screaming like banshees, because, after the explosion, an American soldier, realising that the tank was not on fire, had opened the hatch and blazed away with a sub-machine gun. And that's when he hit these boys. I suppose they'd been celebrating their victory and standing upright, which no soldier would do, but these kids did. So he hit them at about stomach-level. And that's the worst thing that can happen, when the wall of the stomach is shot through and things spill out. And they were screaming. One was screaming like crazy for his mother.'

Even the US soldiers were horror-struck: 'They were shocked when they saw it was kids they had been shooting at. They opened their first-aid kits and called up paramedics but there was nothing anyone could do. They lay there and bled to death, the Hitler Youth who had stormed into battle with a grenade launcher.' Franz Müller, a young survivor of the anti-Hitler movement, thus witnessed once again that inhuman power of enticement which he had resisted at the risk of his own life.

> Obedience was the one thing they learned. When they got an order, there were no questions asked. But we had to restrain them, dampen their enthusiasm. They had even been sent wild by pictures in the press of Hitler awarding Iron Crosses to youngsters. We couldn't really make proper use of them. They were just sacrificed. It made no sense, because they achieved nothing.
>
> *Willi Rabe, Wehrmacht officer, born 1925*

Contemporary eye-witnesses also have oppressive memories connected with the town of Bad Tölz, near Munich. In April 1945 there was great unrest there. The military hospital was hopelessly overcrowded, thousands of retreating Wehrmacht soldiers were streaming through the streets. SS men were preparing to escape across the Alps. Some of them had come from the Dachau concentration camp.

Bad Tölz was the location of the SS *Junkerschule*, which along with institutions in Klagenfurt and Braunschweig was one of the elite training centres for up-and-coming officers of the *Waffen-SS*.

When the inmates of Dachau were marched to the Tegernsee Lake to be murdered, they passed this school. One of them was Zvi Katz, who today lives in Tel Aviv. He remembers how, at the *Junkerschule* in Bad Tölz, new guards joined them, 'young blokes, their faces distorted with hatred, giving us menacing looks. Their threatening gestures told us that these were our executioners.' Zvi Katz managed to escape and only knows at second hand how brutally the young SS men treated his fellow-sufferers, often more cruelly than the concentration camp warders.

Yet the *Junkerschule* provided training not only for young SS officers, but also for members of the *Volkssturm*. Gregor Dorfmeister, then aged sixteen, was drafted with other pupils from Bad Tölz early in March 1945. Under the pen-name of Manfred Gregor, he later set down his experiences in a novel called *Die Brücke* (The Bridge), which was made into a film by Bernhard Wicki. For three solid weeks the boys were confined to barracks for training. 'We had already been taught to handle firearms and turned into potential killers. We got that from the pre-military training in the Hitler Youth, which we were put through every Sunday morning in Bad Tölz, preferably when other people were going to church. That way the Party killed two birds with one stone. Firstly the lads were kept away from church, and anyway handling rifles and pistols was probably more interesting than Holy Communion. We knew what to do with weapons, including hand-grenades and grenade launchers. We really had rehearsed to the utmost for the real thing.'

What can be said about the motives of young Gregor Dorfmeister? 'Perhaps what mattered most was the sense of belonging to a fellowship and of sharing the responsibility for it. That's to say: the moment I go, I'm leaving the others in the lurch.'

He could have no inkling of how severely his principles would be tested – until 30 April. In the grounds of the *Junkerschule* the boys were divided into sections and marched off. Units of the US 7th Army were already close enough to be heard. Dorfmeister and six friends were led by an NCO who posted them at a little bridge over the river Loisach. Initially they were disgruntled: 'Our keenness for the big adventure had already evaporated a bit, because we had assumed the bridge to be completely without interest, completely unimportant. So it was all the more surprising when an American tank actually appeared.' At the first contact with the enemy they became frightened. 'It's a grinding sound, an inhuman, mechanical noise. I mean, when you hear the noise, you can't imagine that there are people inside this contraption. You think: here's something with a mind of its own, something totally destructive coming towards you, and you're helpless against it.'

Then the boys fired. 'I reckon we launched seven or eight grenades at the tank. And one or two were direct hits. But at first the tank just kept on coming. That traumatic instant has burned itself into my memory.' However, the Americans then withdrew temporarily. Dorfmeister and his colleagues celebrated the victory they had just scored over the USA. Yet the true ordeal by fire was not long in coming. 'Suddenly there were two fighter aircraft above us and a real turkey-shoot began. There's no other way to describe it. When the first one of us fell dead, there was nothing but sheer terror and panic.'

The boys fled back towards Bad Tölz. There the Field Gendarmerie wanted to deploy them again, this time on the bridge over the Isar. 'They showed us a sandbagged machine-gun nest. Then I realised what a repulsive and deadly trick they were planning to play on us.' While the gendarmes made their getaway, Dorfmeister and his friends were supposed to take over the defence of the bridge, a totally senseless enterprise in view of the enemy's overwhelming superiority. 'I wasn't falling for that. I even tried to make my two pals understand, but I couldn't convince them. They stayed put. I think they wanted to perform their deed of heroism. I imagine they looked on me as a cowardly creep, when I left.'

He made his way back to his parents' house and exchanged his uniform for civilian clothes. The next morning he found his two comrades – dead. The Americans had marched in during the night. Gregor Dorfmeister was lucky, he was able to free himself from that doomed brotherhood. 'I didn't feel good about it, but I know that if I hadn't gone, I'd probably have been the third body lying there.' That is not quite the end of the story. An old woman came across the bridge, greeted the Americans guarding it, then bent over the dead boys and spat on them. It was an expression of hate for all those who wanted to prolong the war. And it was what led Gregor Dorfmeister, a.k.a. Manfred Gregor, to write his book.

On 11 April the Americans reached the river Elbe at Schönebeck, south of Magdeburg. A short time later they would come to an agreement with the Soviets under which the river would be the demarcation line between the US Army and the Red Army. But before this the Americans fought to establish two bridgeheads east of the Elbe. On 12 April US units west of the Elbe were positioned around Magdeburg. The German army commandant of the city, *Generalleutnant* Raegener, rejected the American demand for a surrender. Thus, on 17 April Magdeburg was attacked by more than 300 bombers and brought under artillery fire.

During the first days of April nests of resistance had been established in various outer suburbs of the city. The intention was that soldiers of the *Waffen-SS* and units of the Wehrmacht, the *Volkssturm* and the Reich Labour Service, as well as 800 *Hitlerjungen* from the Magdeburg company, were to defy the enemy here. Their task was to deny the Americans access to the Elbe for as long as possible. In Berlin there was still uncertainty as to whether or not the US Army intended to march directly towards the capital which lay well to the east of the Elbe. Consequently every house and every block in Magdeburg was bitterly fought over.

Among the *Hitlerjungen*, whose *Volkssturm* units placed themselves in the path of the American divisions, were two sixteen-year-olds, Horst Blanke and Günter Prätorius. Only the day before they had been singing 'We're riding to the eastern lands', 'Führer, command; we follow thee' and the anthem of the Hitler Youth, '. . . for the flag means more than death'. So the boys went into battle without fear or doubt, although it must have been clear to them that any resistance was pointless. 'The belief that we could achieve something by defending Magdeburg had scarcely mattered to us. We were simply following the performance of our duty that had been drummed into us, to stand firm at all costs.' Horst Blanke remembers. 'We had no shortage of reasons to get out of there. In the very first engagements there were many deaths. And the worst thing was, a friend of mine got hit. He didn't get to his foxhole in time. Suddenly he was lying there with his back ripped open. We buried him in the cemetery nearby. Knowing what we know today, we should have said at that point, if not sooner: that's it, no more. But we didn't. Instead we talked about the loyalty of the Nibelungs and how we would fight to the last drop of blood.'

Willi Rabe, who, as a Wehrmacht officer, had to lead a *Volkssturm* unit, is another who tells of the unquestioning readiness for action on the part of many Magdeburg *Hitlerjungen*: 'We had to put the brakes on them. They were inexperienced and had old-fashioned Italian carbines, which they didn't even know how to handle properly. But they wanted to fling themselves into the thick of the battle.' It was all Rabe could do to pull the boys back from suicidal attacks. When, in the end, even the boys' mothers came to their dugout, the absurdity reached its climax. 'They begged me to take care of their sons. So I said: "Take them away with you." "No", they replied, "we can't do that. If we did, we'd be shot."' It was true that parents could expect draconian punishments if they tried to keep their children away from active service. Some paid for this with their lives.

'We had a duty to go on fighting to the end. Regardless of what happened, the word was: the flag means more than death', says Blanke. Often the boys were only brought to their senses by personal disappointment, for instance through 'treason' by their commanding officer, as was the experience of sixteen-year-old Günter Prätorius. 'We were in the suburb of Sudenburg, retreating down a long, straight road. The Americans were above us with their tanks, shooting at us ceaselessly. One of my pals had a loose rifle-strap and he came back without his weapon. So the officer told him he had to go back for his gun; we couldn't spare a single weapon. He went off and what happened was exactly what was to be expected. We didn't get the gun back and our comrade was killed.' Then came the next disappointment. 'We were doing a recce of the front line when we suddenly heard violent explosions in the distance. "That was the Elbe bridges", the NCO said to me. I replied that that surely couldn't be true. "Oh yes, you'll see. That was the two northern bridges in the city."' Those bridges were the only way back across the Elbe for Prätorius and his colleagues. They had been blown up by retreating German troops. 'I had the feeling that we'd just been crossed off the list. Now they'll just expect us to face the music. They've written us off. It was a bitter feeling. It was then that I actually first began to wonder what we were still fighting for. The men in charge had made a run for it and were watching events from the other bank of the Elbe. We were nothing but cannon-fodder.'

While Günter Prätorius was marched off as a prisoner of the Americans, Horst Blanke got away unscathed. A German sergeant asked him his age: 'Sixteen!' That did it, the boy was allowed to go home. This decision might have cost the sergeant his life, but the surrender was only a matter of hours away. At home Blanke waited for the Americans to march in. He opened the door with a polite 'How do you do' when GIs wanted to search the apartment for German soldiers. In the nursery the Americans caught sight of his four-month-old brother. A short time later they returned and presented the family with food and milk – things that were very scarce. 'Then it suddenly hit me. These were the men we had been fighting against!' At a stroke Blanke was suddenly made to see the senselessness of his military service.

By 18 April the Americans had taken the suburbs of Magdeburg on the west bank of the Elbe. They kept to their agreement with the Russians and made no attempt to cross the river. While the Nazi elite made a hasty getaway, German soldiers in the eastern part of the city went on all day shooting at the Americans from across the River Elbe, which once again led to needless destruction. Not until the Russians occupied the area did the guns fall silent.

> For the past few days refugees with horse-drawn wagons and hand-carts or on foot had been heading westwards along the cobbled road past the camp. But now there were more military vehicles and a few soldiers in full equipment among them.
> I stood there and watched the endless column, still not realising what was happening, namely the absolute end of the war, involving the flight and expulsion of millions of people from their homes.
>
> *Hartmut Schreiber, born 1928*

The final climax of the Second World War in Europe was the battle for the centre of power in Hitler's Reich, Berlin. The Red Army assembled a gigantic strike-force near the capital. The array of armaments was large enough for them to place a gun every three yards along the entire front. Three Soviet army groups comprising a total of 2.5 million men stood at the ready, with 6,250 tanks and gun-carriers, 41,000 heavy guns and grenade launchers. With

7,500 warplanes the Soviet air force had control of the skies. General Weidling, who had been appointed commandant of 'Fortress Berlin' on 23 April, had to accept the fact that against this force he could only put up about 44,000 German soldiers, 'supported' by 42,000 members of the *Volkssturm* and 5,000 *Hitlerjungen*.

February and March saw the final call-up of boys born in 1928, for the Wehrmacht and the *Waffen-SS*. But the net was cast wide enough to include some sixteen-year-olds as well, since at the end of February Hitler had agreed to Bormann's request for 6,000 boys born in 1929 to be drafted – as part of the *Volkssturm* – if only for the rear defensive lines in the capital. *Generalfeldmarschall* Wilhelm Keitel instructed the Wehrmacht to begin the compulsory drafting of those born in 1929.

In Berlin, as elsewhere, the auxiliary troops were poorly trained, if at all, and equipped with inadequate weapons. However, while the *Volkssturm*, who had been given some hasty instruction after working hours or at weekends, frequently withdrew from action, the *Hitlerjungen* usually remained in their positions. The death toll exacted by their misguided zeal was correspondingly high. This meant that the Soviet superiority as they approached Berlin was in reality even more apparent than on paper.

> At the age of 17 or 18, we have no idea that we are supposed to be the last contingent in the defence of Berlin. We still believe in ultimate victory and pin our hopes on the miracle-weapons. We don't know, or refuse to believe, that this war was lost long ago.
>
> *Günter Dunsbach, born 1927*

The defence of the Reich capital was now in the hands of a motley assortment of regular formations which had long been far below strength, with volunteer troops of former allies, as well as units with fine-sounding names like 'Army Group Spree' made up of *Volkssturm* and Labour Service personnel. Only the boys were required to hold off well-trained and superbly equipped Russian front line soldiers. The girls of the BDM were no more trained to handle a *Panzerfaust* grenade launcher than their mothers were.

Not until 13 April did the order go out to the civilian population to put Berlin on to a defensive alert. However, the greatest problem for 'Fortress Berlin' was the lack of arms and ammunition. This made no difference to the 'strategists' in the *Führerbunker*. For them there was no question but that 'every block, every house, every floor, every hedge, every shell-crater will be defended to the last!' It was not important for every defender of the capital to have mastered all the technical details of his weaponry, but that each of them should be 'possessed and imbued with a fanatical determination to go on fighting'.

Meanwhile the massive Soviet war-machine had halted its advance 40 miles short of Berlin. The severely depleted divisions of the Wehrmacht and *Waffen-SS*, who confronted the Soviet armies assembled along the River Oder, nevertheless imagined they were capable of blocking the enemy's path to Berlin. Large numbers of youthful semi-soldiers accompanied them into the inferno of the Seelow Hills. One of them was the flak auxiliary Hans Hansen: 'We were actually quite proud to be transported to the Front just like adults. There's no getting around that. That's simply the way it was. At a stroke we had grown up and that's how we felt. Fear had been educated out of us. We weren't allowed to show any feelings, any fear. We had to maintain discipline at all times and get through any situation. But none of us were prepared for what happened next.'

On 16 April 300,000 Red Army troops led the main thrust from the bridgehead at Küstrin towards the Seelow Hills. The inferno began with continuous shelling by more than 20,000 guns. General Kazakov, in command of the 1st White Russian Front, describes how the attack began at 3 a.m.: 'It was an eerie scene, as the whole front was lit up by the muzzle-flashes and the exploding shells from 10,000 guns. The primeval power of this phenomenon left an indelible impression even on us old artillery hands.' In that case, what effect must it have had on the young defenders? 'It was a kind of thunderstorm from hell, something you simply cannot imagine', is how Hans Hansen describes the onslaught. 'You're sitting in a hole, and each minute seems like a quarter of an hour. And the quarter-hours become an eternity. Time stands still. Everything was churned up, and the casualties were terrible. One thing we all knew: this was the end of our childhood – in fact, the end of our youth. Nothing would ever be the same again.'

The battle for the Seelow Hills cost over 50,000 human lives, among them many child-soldiers. By 18 April the road to Berlin lay open to the Red Army. Only a few days later the circle round Berlin was closed, and on 25 April the leading Soviet units reached the Elbe and linked up with the Americans at Torgau.

> Thirty-seven Germans fell into the hands of the second platoon, crying, bleeding and screaming hysterically.
> They were just children, said Lieutenant Slade after the engagement. Before our bazooka shells got to them, they had been fighting like hell, but now they were just a disorganised bunch of fourteen- to sixteen-year-olds.
> *Report of the 100th US Infantry Division, 5 April 1945*

In the capital, too, the final battle had begun with high-flown propaganda. As late as 18 March the man who had organised the Berlin Olympics in 1936, Carl Diem, gave a fiery speech to young people in the Domed Hall of the Olympic complex. 'That speech was larded with quotations celebrating death for the Fatherland, noble self-sacrifice, the fine heroic death', says Reinhard Appel, who was in that audience and is still incensed about it. 'We were idealistic youngsters – sixteen and seventeen years old. Five hundred of us had been brought together, and I reckon that if the Russians had appeared on the Reich sports ground, we would have gone for them straight away with *Panzerfäuste*. And all the time, the adults knew that the war was lost. That speech by Diem was criminal, inhuman.' The speaker held up to the young people the shining example of the tiny band of Spartans fighting to the death against the Persians at Thermopylae: 'Death is a fine thing when the noble warrior falls for the Fatherland.'

Admittedly, the opponents could take it that the sacrifice of the young was an admission by the Germans that they were already defeated, but the Nazi leadership was no longer concerned with outward appearances. All that mattered was maintaining the pretence internally.

For the Nazi regime the deployment of the young had not only a military function but also a psychological one. If even the youngest were fighting for the national cause, the adults could surely not give up hope! That is why, just three months before the capitulation, the government instituted an 'Honouring of Heroes' in scenes intended to suggest that the entire nation would go on fighting until the *Endsieg*, or ultimate victory. On 9 March Joseph Goebbels, as 'Plenipotenitary of Total War Mobilisation' awarded the Iron Cross to a little band of *Hitlerjungen* in the town of Lauban in Lower Silesia. As part of their reward some members of the group were allowed to go to Berlin where on 19 March – as the climax of a largely bomb-free week's holiday – they met 'the greatest military leader of all time'. In the words of the *Völkischer Beobachter*, 'symbolically the whole youth of Germany stepped forward with these twenty lads, who are currently, as the most loyal auxiliaries to our soldiers and to the *Volkssturm*, standing courageously and unafraid on German soil in the highest performance of their duty'.

I was just sixteen when I heard that the leading American tanks had broken through near Brandenburg. And this was the first time that I began to have doubts about a final victory, which of course I had believed in up till then. I remember saying to my mates: what's all this crap about shooting at the Americans?

*Lothar Loewe, born 1928*

When the Americans were at the gates, we felt safe. True, no-one could tell what would happen next. But we were relieved. Most of all, I suppose, we were free from the fear of air raids.

*Kurt Biedenkopf, born 1930, postwar politician*

Shortly after Hitler had issued his so-called 'Nero order': the destruction of infrastructure facilities, 'which the enemy may make use of in continuing the war' (nothing less than applying the 'scorched earth' policy to Germany itself), he received twenty *Hitlerjungen* aged from fifteen to seventeen, accompanied by the *Reichsjugendführer*, Artur Axmann. The newsreel cameras were there as well. Among those to be decorated was the seventeen-year-old Wilhelm Hübner. 'What every *Hitlerjunge* really wanted was to see the Führer, if only at some parade or public appearance. So to stand in front of him in person and shake his hand, that was just the greatest thing that could ever happen to you back then.'

Child-soldiers like this were just what the Nazi propagandists liked. Their idols were war-heroes, their ideal was to die for *Führer, Volk und Vaterland*. 'You are nothing, your *Volk* is everything' and other such slogans had taken root in their heads and hearts. But as the boys stepped forward, their breasts swelling with pride, it did not escape their notice that the man who received them in the garden of the Reich Chancellery, listened to their citations, patted their cheeks and muttered a few weary words of congratulation, was a visibly decrepit Führer. After the parade, the warlord left the courtyard again with his dog and his entourage. On 20 April, the Führer's birthday, the ritual was played out once more. It was Hitler's last appearance in public.

That was the day when Artur Axmann's messenger, a boy named Armin Lehmann, aged sixteen, received the Iron Cross from the Supreme Commander. Even in the face of imminent destruction this seemed to the boy an honour scarcely to be surpassed: 'I imagined my father going to the cinema a week or so later, seeing the newsreel pictures and thinking to himself that maybe his son wasn't a failure after all.' Yet the audience with Hitler had a sobering effect on Lehmann too: 'We thought this was an aged man in front of us.' However, almost apologetically, Axmann pointed out to his messenger that the Führer's gaze was 'nevertheless still very determined'. As Lehmann explains: 'Axmann was absolutely obsessed with the idea of showing Hitler that the youth he led were keeping faith with their Führer.'

After the war the former *Reichsjugendführer* notoriously ducked the question about why, year after year, he had made a 'present' to the Führer of each new crop of youngsters – to serve in a war that had already been lost. Axmann rejected the suggestion that it served to enhance his personal status. It was rather, he claimed, a matter of 'bringing things to an honourable end'. Axmann's view had been: 'We shall never surrender', he told us in his last, lengthy interview. Lehmann believes 'he considered Hitler to be a superman'. By delivering up the young to Hitler, he gained the favour he had always longed for. Axmann was revelling in the closeness to Hitler which had so long been denied him, because Bormann, who ran the Führer's private office, had refused to give him access. It was Axmann who actually saw to the formation of proper Hitler Youth units. 'He did not want the boys' idealism to be dampened by the derogatory remarks of disillusioned army regulars', Lehmann says.

The cynical calculation paid off. Indeed, it was chiefly the *Hitlerjungen* who, in April and May 1945, continued the war with their great fanaticism and high degree of willingness to go into action. Axmann even believed that the HJ should become 'the centre of national resistance'. 'It is your duty to grow stronger when others tire, to stand firm when others fall back. But let your greatest honour be your unshakeable loyalty to Adolf Hitler.'

Now, for the first time in the Reich Chancellery the Führer could hear the thunder of Marshal Zhukov's artillery. On his birthday he proclaimed 'Operation Clausewitz'. The capital of the Reich was now officially in a state of siege. Thus, at Hitler's annual reception on 20 April there was no cause for celebration. 'We even went without champagne', recalls Traudl Junge, Hitler's secretary.

The dictator withdrew to his quarters and again bent anxiously over situation maps, hoping for relief by armies that no longer existed. His health was visibly deteriorating. He was repeatedly given injections against real or imagined diseases. 'All generals are liars!' the warlord had yelled in the face of General Hasso von Manteuffel, on 3 March 1945. The 'greatest military leader of all time' sought and found error in others but never in himself. Idiots and cowards was how he saw the officers of his General Staff – talentless, incompetent and lacking in will, they had failed to translate his brilliant ideas into action.

The final situation conference took place on 22 April. The Soviets were in the heart of Berlin and Hitler was beside himself.

The German troops were unable to offer any serious resistance against the Red Army. The dictator dismissed the top brass from the room. Only General Burgdorf, his senior aide-de-camp, as well as Keitel, Krebs and Bormann were allowed to stay behind.

When the doors closed again Hitler lost control completely. His whole body trembling, he screamed, in a voice that repeatedly cracked with emotion, about treason and cowardice, incompetence and disobedience. The *Waffen-SS* and the Wehrmacht had failed, he said. He now stood alone. Anyone who wanted to go should leave him now. This outburst of rage was over as suddenly as it had begun. Hitler dropped exhausted into a chair and groaned : 'Now all is lost. It's all over. I shall shoot myself.'

For minutes there was a paralysed silence. For the first time Hitler had admitted that the war was lost, for the first time he had spoken openly of killing himself. He could no longer win his war. A whole continent lay largely in ruins. The war had claimed 50 million victims. Most of Europe's Jews had been murdered. Now Hitler's annihilating fury was directed against his own people. They had been the tool of his mania for destruction and yet, in his eyes, they had ultimately failed him. Like many of his other ideas, there was nothing new or surprising about this. As early as November 1941, long before the first big defeats, he had said: 'In this, too, I am as cold as ice. If the German people is no longer strong enough or willing enough to sacrifice its own blood in the cause of its existence, then it must pass away and be destroyed by another, stronger power. I will shed no tears for the German people.'

The madness was to last a further ten days in the capital, and sixteen days in the rest of the Reich, until the destructive and self-destructive war reached its end. From the bunker, surrounded by his last 'loyal retainers', Hitler went on trying somehow to exert an influence on military events. Within yard-thick concrete walls, cut off from the horrors of reality, decisions were taken which could not be put into effect. A 'Führer order' dated 23 April reveals what Hitler was placing his hopes on: 'Soldiers of the Wenck Army! An order of great moment has set you on an eastward march. Your task is clear: Berlin is still German. Berlin awaits you, Berlin longs with a fervent heart for your arrival.'

The army which Hitler was banking on existed for the most part on paper only. Of the seven divisions – named after such diverse historical figures as Clausewitz, Scharnhorst, Ulrich von Hutten, Theodor Körner, Albert Leo Schlageter and Friedrich Ludwig Jahn – only three were fully established. Nearly 90 per cent of the personnel consisted of eighteen-year-old officer cadets with no combat experience, and men from the Labour Service. In many units only half the men were armed.

Posters on Berlin's advertising pillars went on sounding off about the 'final victory'. Promises like this contrasted noticeably with graffiti on the bombed-out buildings: messages from bomb victims for those who had stayed behind, informing them of their new addresses. Those who were out on the streets had to beware, not only of falling debris or shells from the attackers, but also of SS patrols. They were still searching for deserters and those of any age who were capable of bearing arms, but who refused to put their lives at stake for Hitler. The accusation of cowardice, draft-dodging or treason was fatal. The summary courts-martial worked quickly. Mere suspicion was often enough. In order to prevent the very idea of desertion from entering the heads of others, the executions were carried out publicly. Young people in particular had to be reminded of their duty. Reinhard Appel describes an event that took place in the Olympic complex: 'We had to witness the shooting of six soldiers. Three of them were our age. They were summarily shot for being absent without leave. We went up the hill and had to watch them being executed. It was obvious what happened to anyone who left his unit.'

That was how the still intact network of Gestapo, Security Service and their informers, exacted their daily tribute. 'I was too cowardly to fight for my wife and child. That is why I am hanging here. I am a *Schweinehund*.' Such executions took place in many parts of the city. In the ultimate compounding of their torment, the victims were forced to write the words themselves on the white board which the murderers would then hang round their necks as a deterrent, before hanging them with a wire noose from the nearest lamp-post, and relishing their agonised death throes. 'Shortly before the ending of Hitler's criminal war two young German soldiers were hanged here by dehumanised SS bandits' –

these words on a memorial plaque at Berlin's Friedrichstrasse Station recall the many men who lost their lives in this way in the last days of fighting.

Where there is such a gaping chasm between desire and reality, even propaganda finds itself in difficulties; the *Völkischer Beobachter* appeared for the last time, and from then on Berliners read the 'combat news for the defenders of Greater Berlin' with the silly title of *Der Panzerbär* ('the Armoured Bear', the bear being the emblem of the city). But this sheet preached windily about 'Berlin, bulwark against Bolshevism', or described the capital as 'a mass grave for Soviet tanks'. All that had changed were the title and layout of the paper; the simple-minded slogans and fraudulent content remained the same: appeals to hold out, rousing calls to the *Volkssturm* and the Hitler Youth.

---

Of course we were sorry for them. We could see they weren't soldiers, they were simply little mothers' boys, as we would say; absolute children who had hurriedly been put into uniform and taught to defend themselves, so as to prolong for a little while the existence of Hitler and his leading Nazis. And they did actually put up quite a lot of resistance to our troops.
*Mikhail Y. Pozelsky, born 1917, Soviet cameraman at the Battle of Berlin*

When the Russians saw us, they kept shaking their heads. They couldn't believe that we were just kids.
*Theodor Reichert, born 1929*

---

In the afternoon of 24 April the Red Army captured Tempelhof Airport after a heavy bombardment. The battle for the beleaguered city went on for another eight long days. Once again the people were told a lie. On 27 April Goebbels announced on Reich Radio: 'The situation has altered decisively in our favour. The great turnround in the war can be expected at any moment. Berlin must be held regardless of casualties, until the Wenck Army arrives.'

The 'Wenck Army' would never arrive. The commander of the 12th Army, on which Hitler was placing his hopes, knew that an attack on Berlin was no longer possible. He did not want to lead his young soldiers to their destruction and defied Hitler's orders. Instead, he made it possible for the remains of the 9th Army, bottled up by the Russians near Halbe, to break out of the pocket, and marched his divisions, along with thousands of civilian refugees, westwards to the Elbe. At Tangermünde the 9th and 12th Armies and the refugees were able to cross the river to the safety of American imprisonment. Walter Wenck was one of the few German generals who frankly admitted that by this time Berlin was already lost. But in his catacombs Hitler would not accept reality.

The *Hitlerjungen* had even less of a grasp of the facts than their Führer. Dogged and fearless in their blinkered view they went into battle with one goal in mind: to knock out as many Russian tanks as possible with their *Panzerfaust* grenade launchers. Artur Axmann invented a name for them – 'tank-crackers'. Hans-Dietrich Nicolaisen still remembers exactly how he was sent into action: 'We were armed with a French rifle that was too long. We had to stuff the ammunition into our coats somehow. We had no ammunition pouches. Then each of us had a Panzerfaust. We had to shove the detonators for it in our trouser-pockets. The grenades we stuck into our belts. And thus equipped we set off.'

However, not even the poor weaponry could deter the youngsters. Combatants aged fourteen and fifteen stood in the way of the Russians, often to the latters' astonishment, as the Soviet army cameraman Mikhail Pozelsky describes: 'You couldn't call them soldiers. They were boys of fourteen, fifteen, maybe sixteen, little lads who lived at home with their mothers. They may not have been soldiers but they behaved as if they were. They wore army greatcoats which hung loosely on them, because they were much too big, not made for them.' Despite their dispirited appearance, the Russians knew that the young warriors were not to be underestimated. At Berlin's Anhalt Station Pozelsky's Red Army colleague Vassily Manturov personally experienced the danger posed by the *Hitlerjungen*: 'I myself was shot at and wounded by one of them with a *Panzerfaust*. It was a little boy who shot me, a lad from a Hitler Youth unit.'

The combative spirit of the youngsters amazed their own older comrades as well. 'They went for the tanks with a fearlessness that is simply indescribable', says Gerd Häffner. 'And they really were just children. I was seventeen, but they were fifteen or younger. Without a thought for themselves they walked into certain death. And at many points they actually forced the Russians to pull back. But then the children in their HJ uniforms were left lying in the street.'

We just felt very sorry for these children, d'you see? If an adult, with all his experience of life, with his awareness, deliberately gets involved in that sort of thing, OK – but a boy like that just cannot comprehend what's coming to him.
       *Vassily S. Manturov, born 1922, Red Army infantryman*

There were a lot of terrified lads, who were still just children. One could only pity them. Many of them we didn't even take prisoner. We sent them straight home.
       *Makhmut A. Gareyev, born 1925, Soviet general*

Still the propaganda went on talking about the victorious turning-point of the war, of miracle-weapons and of a relief army marching towards Berlin. Still the picture was painted of a Führer in the very front line, defying the Russians alongside his own troops.

The situation around the Reich Chancellery was menacing. On the morning of 29 April a violent artillery bombardment began. The occupants of the Führer-bunker wondered how long the concrete roof would hold. A short time later came the report: 'The Red Army is 500 yards from the Reich Chancellery.' The advance could perhaps be stopped once more.

In the Führer-bunker the commandant of the city, General Weidling, prepared his plan for a breakout. Part of Hitler's entourage were able to escape, led by *Hitlerjungen* by a secret route to the bridges over the River Havel at Pichelsdorf. It was here that poorly equipped HJ units were still holding greatly superior Soviet forces at bay. Of the original 5,000 young HJ soldiers sent into action in Berlin, only a few hundred were now still alive. Completely exhausted and with no prospect of being relieved, they went on fighting. Axmann had promised Hitler that with 'his' youth he would hold the bridges as an escape route for a possible breakout to the west. It was a suicide mission. Lothar Loewe was sixteen years old when he witnessed the events at one of these bridges. 'We knew it was the needle's eye which they had to get through, and that it was exposed to the full weight of Russian fire.' He and his comrades got a taste of it on the Charlotte Bridge. 'It was a bloodbath there, with hundreds of dead and wounded. They were caught between the steel sides of the bridge and the advancing column rolled over them. I was sitting in a motorcycle-sidecar and could see the whole thing. It's a sight I'll never forget. The blood ran in streams; people were crushed to pulp.'

Eberhard Pohland, also a *Hitlerjunge* at the time, has traumatic memories of the action at the Picheldorf bridges. 'There was nothing but gunfire. There was shooting from every side and every direction. Dead and severely wounded were lying everywhere. Others were cowering in the angles of steel girders. I remember one guy had his stomach ripped open and everything was spewing out. It was horrible.'

With rifles and *Panzerfäuste*, but most of all with sheer determination, the *Hitlerjungen* had held the bridges for days on end. For this Artur Axmann was again highly decorated: with the Gold Cross of the German Order and with the Iron Cross. 'Without your boys it would have been impossible to carry on the battle at all, not only in Berlin, but in the whole of Germany', were Hitler's words of praise. To the survivors this was a mockery. 'I could shoot that Axmann', says the *Hitlerjunge* Axel Eckenhoff, who fought at the Schilling Bridge. 'It was criminal.' The unnecessary and inhuman sacrifice of young lives, and the way Axmann admitted so little after the war, still enrages Reinhard Appel today: 'It was such a deceitful thing for the *Reichsjugendführer* to say, that the lads had successfully defended the bridges over the Havel and thus given many people the chance to escape beyond the Elbe. But it was all fairy-tales. For whom and for what did we defend those bridges? So that someone like Himmler, the murderer of the Jews, could escape. And for that we were meant to give our lives, for men who killed Jews? It sickens me!'

> Wherever the enemy may break through, he will come up against our home defence front. We will continue our fight until the hour of the German soldier strikes again, until our Wehrmacht finally drives the enemy out of German territory. It is for that hour that we fight. Our struggle is our victory! Werewolves, go get 'em!
>
> *Hitler Youth leaflet in Lower Saxony, April 1945*

While the noose was tightening around the centre of power in Berlin, the advocates of 'total war' were already planning beyond the inevitable surrender. As early as 1 April a rallying-call on radio had announced the existence of a 'spontaneous underground movement' named 'Werewolf'. In fact, this 'organisation born out of a spirit of nationalism' had already been conceived in the autumn of 1944, to carry out terrorist strikes behind enemy lines. Under the command of SS-*Obergruppenführer* Hans Adolf Prützmann, children and young people, predominantly, were to wage a pitiless guerrilla war as partisans behind the enemy's back. The fanatics, who were all for holding out, distributed leaflets among adolescents, calling on them 'to stay in position on the resistance front. You must strike at the enemy wherever you find him.' Acts of sabotage against the Allies were planned, as was action against German 'traitors'. The role of the 'Werewolf' was to intimidate friend and foe alike. 'The Werewolf is here', fly-posters announced all over the Reich. 'Anyone who surrenders will be shot!'

> It is to be feared that the fanatics in this country may try to fight on in a long and bitter guerrilla war. That is a dire prospect, and I believe we should do everything possible to prevent it.
>
> *General Eisenhower, Allied Supreme Commander, to the US Chief of Staff*

> In essence the danger proved to be a hallucination – a
> hallucination of the Germans as much as of their enemies.
> *Historical Report (May/June 1945) of the US 3rd Army
> concerning the alleged 'Werewolf' threat*

The individual guerrilla groups who, according to the plans,
were to be centrally controlled from Hülchrath Castle near
Düsseldorf, were commanded by seasoned members of the
Wehrmacht or the SS, many of whom had been trained in special
skills. The combatants entrusted to their care were 'easy meat'.
For many of the youngsters brought up on years of Nazi
propaganda, it was obvious that they had to perform their final
duty for the Führer here. The brutality with which they were
introduced to their new assignment is etched in the memory of
Werner Kauth, who was then sixteen: 'You have to be so tough
that you could see your own mother and father hanged from a
tree. That's how they trained us.'

At no point in time did the 'Werewolves' have any military
significance. They were never able to develop an organisational
structure. Nonetheless, the legendary existence of an underground
army had such an effect on the Allies that, even after the German
surrender, they were highly suspicious of the civilian population.
In what later became the Soviet Zone, the Werewolf label was
even used to condemn undesirably independent political figures.

The most spectacular case of a Werewolf attack was the
assassination of Franz Oppenhof, the man whom the Americans had
appointed as city mayor of Aachen. 'The new *Oberbürgermeister*
must be shot. He has displayed an attitude that is hostile to the
Reich.' Following this death order issued by Himmler's
headquarters in January, Operation 'Carnival' was launched on 25
March. Four 'freedom fighters' shot the 'ignominious mercenary
of the Americans', as the *Völkischer Beobachter* reported with relish
at the end of the month. All in all, in the last year of the war the
'spirit of German youth' was thought worthy of high praise by the
Nazi party organ. Under the headline 'Intransigent to the Last' on
21 February, the blinkered obduracy of a BDM girl was given

expansive treatment. Even during 'non-stop questioning' by the Americans, the seventeen-year-old had merely repeated the liturgy of propaganda slogans about the 'final victory'. According to Hitler's mouthpiece, the Americans stood 'stunned in the face of the magnificent spirit' of this bemused teenager.

> Whenever heaven is promised, then the whole thing ends in hell. And that is not only true of Nazism.
>
> *Karl-Heinz Böckle, born 1929*

Thus did the Nazi madness continue to devour its children. In the final days in Berlin even twelve-year-old *Pimpfe* took part in the battle. Charlottenburg, Prenzlauer Berg, Spandau, the Olympic Stadium – these names symbolise their senseless sacrifice. 'The youngest of them, the fourteen-, fifteen- and sixteen-year-olds, are fighting with the same passion and contempt for death as our soldiers showed in the earlier campaigns of the war', blustered the propaganda.

However, the time of self-deception finally came to an end on 30 April. Hitler knew that the Russians would soon reach the Reich Chancellery and was brooding about how he could abdicate responsibility for the loss of so many millions of lives. Axmann advised him once more to flee, in which case *Hitlerjungen* were again to be deployed. 'Axmann had the notion that a small platoon with Hitler in the midst of them could get through the encirclement by underground routes, and suggested they be put at the Führer's disposal as a shield', Axmann's messenger, Armin Lehmann, tells us.

But Hitler turned down the offer. He had made up his mind not to run the risk of falling into enemy hands. Towards 2.30 a.m. he summoned all the twenty officers and women remaining in the bunker, and silently shook hands with each of them. Eva Hitler embraced the ladies present. Then both of them left the room. It was clear to everyone that the suicide of which Hitler had spoken in the final days was now imminent. The occupants of the bunker talked to each other informally, without regard to rank or position.

In the early hours of the morning Stalin's troops had reached Potsdamer Platz; the Tiergarten park was already occupied. The Red

Army was only a few yards from the Führer-bunker. However, on Stalin's orders they were first to capture the Reichstag, which he mistakenly believed to be the political heart of the German Reich, and to hoist the Red Flag there on 1 May. But none of this mattered to Hitler any longer. In the evening of 29 April he had sealed the bond of matrimony with Eva Braun, who had waited so long for this moment. Afterwards he set out two wills. The private will was of no consequence, while the political one bore witness to his continuing madness. In the afternoon of 30 April at about 3.30 p.m. a single shot rang out in the bunker under the Reich Chancellery, scarcely audible amidst the din of the Russian artillery barrage. In his private room Hitler sat slumped on the bloodstained sofa. On his right, leaning back, was Eva Hitler. Both were dead. Eva Hitler had poisoned herself with potassium cyanide. Adolf Hitler had first bitten on a cyanide capsule and then shot himself in the right temple.

SS men and personal staff carried the bodies up the narrow staircase from the bunker into the garden of the Reich Chancellery. 'It was as if a spell had been lifted from us', recalls Hitler's secretary, Traudl Junge. One of Hitler's adjutants named Günsche poured petrol over the corpses. A screwed-up piece of paper was set alight and thrown on to the pyre. Hitler had specifically ordered the cremation. Unlike Mussolini, whose hanged body for several days provided a target for the curiosity and wrath of his enemies, Hitler did not want his corpse to fall into the hands of his opponents.

On 1 May Greater German Radio announced its version of events. Adolf Hitler 'in his command-post in the Reich Chancellery, fighting to his last breath, has died for Germany'. It was one of the last lies of the regime. What effect did this report of Hitler's death have on the boys who were still fighting in his name? 'Up until then we had always said: we'll win because we've got the Führer, and the Führer will see us right, the Führer and his miracle-weapons', remembers the former 'Werewolf' Erich Loest. 'Now the Führer was dead, and with him had gone any hope that the war could still be won. It was all over, finished. Now only one thing mattered: to try and survive.' For the *Hitlerjunge* Lothar Loewe this was how things looked: 'Hitler is dead, and that means the Hitler Youth is dead. No Hitler, no Hitler Youth. Actually his death didn't make a particular impression on me, and somehow I had the feeling that now I was free.' Another *Hitlerjunge*, Gerd Häffner, says: 'I felt absolutely nothing any more. At that moment I felt a kind of relief. But certainly nothing like regret. No, nothing else really.' But still the fighting in Berlin continued, for three long days. Hundreds of soldiers and *Hitlerjungen* still had to pay with their lives.

> If there was any sense to it all, then it was this: to go home, clear away the debris, mental as well as physical, to learn something and to help put our country to rights again.
>
> *Hellmuth Buddenberg, born 1924*

On 2 May the Reich capital surrendered. On 8 May the dreadful chapter finally ended and all illusion with it. For many young people the nadir, the zero point, turned into a catharsis. 'You are alive. The war, your war, is over for you. It was a feeling of great happiness', recalls Erich Loest, who was then nineteen. 'We were really in a state of total physical and psychological exhaustion', says Peter Boenisch, eighteen at the time. 'Then, when the growing realisation came to us that it had all been pointless and in vain, that one's friends had died for nothing, that one's brother had died for nothing, we were utterly embittered.' Gregor Dorfmeister, who was just sixteen then, explains: 'I often come up against the question of our motivation, and a "cool" teenager of today naturally asks, why were you so stupid as to go along with it? I can only reply: thank God you are able to ask that question today. We couldn't have asked it then.'

'Everything we believed in then turned out to be worthless, *worthless*. We were left with nothing', says Hans Jürgen Habenicht, who was then sixteen.

> The 8th of May saw the end of my schizophrenia. As I lived through it I decided in future to keep my integrity, and never again to divorce the things I did politically from my own personal standards.
>
> *Jörg Zink, born 1922*

In the end, beside each individual story must be set the great number of dead. Of all the males born between 1919 and 1928, nearly 1.9 million lost their lives in action – one third of total military losses on the German side. Further statistics bear witness to the madness: someone drafted in 1939 had on average just over four more years to live. For those recruited in 1945 (half of whom were born in 1926 or later) the average life expectancy was only a month.

> They had to pick on us boys. We were expendable!
> *Hans-Karl Behrend, born 1929*

After the war, a new dating system began for those who survived, starting with Year Zero. Yet the trauma of the previous epoch persisted. Anyone who has had the opportunity of speaking to hundreds of contemporary eye-witnesses comes away with the phrase many of them used in summing it all up: 'We acted in good faith and were misused in a dreadful cause.'

The poet and playwright Wolfgang Borchert, who was exactly eighteen when the war ended, wrote of his own war experiences: 'We are a generation with no home and no farewell. Our sun is meagre, our love cruel, our youth is without youth.' Inwardly deeply affected, the young writer expressed what was true for many child-soldiers of his age: the inhuman regime never allowed them to become human. As Borchert summed it up after the war ended: 'We are the generation without attachments, without a past, without acknowledgement.' That generation is still living. They can still tell us what happened. We can still draw lessons from their fate. Their memories are a precious legacy – a necessary plea against oblivion.

# INDEX